"Reels and Revelations Through TV and Movie Trivia from the 1960s to the 2000s"

Contents

1960s - A New Wave of Television and Cinema	02
	03
The Dawn of Color Television	08
Classic 60s Sitcoms and Their Legacy	14
The Rise of Sci-Fi: "Star Trek" and Beyond	20
Spy Fever: "The Man from U.N.C.L.E." and "Mission: Impossible"	22
	23
The Golden Age of Cartoons	29
The Great Escape	32
Iconic TV Dramas of the 60s	37
Psycho	41
Guess the 60s Movie	44
To Kill a Mockingbird	46
TV Cult Classics	51
2001: A Space Odyssey	
1970s - The Decade of Diversification in TV and Cinema	55
The Sitcom Evolution: From "All in the Family" to "MASH"	56
The Birth of the TV Miniseries: "Roots" and Its Impact	60
Blockbuster Cinema: "Jaws" and "Star Wars"	64
Guess the 70s Movie	78
Rocky	82
The Horror Boom: On Screen and In Culture	87
The Rise of Saturday Morning Cartoons	90
The Godfather	95
Grease	

1980s - The Explosion of Pop Culture in TV and Cinema	99
The Sitcom Renaissance: "Cheers" to "The Cosby Show"	100
Music Television: MTV Changes the Game	103
The Teen Movie Explosion: John Hughes and the Brat Pack	108
The Golden Age of Action Heroes	112
Sci-Fi and Fantasy: "E.T." to "Back to the Future"	118
Soap Operas and Prime Time Dramas: "Dallas" and "Dynasty"	131
Guess the 80s Movie	135
Animation Breakthroughs: From "The Simpsons" to "Who Framed Roger Rabbit"	146
1980s Pop Culture Quiz	152
1990s - The Broadening Horizons of TV and Cinema	156
The Reality TV Revolution: "The Real World" and Beyond	157
The Animation Renaissance: Nickelodeon and Cartoon Network	160
The Era of Must-See TV: "Friends" and "Seinfeld"	178
The Indie Film Movement: Sundance to Mainstream (Pulp Fiction)	188
Blockbusters and CGI: A New Era of Filmmaking	199
Cult Classics: "The X-Files" and "Buffy the Vampire Slayer"	210
The Rise of Premium Cable: HBO's Golden Age	215
Teen Dramas and Sitcoms: "Dawson's Creek" to "The Fresh Prince of Bel-Air"	221
90s Movie Star Quiz	227

2000s - The Digital Revolution in TV and Cinema ... 233
TV Drama: "The Wire" to "Breaking Bad" ... 234
Reality TV Domination: "Survivor" to "American Idol" ... 247
The Fantasy and Superhero Surge: "Harry Potter" and "The Dark Knight" ... 254
The Sitcom Evolution Continues: "The Office" to "30 Rock" ... 273
The Rise of Streaming Services: A New Way to Watch ... 280
Animated Success: "Shrek" to "Finding Nemo" ... 284
Epic Film Trilogies: "The Lord of the Rings" and Beyond ... 293
Sailing into the New Millennium: The "Pirates of the Caribbean" Saga ... 302
Cult TV Hits: "Lost" and "Firefly" ... 307
Swinging into the New Millennium: Spider-Man's Cinematic Web ... 310
"Mamma Mia! Here We Go Again: A Joyous Journey Through Song" ... 316

Introduction

Welcome to your ultimate guide to traversing the captivating landscape of television and cinematic achievements from the colorful 1960s all the way through the groundbreaking 2000s. As you delve into the pages of this compendium, you're set to embark on a thrilling expedition through time, where legendary characters were born, revolutionary plots were unveiled, and filmmaking itself underwent extraordinary transformations. This compendium is crafted for both avid cinephiles and television enthusiasts, offering a rich exploration of the periods that have defined and reshaped the world of visual storytelling. Here, we celebrate the monumental moments, the evolution of genres, and the timeless stories that have left an indelible mark on audiences worldwide.

This meticulously assembled collection of trivia unveils the enchantment of each decade, spotlighting the significant trends, thematic revolutions, and technological breakthroughs that have influenced the realms of TV and cinema. From the technicolor innovations of the sixties that revolutionized television viewing to the digital effects of the 2000s that heralded a new era for cinematic spectacles, this book spans a comprehensive spectrum. Brimming with questions and answers, intriguing trivia tidbits, and captivating facts, "Reels and Revelations" is designed to enlighten, entertain, and spark a profound appreciation for the pivotal contributions to the legacy of television and film. Whether you're a trivia aficionado keen on challenging your knowledge or a casual fan interested in a nostalgic journey through the classics, this exploration of decades of TV and movies offers a mesmerizing passage into the wonders of the screen.

The 1960s: A New Wave of Television and Cinema

The 1960s heralded a transformative era for television and cinema, marking the dawn of color broadcasting and introducing a revolutionary cultural shift mirrored in the content and storytelling of the time. This decade was a period of vibrant change and innovation, where television began to reflect the dynamic social movements, bringing the British Invasion not only to music but also to the small screen, and launching iconic sitcoms that continue to influence the genre. As the world of sci-fi expanded with groundbreaking shows like "Star Trek," spy fever took over with classics such as "The Man from U.N.C.L.E." and "Mission: Impossible," setting the stage for a decade of intrigue and adventure. The golden age of cartoons and the rise of cult classics defined a generation, offering a new dimension of entertainment and creativity.

Meanwhile, the film industry experienced its own evolution with movies that challenged societal norms, embraced new filmmaking techniques, and showcased the decade's tumultuous spirit. The 1960s were not just about the escalation of genres but also about setting new narratives that spoke to a global audience, making it a seminal decade for both television and cinema. It was a time when the medium became a mirror to the world's changing dynamics, offering an escape, a reflection, and a critique all at once. As we delve into the iconic TV dramas, cult classics, and seminal movies of the 1960s, we celebrate a decade of unparalleled creativity and the birth of many firsts in the realm of visual storytelling.

The Dawn of Color Television

As the 1950s laid the foundation for the advent of color television, it was during the vibrant and transformative 1960s that color broadcasting truly came into its own, captivating audiences and reshaping the television landscape. The early experiments and technological battles of the previous decade culminated in a burst of color that swept across the nation's screens, making the 1960s a pivotal era for the medium. With the technical hurdles largely overcome and color sets becoming more affordable, networks expanded their color programming, bringing a new dimension to the viewer's experience.

This era witnessed iconic shows making their debut in living color, enhancing the storytelling and visual appeal of television. The British Invasion, which had taken the music world by storm, extended its reach to television, with bands like The Beatles appearing in color on "The Ed Sullivan Show," leaving an indelible mark on American pop culture. This period also saw the rise of classic 60s sitcoms such as "I Dream of Jeannie" and "Bewitched," whose magical and whimsical elements were brought to life with the use of color, creating a lasting legacy and setting the standard for future sitcoms.

The 1960s were also significant for the rise of science fiction and spy genres on television, with groundbreaking series like "Star Trek" and "The Man from U.N.C.L.E." utilizing color to enhance their futuristic gadgets and exotic locales, captivating audiences with their vivid storytelling and imaginative worlds. "Star Trek," in particular, leveraged color television to bring its optimistic vision of the future to life, with its colorful uniforms, alien worlds, and technicolor special effects, setting a new benchmark for the sci-fi genre.

Moreover, the decade was known as the Golden Age of Cartoons, with classics like "The Flintstones" and "The Jetsons" making their vibrant debut, enchanting both children and adults with their colorful animation and becoming staples of American television. The era's iconic TV dramas and cult classics, including "The Twilight Zone" and "The Outer Limits," also benefited from the transition to color, adding a new layer of depth and realism to their storytelling.

The 1960s' transition to color television was more than a technological advancement; it was a cultural revolution that transformed the way stories were told and experienced. This era laid the groundwork for the visually rich and immersive television and cinema that would follow, making color broadcasting one of the most significant milestones in the history of visual media.

Trivia Tidbits

NBC's Peacock Logo: NBC adopted its colorful peacock logo in 1956 to highlight its progress in color broadcasting. By the 1960s, this logo became synonymous with the network's commitment to color TV, famously introduced with the phrase, "The following program is brought to you in living color on NBC." First Coast-to-Coast Color Broadcast: The 1965 Rose Bowl Parade was the first program broadcast in color from coast to coast, showcasing the parade's vibrant floats and festivities to viewers across the United States, marking a significant moment in the history of color television.

Color TV Sales Surge: By 1968, the sale of color television sets finally surpassed that of black-and-white units in the U.S., signifying a pivotal shift in consumer preference and the beginning of the end for black-and-white broadcasting.

"Bonanza" and Color Broadcasting: The popular western series "Bonanza" was one of the first series to be broadcast in color, specifically to promote the sale of color television sets manufactured by RCA, the parent company of NBC. Its colorful portrayal of the Ponderosa ranch and its surroundings played a significant role in popularizing color TV.
The Beatles' Color Debut: The Beatles' appearances on "The Ed Sullivan Show" in the early 1960s were initially broadcast in black and white.

"Star Trek" and Racial Inclusion: "Star Trek" not only leveraged color technology for its futuristic storytelling but also for its progressive depiction of racial and cultural diversity, including television's first interracial kiss in 1968, using the medium to promote social change.
Color Television as a Luxury Item: In the early 1960s, a color TV set was a luxury item, costing the equivalent of about $3,000 in today's money, making it a status symbol among consumers.
The Color Transition of News Broadcasts: It wasn't until the late 1960s that news broadcasts began transitioning to color. The 1968 Democratic and Republican National Conventions were among the first major news events to be broadcast in color, marking a new era for news coverage.

Psychedelic Shows and Color TV: The late 1960s saw the rise of psychedelic shows like "Rowan & Martin's Laugh-In," which utilized color television's capabilities to enhance its fast-paced, colorful, and zany visual style, appealing to the youth culture of the time.
Global Adoption Varied Widely: While the U.S. spearheaded the color TV revolution, the adoption of color broadcasting varied globally, with some countries not fully transitioning until the 1970s or even the 1980s, highlighting the technological and economic disparities in global television broadcasting.

Questions

1. What significant event in 1965 showcased the potential of color broadcasting to a nationwide audience in the United States?
   - A) The first live color broadcast of a presidential speech
   - B) The coast-to-coast color broadcast of the Rose Bowl Parade
   - C) The color debut of "The Twilight Zone"

2. Which show became the first major sports event to be broadcast in color, helping to popularize color TV among American viewers?
   - A) The Super Bowl
   - B) The World Series
   - C) The Olympic Games

3. What was a major factor in the surge of color TV sales in the late 1960s?
   - A) Decrease in the price of color TV sets
   - B) The mandatory transition from black-and-white to color broadcasting by the FCC
   - C) The introduction of portable color TVs

4. Which iconic music group's color broadcast on "The Ed Sullivan Show" marked a pivotal moment in television history, symbolizing the cultural embrace of color TV?
   - A) The Beatles
   - B) The Rolling Stones
   - C) The Beach Boys

5. When did the sale of color television sets finally surpass that of black-and-white units, marking a significant milestone in the adoption of color TV?
   - A) 1966
   - B) 1968
   - C) 1970

Answers

1. B) The coast-to-coast color broadcast of the Rose Bowl Parade
2. B) The World Series
3. A) Decrease in the price of color TV sets
4. A) The Beatles
5. B) 1968

Did you know? American television networks often accommodate the country's multiple time zones by broadcasting programs simultaneously across different regions. This ensures viewers across the nation can watch popular shows or live events like sports games in real-time, regardless of their local time zone.

Did You Know? The Beatles arrived in America for the first time on February 7, 1964. They landed at John F. Kennedy International Airport in New York City to a frenzy of fans and media. This event marked the beginning of what would become known as the "British Invasion" of music into the United States

Did you know? that the New York Yankees hold the record for the most World Series championships? The Yankees have won the World Series 27 times

Classic 60s Sitcoms and Their Legacy

The 1960s was a transformative decade for American television, especially in the realm of sitcoms. This era, characterized by immense social and cultural changes, witnessed the rise of classic sitcoms that not only entertained but also subtly mirrored and sometimes challenged the societal norms of the time. The legacy of these sitcoms extends far beyond their original air dates, as they set the stage for future generations of television programming, reshaping the landscape of American comedy.

At the dawn of the 1960s, sitcoms began to evolve from the idealized family portraits of the 1950s to more diverse and complex narratives. Shows like "The Dick Van Dyke Show" broke new ground by depicting a working husband and a stay-at-home wife with aspirations and interests outside of the home, offering a more nuanced portrayal of marriage and work-life balance. Its clever writing, coupled with the charismatic performances of its cast, set a high standard for sitcoms in terms of both humor and storytelling.

Meanwhile, "I Dream of Jeannie" and "Bewitched" introduced elements of fantasy and magic into the sitcom domain. These shows, while seemingly light-hearted and whimsical, subtly pushed against the constraints of traditional gender roles, with female protagonists possessing powers that often put them at odds with the expectations of a male-dominated society. Their popularity indicated audiences' appetite for stories that bent the rules of reality and allowed for a temporary escape from the everyday.

Another significant shift was the move towards addressing social issues through comedy, a trend exemplified by "The Andy Griffith Show." Set in the fictional town of Mayberry, the series offered a nostalgic view of American life but didn't shy away from tackling topics such as morality, justice, and community spirit. Its enduring appeal lies in its ability to blend humor with heartfelt storytelling, creating a sense of idealism without ignoring the complexities of human nature.

The late 1960s saw the debut of "The Brady Bunch," a sitcom that reflected the changing American family structure by showcasing a blended family navigating life's ups and downs. The show's premise, revolutionary at the time, paved the way for future sitcoms to explore non-traditional family dynamics, highlighting themes of unity, acceptance, and the challenges of blended familial relationships.

Perhaps one of the most enduring legacies of 1960s sitcoms is their role in pioneering the inclusion of diverse voices and perspectives in mainstream television. "Julia," starring Diahann Carroll as a widowed African American mother and professional nurse, broke new ground as one of the first sitcoms to feature an African American woman in a non-stereotypical role. Its success demonstrated the potential for sitcoms to contribute to broader societal conversations about race, representation, and equality.

These classic 1960s sitcoms left an indelible mark on American pop culture, influencing countless creators and shaping the future of television comedy. Their innovative approaches to storytelling, character development, and social commentary created a blueprint that has been revisited and reimagined by subsequent generations of sitcoms. As we look back on this golden era of television, it's clear that the legacy of these groundbreaking shows lies not just in their ability to entertain, but in their enduring impact on the fabric of American society, challenging audiences to see the world—and each other—in a more nuanced light.

Trivia Tidbits

- "The Dick Van Dyke Show" was one of the first to feature a working woman prominently, reflecting changing gender roles.
- "I Dream of Jeannie" featured the first instance of a woman in a leading role living independently from a man on American TV.
- "Bewitched" subtly addressed issues of prejudice and tolerance through its supernatural metaphor, paralleling the Civil Rights Movement.

- "The Andy Griffith Show" often used its rural setting to explore and critique contemporary social issues under the guise of simplicity and nostalgia.
- "The Brady Bunch" is credited with introducing the concept of a blended family to mainstream America, a rarity in television portrayals at the time.
- "Julia" was groundbreaking for being the first American sitcom to star an African American actress in a non-stereotypical role.
- "The Dick Van Dyke Show" is notable for its behind-the-scenes talent, with creator Carl Reiner drawing heavily from his own life in show business.
- The set of "I Dream of Jeannie's" bottle interior was designed in vibrant pink, symbolizing the show's embrace of psychedelic pop culture.
- "Bewitched" went through two Darrins (Dick York and then Dick Sargent), an early instance of a major character being recast on a popular show.
- "The Andy Griffith Show's" fictional town of Mayberry was based on Andy Griffith's real hometown of Mount Airy, North Carolina.
- "The Brady Bunch" never showed Carol and Mike Brady's bedroom with a single bed for the couple, sidestepping then-controversial representations of marital intimacy.
- "Julia" received both praise and criticism for its portrayal of African American life, sparking conversations about representation on television.
- Episodes of "The Dick Van Dyke Show" often concluded with moral lessons, a nod to the sitcoms of the previous decade but delivered with a modern twist.
- "Bewitched" and "I Dream of Jeannie" reflected the era's fascination with space and the supernatural, tapping into the zeitgeist of the 1960s' space race and counterculture.

- "The Brady Bunch" initially received mixed reviews from critics but grew in popularity through syndication, becoming a cultural icon and a symbol of 1960s and 70s Americana.

The Dick Van Dyke Show

"The Dick Van Dyke Show," premiering in 1961 and concluding in 1966, was a pivotal sitcom that reflected and subtly shaped the cultural landscape of the 1960s in America. Set against the backdrop of the suburban home in New Rochelle, New York, and the bustling workplace of the fictional Alan Brady Show in Manhattan, the series masterfully balanced home life and work life, presenting a more complex and relatable view of American adulthood.

Rob Petrie (played by Dick Van Dyke) is the head writer for the Alan Brady Show, navigating the quirks of the entertainment industry alongside fellow writers Sally Rogers (Rose Marie) and Buddy Sorrell (Morey Amsterdam). At home, Rob's interactions with his wife Laura (Mary Tyler Moore), a former dancer turned homemaker, and their son Richie, highlighted the dynamics of a modern, loving family, breaking away from the stereotypical patriarchal family model prevalent in earlier sitcoms.

The show was revolutionary for several reasons:

- Pioneering Portrayal of Work-Life: It was among the first sitcoms to feature both the protagonist's work and home environments, offering a dual perspective on the lead character's life and challenges.
- Breaking Gender Norms: Mary Tyler Moore's portrayal of Laura Petrie was groundbreaking. Laura was intelligent, witty, and occasionally the breadwinner, challenging the era's gender norms and paving the way for more dynamic female characters in television.

- **Meta-Comedy Elements:** The show often utilized meta-comedy, with the fictional Alan Brady Show serving as a show-within-a-show, allowing for a satirical look at the television industry itself.

Physical Comedy and Dance

One of the most memorable aspects of "The Dick Van Dyke Show" is its opening sequence, where Dick Van Dyke navigates a set of living room furniture. In one version, he deftly sidesteps the ottoman; in another, he famously trips over it. This moment, emblematic of Van Dyke's physical comedy, became one of the show's signature gags.

Throughout the series, Van Dyke's character, Rob Petrie, finds numerous opportunities to showcase his dance skills. Notable episodes include "The Twizzle," where Rob invents a new dance craze, and "The Secret Life of Buddy and Sally," featuring an impromptu soft-shoe routine in the writers' room.

Van Dyke utilized his background in physical comedy to enhance many scenes, incorporating falls, stunts, and slapstick humor that added a dynamic visual element to the show's comedy. His ability to convey humor through movement and physical expression set a high bar for comedic performance.

Cultural Impact

"The Dick Van Dyke Show" had a profound influence on the structure and tone of future sitcoms. Its successful integration of work-life and home-life narratives into a cohesive comedic framework inspired shows like "The Mary Tyler Moore Show" and "30 Rock."

The series was celebrated for its sophisticated writing, blending witty dialogue with situational comedy and character-driven humor. Creator Carl Reiner, who based the show on his own experiences as a writer, set new standards for sitcom writing that valued cleverness and relatability.

While primarily a comedy, the show did not shy away from social issues. Episodes like "That's My Boy??" subtly addressed concerns about racial prejudice, and Laura Petrie's character, often seen wearing pants, quietly challenged the era's gender norms regarding women's attire and roles.

The show received 15 Emmy Awards, a testament to its excellence and influence.

The Rise of Sci-Fi: "Star Trek" and Beyond

The 1960s marked a significant period in the evolution of science fiction on television, with "Star Trek" leading the charge. Premiering in 1966, "Star Trek" was a visionary creation by Gene Roddenberry that presented a future where humanity had overcome its differences and was exploring the vastness of space as part of a united Federation of Planets. The series was groundbreaking, not only for its imaginative storytelling and special effects but also for its approach to tackling social and ethical issues through the lens of science fiction. It presented a diverse crew aboard the USS Enterprise, working together in harmony, which was a bold statement during the turbulent 1960s.

"Star Trek" set a new standard for the genre, inspiring a plethora of science fiction series that followed. It explored complex themes such as racism, war, and the human condition, wrapped in the engaging packaging of space exploration and adventure. The show's optimistic view of the future, where technology and humanity coexist for the greater good, captured the imaginations of viewers around the world, spawning a franchise that continues to this day.

Trivia Tidbits:

- Cultural Impact: "Star Trek" introduced the Vulcan salute and the phrase "Live long and prosper," both of which have become ingrained in popular culture.
- Technological Predictions: The original series famously predicted several future technologies, including automatic doors, cell phones (communicators), and tablet computers (PADDs).
- Diverse Cast: "Star Trek" featured one of television's first multi-racial casts, including the groundbreaking character Lt. Uhura, a significant role for an African American woman at the time.
- First Interracial Kiss on TV: In the episode "Plato's Stepchildren," "Star Trek" showcased the first interracial kiss on American television between Captain Kirk and Lt. Uhura.
- Fan Influence: The show's cancellation after three seasons led to an unprecedented letter-writing campaign by fans, illustrating the early power of fan-based movements in influencing television programming.
- Tribble Trouble: The episode "The Trouble with Tribbles" is one of the most beloved in the "Star Trek" series, introducing the furry, rapidly reproducing creatures known as Tribbles. This episode is celebrated for its humor and has inspired multiple follow-up stories in the franchise.
- Spock's Influence: Leonard Nimoy's character, Spock, became a cultural icon, embodying the struggle between logic and emotion. His Vulcan nerve pinch and mind meld became legendary elements of the series.

- Klingon Language: "Star Trek" introduced the Klingons, a warrior race whose language, developed in later series, has become a fully constructed spoken language, complete with its own dictionary and learning materials.
- Environmental Messages: The episode "The Devil in the Dark" explored themes of environmentalism and misunderstanding, showing a creature killing miners not out of malice but in defense of its offspring, highlighting the importance of empathy and understanding.

"Beam Me Up, Scotty"

- Despite its popularity in culture, the exact phrase "Beam me up, Scotty" is never actually spoken in the original series. Variations of the phrase are used, but the exact line became famous as a misquotation.
- Gene Roddenberry's Vision: Creator Gene Roddenberry envisioned "Star Trek" as a "Wagon Train to the stars," using the platform to explore social issues under the guise of science fiction, which allowed for discussions on race, equality, and peace that were progressive for its time.
- NASA's Real-Life Influence: "Star Trek" has inspired countless individuals to pursue careers in science and space exploration. NASA even named its first Space Shuttle Enterprise, after the starship from the series.
- Syndication Success: Though not a hit during its original broadcast, "Star Trek" found a massive audience in syndication, leading to its status as a cult classic and sparking the development of an extensive franchise.
- The Gorn: One of the series' most memorable antagonists, the Gorn, appeared in only one episode, "Arena." Despite its limited screen time, the reptilian creature left a lasting impact due to its unique appearance and the episode's message about overcoming prejudice and finding common ground.

- Nichelle Nichols' NASA Recruitment: Nichelle Nichols, who played Lt. Uhura, worked with NASA after the series ended to recruit minority and female personnel for the space agency, including astronauts Sally Ride, the first American woman in space, and Guion Bluford, the first African American in space.

Captain James T. Kirk (William Shatner): The charismatic and daring captain of the USS Enterprise, James T. Kirk, is known for his leadership qualities, moral conviction, and willingness to bend the rules for the greater good. His command style and decisions often reflect the tension between duty and personal ethics, making him a quintessential hero of the space frontier.

Spock (Leonard Nimoy): Serving as the science officer and first officer aboard the USS Enterprise, Spock is a Vulcan-human hybrid whose character embodies the conflict between logic and emotion. His Vulcan heritage urges him towards rationality and control, while his human side occasionally reveals deeper passions and empathy. Spock's struggle for identity and balance between these two worlds resonates with audiences, making him one of the most iconic characters in science fiction.

Dr. Leonard "Bones" McCoy (DeForest Kelley): The Enterprise's chief medical officer, Dr. McCoy, is known for his Southern charm, compassion, and often humorous pessimism. His catchphrases, like "I'm a doctor, not a(n) [occupation]," highlight his down-to-earth personality and medical expertise. McCoy frequently serves as the emotional counterpoint to Spock's logic, embodying the humanistic and ethical perspectives in the series.

Lt. Nyota Uhura (Nichelle Nichols): As the communications officer of the Enterprise, Uhura is groundbreaking for being one of the first African American female characters on American television in a significant, non-stereotypical role. Her presence and professionalism on the bridge crew contributed to the show's vision of an inclusive and diverse future.

Hikaru Sulu (George Takei): The Enterprise's helmsman, Sulu, is known for his expertise in astrophysics and fencing, showcasing the diverse interests and skills of the crew members. His character represents Asian Americans in a future where race and ethnicity are no longer barriers to achievement and camaraderie.

Pavel Chekov (Walter Koenig): Introduced in the show's second season, Chekov serves as the Enterprise's navigator. Portrayed as a young and enthusiastic officer, his Russian heritage was particularly significant during the Cold War era, symbolizing the show's message of global unity and cooperation.

Montgomery "Scotty" Scott (James Doohan): The Enterprise's chief engineer, affectionately known as "Scotty," is renowned for his technical genius and his Scottish accent. His catchphrase, "I'm givin' her all she's got, Captain!" encapsulates his dedication and miraculous ability to solve nearly impossible engineering challenges under pressure.

"The City on the Edge of Forever" (Season 1, Episode 28): Often cited as one of the greatest "Star Trek" episodes, "The City on the Edge of Forever" is celebrated for its profound narrative depth, emotional impact, and ethical quandaries. The story involves Dr. McCoy accidentally injecting himself with a substance that causes him to go mad and leap through a portal to 1930s Earth. Kirk and Spock follow, only to discover that McCoy's actions have altered history, preventing the formation of the Federation. Kirk falls in love with Edith Keeler (played by Joan Collins), a pacifist whose survival would lead to Nazi Germany winning World War II due to delayed U.S. involvement. Kirk is faced with the heartbreaking decision to allow Keeler to die, thus restoring the timeline. This episode is a poignant exploration of sacrifice, the greater good, and the harsh realities of time travel.

"Balance of Terror" (Season 1, Episode 14): "Balance of Terror" introduces the Romulans, establishing much of the lore surrounding this enigmatic race and setting up a longstanding rivalry within the "Star Trek" universe. The episode plays out as a tense submarine-style warfare narrative in space, showcasing a battle of wits between the Enterprise, under Kirk's command, and a Romulan warbird, commanded by an equally honorable and skilled Romulan captain. It addresses themes of prejudice, duty, and the tragedy of war, as neither side truly wishes for conflict but is bound by duty to their respective nations. The episode is a masterclass in suspense, strategy, and the exploration of military ethics.

"Amok Time" (Season 2, Episode 1): This episode is significant for delving into Vulcan culture, particularly the Pon Farr, a time of mating frenzy that Vulcans experience. Spock must return to Vulcan to undergo this ritual, but the situation quickly escalates into a battle to the death between Spock and Kirk, orchestrated by Spock's betrothed, T'Pring, who wishes to choose a different partner. "Amok Time" is notable for its exploration of Spock's character, revealing the complexities and struggles of his Vulcan heritage and his friendship with Kirk. It's a compelling look at the clashes between tradition and personal desire, as well as the lengths to which one may go to uphold cultural customs.

These episodes stand out not only for their storytelling but also for how they expanded the "Star Trek" universe, deepened character development, and explored ethical dilemmas, setting high standards for all science fiction television that followed.

Spy Fever: "The Man from U.N.C.L.E." and "Mission: Impossible

The 1960s were a golden era for spy-themed entertainment, fueled by the Cold War's tensions and intrigue. This fascination with espionage found a prominent place on television, notably through two iconic series: "The Man from U.N.C.L.E." and "Mission: Impossible." These shows captured the imagination of audiences, offering a blend of suspense, action, and the exotic allure of international espionage, all while reflecting and amplifying the era's spy fever.

"The Man from U.N.C.L.E." (1964-1968): This series introduced viewers to the stylish and suave secret agents Napoleon Solo (Robert Vaughn) and Illya Kuryakin (David McCallum) of the United Network Command for Law and Enforcement (U.N.C.L.E.). Tasked with protecting the world from the threats posed by the nefarious organization THRUSH, Solo and Kuryakin traveled the globe, employing a mix of cunning, cool gadgets, and charisma. The show was notable for its light-hearted approach to espionage, combining action with humor and setting a precedent for buddy-cop dynamics in future television series and films. Its portrayal of an American and a Russian working together was particularly poignant during the Cold War, symbolizing a hopeful vision of international cooperation.

"Mission: Impossible" (1966-1973): With its innovative plot structures and the iconic "Your mission, should you choose to accept it" message that self-destructed, "Mission: Impossible" brought a new level of sophistication and complexity to TV espionage. The series focused on the Impossible Missions Force (IMF), a team of elite agents led by the cool-headed Jim Phelps (Peter Graves, from the second season onward), engaging in covert operations to thwart dictators, evil organizations, and other threats to global peace. The show was celebrated for its intricate plots, use of cutting-edge technology, and the famous theme song by Lalo Schifrin, which became synonymous with suspense and action. The series' emphasis on teamwork and the unique skills of each team member, from master of disguise to electronics expert, showcased a different aspect of spy work, moving away from the lone agent trope.

Trivia Tidbits:

- Crossover Appeal: David McCallum's Illya Kuryakin became a pop culture icon and sex symbol, unexpectedly catapulting the actor to international fame.
- Cameo Connections: "The Man from U.N.C.L.E." featured cameo appearances by notable stars, including William Shatner and Leonard Nimoy in the same episode, before they became famous for "Star Trek."
- Gadgets Galore: Both shows were renowned for their imaginative use of gadgets and technology, from the pen communicators in "The Man from U.N.C.L.E." to the intricate devices used by the IMF in "Mission: Impossible."
- Innovative Filmmaking: "Mission: Impossible" was praised for its groundbreaking use of the cold open and the dossier scene, innovations that have since become standard in the spy genre.
- Cultural Impact: Both series had a significant impact on popular culture, inspiring a host of imitations, parodies, and a revival in interest in the spy genre, including modern movie adaptations and reboots that continue to entertain audiences worldwide.

Both shows introduced several novel elements to the spy genre, influencing countless imitators and setting new standards for action and adventure on television.

The Man from U.N.C.L.E.

- International Cooperation: Set against the backdrop of the Cold War, "The Man from U.N.C.L.E." featured agents from the United States (Napoleon Solo, played by Robert Vaughn) and the Soviet Union (Illya Kuryakin, played by David McCallum) working together for a secretive international organization. This premise of international cooperation was a refreshing narrative, promoting unity during a period of global tension.
- Gadgets and Tech: Inspired by the James Bond films, the series made extensive use of futuristic gadgets and technology, which became a hallmark of the spy genre. From communicators concealed as everyday items to tricked-out vehicles, the innovative tech added an element of fantasy and excitement to the missions.
- Humor and Camp: While dealing with serious themes of espionage and global threats, "The Man from U.N.C.L.E." also incorporated a lighter tone, with witty banter between characters and campy, over-the-top villains. This blend of humor and action helped broaden its appeal beyond traditional action-adventure fans.

Mission: Impossible

- The Impossible Missions Force (IMF): "Mission: Impossible" introduced the concept of the IMF, a team of experts from various fields, each bringing unique skills to the table. This emphasis on teamwork and the combination of different talents to achieve a common goal was a novel approach in the spy genre.

- Intricate Plots and Deception: The show was renowned for its complex plots that often involved elaborate deceptions, disguises, and carefully planned operations. The famous phrase "Your mission, should you choose to accept it" became synonymous with the setup for these intricate missions, which usually involved outsmarting highly intelligent adversaries.
- Use of Masks and Disguises: A signature element of "Mission: Impossible" was the use of lifelike masks and disguises, allowing team members to assume any identity necessary to complete their mission. This not only added a layer of suspense and surprise but also showcased the theme of identity and deception.
- The Self-Destructing Message: At the start of each episode, the team leader would receive mission details via a recording that would "self-destruct" after being played. This concept became an iconic aspect of the show, emphasizing the secretive and dangerous nature of their work.

The Golden Age of Cartoons

The 1960s heralded what many consider the Golden Age of Saturday Morning Cartoons, a time when animation enjoyed unprecedented popularity and creativity. This era introduced a plethora of animated series that have since become cultural icons, captivating children and adults alike with their imaginative stories, memorable characters, and innovative animation techniques. The decade saw the emergence of cartoons that not only entertained but also subtly imparted lessons on friendship, courage, and morality.

Hanna-Barbera Productions dominated the scene, churning out a multitude of series that defined the era. Shows like "The Flintstones", the first prime-time animated show aimed at adults as well as children, and "The Jetsons", offering a whimsical look at the future, reflected contemporary American culture through the lens of animation. "Scooby-Doo, Where Are You!" combined mystery with comedy, creating a formula that has been replicated numerous times since. These shows, among others, exemplified Hanna-Barbera's knack for creating enduring franchises.

"Looney Tunes" and "Merrie Melodies" also gained popularity during this period, with Warner Bros. repackaging these classic shorts for television audiences. Characters like Bugs Bunny, Daffy Duck, and Porky Pig became household names, known for their slapstick comedy and witty banter. The clever writing and timeless humor of these shorts appealed to a wide audience, further cementing their place in animation history.
The 1960s also saw the rise of superhero cartoons, with "The Marvel Super Heroes" and "Spider-Man" bringing comic book heroes to the small screen. These shows capitalized on the growing popularity of comic books, offering children new role models and fantasies of heroism and adventure.

The Flintstones

"The Flintstones" is set in the prehistoric town of Bedrock and follows the daily lives of the Flintstone family and their neighbors, the Rubbles. Fred Flintstone, his wife Wilma, their daughter Pebbles, and pet dinosaur Dino navigate life's modern-day challenges with Stone Age solutions, resulting in humorous situations and puns related to their era.

- Historic Primetime Slot: "The Flintstones" was the first animated series to hold a primetime slot on television, breaking ground for future animated shows.
- Inspiration: The show was inspired by "The Honeymooners," a popular live-action sitcom from the 1950s, with Fred and Barney often compared to Ralph and Ed.
- Product Placement: It famously featured characters in ads for Winston cigarettes in its early seasons, reflecting the era's lax attitudes towards advertising and smoking.
- First Animated Couple in Bed: Fred and Wilma were the first animated couple shown sharing a bed on television, challenging the norms of the time.
- Spin-offs and Films: The show's popularity led to numerous spin-offs, live-action films, and specials, cementing its place in pop culture.
- Theme Song Recognition: The iconic theme song, "Meet the Flintstones," introduced in the third season, quickly became one of the most recognizable television theme songs, epitomizing the show's fun and catchy appeal to audiences of all ages.
- Innovative Sound Effects: "The Flintstones" utilized unique sound effects to mimic modern appliances and vehicles operated by animals, contributing to the show's humorous prehistoric setting. These sounds became characteristic of the show's inventive approach to storytelling.
- Celebrity Cameos: The series featured caricatures of popular celebrities of the time, such as "Ann-Margrock" (Ann-Margret) and "Stony Curtis" (Tony Curtis), allowing for a blend of pop culture references and prehistoric puns that delighted viewers.
- Crossover Episodes: In a notable crossover, "The Flintstones" met "The Jetsons" in the 1987 made-for-TV movie "The Jetsons Meet The Flintstones," uniting two of Hanna-Barbera's most beloved families in a time-travel adventure.

- Addressing Social Issues: Despite its prehistoric setting, "The Flintstones" occasionally tackled social issues and family dynamics in a manner that was relatable to contemporary audiences, making it more than just a cartoon but a reflection of American society.
- Merchandising Boom: The success of "The Flintstones" led to an extensive range of merchandise, from toys and breakfast cereals to comic books and video games, demonstrating the show's significant impact on popular culture and consumer products.
- Syndication Success: After its original primetime run, "The Flintstones" achieved remarkable success in syndication, reaching new generations of viewers and securing its status as a timeless classic.
- International Appeal: The show was dubbed into numerous languages and enjoyed popularity around the world, showcasing its universal appeal and the global reach of American animated television.
- Animation Technique: "The Flintstones" was produced using traditional hand-drawn animation techniques, with each episode requiring thousands of drawings, highlighting the labor-intensive process of animation before the advent of computer-assisted techniques.
- Emmy Nomination: "The Flintstones" was the first animated TV series to be nominated for a Primetime Emmy Award (Outstanding Comedy Series in 1961), underscoring its groundbreaking nature and the industry's recognition of its quality and appeal to a broad audience.

The Jetsons

"The Jetsons" depicts the life of a futuristic family living in the space age, with elaborate gadgets, flying cars, and robots, focusing on George Jetson, his wife Jane, their children Judy and Elroy, and their dog Astro.

- Futuristic Vision: The show's depiction of futuristic technology, like video calls and robot servants, was remarkably prescient, predicting many modern-day devices.
- Short Original Run: Despite its impact, "The Jetsons" originally aired for only one season (24 episodes) in the 1960s but was revived in the 1980s due to renewed interest.
- Theme Song: The catchy theme song, detailing the members of the Jetson family, has become iconic, easily recognizable by multiple generations.
- First Broadcast in Color: "The Jetsons" was ABC's first series to be broadcast in color, highlighting its futuristic theme.
- Cultural Influence: The show has influenced other futuristic media and is often referenced in discussions about future technology and design.

Scooby-Doo, Where Are You!

This series introduced Scooby-Doo, a talking Great Dane, and his four teenage friends - Fred, Daphne, Velma, and Shaggy - as they travel in their van, the Mystery Machine, solving mysteries involving supposedly supernatural creatures through real-world logic.

- Mystery Format: The show popularized the formula of a group of teenagers solving mysteries with a pet, inspiring numerous adaptations and similar series.
- Scooby's Full Name: Scooby-Doo's full name is Scoobert "Scooby" Doo.
- Inspirations: The series was partly inspired by the success of the animated show "The Archie Show" and the live-action series "The Many Loves of Dobie Gillis."
- Cultural Icon: Scooby-Doo has become a cultural icon, leading to an extensive franchise including direct-to-video films, spin-offs, and live-action movies.

- Voice Actor Legacy: Don Messick, the original voice of Scooby-Doo, voiced the character for over two decades, contributing significantly to the character's enduring popularity.

Spider-Man (1967)

This animated series follows Peter Parker, who gains spider-like abilities after being bitten by a radioactive spider and becomes the superhero Spider-Man, battling a variety of villains in New York City while dealing with the challenges of his personal life.

- First Animated Appearance: This was Spider-Man's first appearance in an animated format, introducing the character's adventures to a wider audience.
- Theme Song: The theme song from the series, "Spider-Man, Spider-Man, does whatever a spider can," has become legendary.
- Limited Animation: Due to budget constraints, the show often reused animation and backgrounds, a common practice in television animation at the time.
- Influential Villains: The series featured many of Spider-Man's iconic villains, contributing to their popularity in the wider Marvel Universe.
- Legacy: The 1967 "Spider-Man" series set the stage for numerous future adaptations of the character in various media, including multiple animated series and blockbuster films.

Did you know? The comics for Spider-Man were written by writer Stan Lee and artist Steve Ditko. Their collaboration introduced the iconic superhero to the world in 'Amazing Fantasy' #15, published by Marvel Comics in 1962.

The Great Escape

"The Great Escape" is a 1963 American World War II epic film directed by John Sturges and based on the 1950 non-fiction book of the same name by Paul Brickhill. The film is a dramatization of the true story of a mass escape from the German prisoner-of-war camp Stalag Luft III by Allied prisoners. It is celebrated for its portrayal of ingenuity, teamwork, and the human spirit's resilience.

The film chronicles the planning and execution of an escape by Allied POWs, who aim to divert German resources and make their way back to Allied territory. The prisoners, comprising primarily British, American, Canadian, and Australian officers, dig three tunnels named "Tom," "Dick," and "Harry" as part of their elaborate escape plan. Despite numerous challenges, including the discovery and destruction of tunnels, the group perseveres. The climax of the escape sees 76 men breaking free, although their subsequent attempts to evade capture are met with varying degrees of success.

"The Great Escape" had a profound impact upon its release and remains a classic, influencing not only the war film genre but also popular culture. Its depiction of camaraderie, determination, and the strategic outwitting of enemy forces captured the imagination of audiences worldwide. The film's score, composed by Elmer Bernstein, including its iconic theme, became instantly recognizable and has been used in various contexts to evoke the spirit of adventure and freedom.

Did you know? The phrase 'Tom, Dick, and Harry' is often used colloquially to refer to unspecified or ordinary individuals. Its origins date back to 17th-century England, where 'Tom,' 'Dick,' and 'Harry' were common names, representing the average or common man.

The Stars:

- Steve McQueen as Captain Virgil Hilts: Often remembered for his iconic motorcycle chase scene, McQueen's portrayal of the "Cooler King" added a rebellious and indomitable spirit to the film's ensemble. His performance helped cement his status as a Hollywood icon.
- James Garner as Flight Lieutenant Robert Hendley: Garner's character, the "Scrounger," uses his wits and charm to acquire necessary materials for the escape, showcasing Garner's versatility and charisma.
- Richard Attenborough as Squadron Leader Roger Bartlett: As the architect of the escape plan, Attenborough's character is pivotal. He embodies the leadership and determination of the prisoners, bringing depth and gravitas to the role.
- Charles Bronson as Flight Lieutenant Danny Velinski: Known as "The Tunnel King," Bronson's character deals with claustrophobia while being one of the key figures in tunnel digging. His performance adds a poignant element to the film, highlighting the personal struggles of the prisoners.
- Donald Pleasence as Flight Lieutenant Colin Blythe: Pleasence plays the "Forger," who is crucial in creating documents for the escapees. His portrayal underscores the importance of each prisoner's skills and contributions to the collective effort.

Trivia Tidbits

- Real-Life Inspiration: The character of Squadron Leader Roger Bartlett (Richard Attenborough) is based on Roger Bushell, the real-life mastermind of the escape, who led the planning and execution of the breakout from Stalag Luft III.

- Steve McQueen's Motorcycle Stunt: One of the film's most memorable scenes is McQueen's motorcycle jump over a barbed wire fence. While McQueen did perform many of his own motorcycle stunts, the iconic jump was executed by stuntman Bud Ekins due to insurance reasons.

- Filming Location: Although set in Germany, most of "The Great Escape" was filmed in Bavaria, Germany, near the town of Füssen, and on specially constructed sets to replicate Stalag Luft III.

- International Cast: To reflect the diverse nationalities of the POWs in Stalag Luft III, the film featured an international cast, including actors from the UK, the US, Canada, Australia, and even Charles Bronson, who was of Lithuanian descent, playing a Polish character.

- The Great Escape March: The film's score, especially "The Great Escape March," has become synonymous with the theme of adventure. Its composer, Elmer Bernstein, was nominated for an Academy Award for Best Original Score.
- Escape Tunnel Reality: In the true story, none of the tunnels were actually named "Tom," "Dick," or "Harry." These names were created for the book and the film. The real tunnels had code names based on colors.
- Limited Historical Accuracy: While the film captures the spirit of the actual event, several liberties were taken for dramatic effect. For example, the Americans were segregated from the British and Commonwealth officers in the camp long before the escape took place.
- Cameo by the Author: Paul Brickhill, who wrote the book "The Great Escape," was originally a prisoner in Stalag Luft III and contributed to the escape efforts, although he did not escape himself. He makes a cameo appearance in the film.

- James Garner's War Experience: Garner's role as the "Scrounger" echoed his own World War II experience, where he was awarded two Purple Hearts for his service. His personal history lent authenticity to his portrayal.
- No Escape for Women: Although the film does not feature any female characters, the real-life escape efforts at POW camps often involved the assistance of women from the local population, a detail omitted in the film's narrative.

Iconic TV Dramas of the 60s

The 1960s was a decade marked by social upheaval and cultural shifts, mirrored in the television landscape through a series of groundbreaking and iconic TV dramas. These series pushed the boundaries of storytelling, delved into complex issues, and in many ways, reflected the changing society of the time. From legal dramas to science fiction, the 1960s introduced viewers to new genres and narrative depths that would influence the future of television.

Perry Mason

A legal drama series based on the character of the same name by Erle Stanley Gardner, "Perry Mason" featured Raymond Burr as a brilliant and unflappable defense attorney who specialized in seemingly indefensible cases. With the help of his secretary Della Street and private investigator Paul Drake, Mason often uncovered the truth, exonerating his clients in dramatic courtroom reveals.

"Perry Mason" set the standard for legal dramas, establishing a formula that combined mystery and legal procedure. Its focus on courtroom strategy and justice resonated with audiences, paving the way for countless legal dramas that followed.

- Raymond Burr's Casting: Initially, Burr auditioned for the role of the district attorney, but his portrayal impressed producers so much that he was cast as Perry Mason instead.
- Erle Stanley Gardner's Involvement: Gardner, the creator of Perry Mason, was closely involved with the show and even appeared in the final episode as a judge.
- First Televised Case: The first episode, "The Case of the Restless Redhead," aired in 1957, setting the stage for the series' long run.
- A Total of 271 Episodes: "Perry Mason" aired for nine seasons, making it one of the longest-running legal dramas of its time.
- Signature Theme Music: The show's theme, "Park Avenue Beat," composed by Fred Steiner, became iconic and synonymous with legal drama.
- Della Street's Role: Barbara Hale played Della Street, Mason's loyal secretary, and was one of the few characters to appear in every episode.
- Real Courtroom Procedures: The show was praised for its realistic depiction of courtroom procedures and legal strategies.
- Revival and Films: After the original series ended, Raymond Burr reprised his role in 26 TV movies from 1985 until his death in 1993.
- Impact on Legal Careers: "Perry Mason" inspired many viewers to pursue careers in law, influencing a generation of legal professionals.
- No Emmy for Burr: Despite the show's success and Burr's acclaimed performance, he never won an Emmy for his role as Perry Mason.

Did you know? The Emmy Awards, which honor excellence in television, were first presented on January 25, 1949. The inaugural ceremony took place at the Hollywood Athletic Club.

The Twilight Zone

Created by Rod Serling, "The Twilight Zone" was an anthology series that blended science fiction, fantasy, and horror with social commentary. Each episode presented a standalone story, often with a surprising twist, exploring themes of human nature, technology, and morality.

"The Twilight Zone" was groundbreaking in its use of speculative fiction to comment on social issues and moral dilemmas, challenging viewers to think critically about the world around them. Its legacy endures in the continuing popularity of anthology series and its influence on genre storytelling.

- Rod Serling's Writing: Serling wrote or co-wrote 92 of the show's 156 episodes, often drawing from his own experiences and concerns about social issues.
- Famous Guest Stars: Many then-unknown actors who would later become famous, including William Shatner and Robert Redford, appeared in episodes.
- "To Serve Man": One of the most memorable episodes, featuring a twist ending that has become part of pop culture.
- Critical Acclaim: The show won three Emmy Awards and received critical praise for its storytelling and innovative concepts.
- Iconic Opening Narration: Rod Serling's opening and closing narrations are among the most recognizable elements of the show.
- Reboots and Revivals: "The Twilight Zone" has been revived several times, including series in the 1980s, 2000s, and 2019, keeping its legacy alive.
- The Twilight Zone Tower of Terror: The show inspired a popular ride at several Disney parks, blending the show's eerie atmosphere with thrill-seeking.

- Banned Episode: "The Encounter," an episode dealing with racial tensions, was pulled from syndication for decades due to its controversial content.
- Influence on Other Series: Its anthology format and twist endings influenced many subsequent series, from "Black Mirror" to "The Outer Limits."
- Serling's Social Commentary: Serling used the show to comment on societal issues like racism, war, and censorship, often bypassing television censors with science fiction allegories.

The Fugitive

"The Fugitive," starring David Janssen as Dr. Richard Kimble, followed the story of a man wrongfully convicted of his wife's murder. On the run from the law, specifically Lieutenant Philip Gerard, Kimble searches for the one-armed man he believes to be the real killer, encountering various characters and scenarios along the way.

The series was innovative for its time, combining elements of crime drama with a serialized narrative that kept audiences engaged throughout its run. "The Fugitive" concluded with one of the most-watched episodes in television history, setting a precedent for series finales.

- Inspiration from a Real Case: The concept was loosely inspired by the real-life case of Dr. Sam Sheppard, accused of murdering his wife.
- Record-Breaking Finale: The series finale in 1967 was the most-watched television episode at the time, with a 72% share of the viewing audience.
- Innovative Use of Narration: William Conrad's narration added depth and urgency to the storytelling, a notable feature of the series.

- Critical Acclaim: The show received multiple Emmy Awards, including Outstanding Dramatic Series.
- David Janssen's Commitment: Janssen appeared in nearly every scene of every episode, an unusually demanding role for a TV actor.
- First to Win an Emmy for Lead Actor: Janssen was the first actor to win an Emmy for a role in a television series that was still airing.
- Impact on Future Storytelling: The serialized format influenced the development of story arcs in television drama.
- One-Armed Man: The real identity of the one-armed man, Fred Johnson, became one of TV's most famous plot points.
- Film Adaptation: In 1993, "The Fugitive" was adapted into a successful film starring Harrison Ford as Dr. Richard Kimble.
- Cameo in the Remake: Barry Morse, who played Lt. Philip Gerard, made a cameo appearance in the 2000 TV series remake of "The Fugitive."

These iconic TV dramas of the 1960s not only entertained audiences but also challenged them to consider deeper questions about justice, morality, and the human condition. Their innovative storytelling, memorable characters, and willingness to address contemporary issues solidified their place in television history and set the stage for future generations of TV dramas.

Did you know? Before becoming a Hollywood star, Harrison Ford worked as a carpenter. In fact, his carpentry skills helped him secure a role in the film industry. While working on a door for director George Lucas, Ford was asked to read lines for auditions, eventually leading to his breakout role as Han Solo in the 'Star Wars' franchise.

Psycho

"Psycho," directed by Alfred Hitchcock and released in 1960, is one of the most influential films in the horror genre and a landmark in cinematic history. Based on the 1959 novel of the same name by Robert Bloch, the film's storyline, innovative cinematography, and masterful direction contributed to its fame and enduring legacy.

"Psycho" begins with Marion Crane (Janet Leigh), a secretary who embezzles $40,000 from her employer to start a new life with her boyfriend, Sam Loomis (John Gavin). On the run, she stops at the Bates Motel, where she meets the polite but peculiar Norman Bates (Anthony Perkins), who manages the motel and lives with his domineering mother. Marion's decision to stay at the Bates Motel leads to her unexpected and brutal murder in the shower, a scene that becomes the film's pivotal moment. As the investigation into Marion's disappearance unfolds, the dark secrets of Norman Bates and his "mother" are shockingly revealed, culminating in one of cinema's most unforgettable twists.

Why It Was So Famous
- The Shower Scene: Perhaps the most iconic scene in film history, Marion Crane's murder in the shower set new standards for violence and suspense in mainstream cinema. Its editing, musical score, and visual impact left an indelible mark on audiences and filmmakers alike.
- Music Score: Bernard Herrmann's score, especially the screeching violins during the shower scene, intensified the film's suspense and terror, becoming instantly recognizable and widely acclaimed.

- Twist Ending: "Psycho" was one of the first films to feature a major twist that genuinely surprised audiences, challenging narrative conventions and expectations.
- Cinematic Techniques: Hitchcock's use of innovative camera angles, lighting, and editing techniques, such as the first use of the dolly zoom effect, contributed to the film's intense psychological atmosphere.
- Promotion and Release Strategy: Hitchcock's marketing strategy, including forbidding late admissions to theaters and insisting on the secrecy of the plot, fueled public curiosity and became a major factor in the film's success.

Hidden Things and Interesting Facts

- Mother's Corpse: The corpse of Norman Bates's mother was created by combining a molded skull with a wig and applying makeup for a decomposed effect, contributing to the film's chilling climax.
- Shower Scene Complexity: The shower murder scene, lasting only a few minutes on screen, took seven days to film and included over 70 camera setups for 45 seconds of footage.
- Psychoanalysis Theme: The film delves into themes of identity, psychosis, and the Oedipal complex, with Norman Bates's split personality reflecting Hitchcock's interest in psychoanalysis.
- Based on a Real Criminal: The character of Norman Bates was loosely inspired by Ed Gein, a real-life murderer and body snatcher, which added a layer of realism to the horror.
- The First Flush: "Psycho" is credited with showing the first toilet flush in American cinema, breaking a taboo and adding to the film's daring reputation.
- Use of Chocolate Syrup: For the black-and-white film, Hitchcock used chocolate syrup as blood in the shower scene for its realistic texture and color on screen.

- Limited Budget: Despite its success, "Psycho" was shot with a modest budget, leading Hitchcock to use the crew from his TV series "Alfred Hitchcock Presents" and shoot in black and white.
- Casting Against Type: Janet Leigh, known for her roles as the wholesome and virtuous woman, was cast against type as Marion Crane, adding shock value to her character's demise.
- Multiple Endings: Hitchcock filmed several different endings to maintain secrecy and prevent leaks about the film's climax.
- Influence on the Horror Genre: "Psycho" is often cited as the precursor to the "slasher" film genre, influencing countless horror films with its blend of psychological insight and visceral terror.

"Psycho" remains a masterpiece of cinema, revered for its ability to manipulate audience emotions and its innovative contributions to the horror genre. Its legacy endures, fascinating filmmakers and audiences with its deep psychological themes, unforgettable imagery, and masterful storytelling.

Alfred Hitchcock's impact on cinema, particularly through "Psycho" and his other works, is profound and multifaceted, solidifying his reputation as a master of suspense and a pioneering filmmaker. His innovative techniques, storytelling prowess, and unique vision have influenced generations of filmmakers and reshaped the landscape of the thriller and horror genres.

- Master of Suspense: Hitchcock earned the title "Master of Suspense" through his unparalleled ability to create tension and anticipation in his films. With "Psycho," he took this to new heights, crafting scenes that left audiences on the edge of their seats, particularly through the use of unexpected plot twists and masterful pacing.

- Innovative Cinematography and Editing: Hitchcock's innovative use of camera techniques, such as the dolly zoom effect in "Vertigo" and the rapid montage editing of the shower scene in "Psycho," revolutionized cinematic storytelling. These techniques have been studied and emulated by filmmakers seeking to create their own suspenseful and visually compelling narratives.
- Psychological Depth: Hitchcock's films often explore complex psychological themes, delving into the human psyche's dark and troubled aspects. "Psycho," with its exploration of Norman Bates's split personality and its underlying psychoanalytic themes, stands as a prime example of his interest in character psychology and its impact on storytelling.
- Influence on the Horror Genre: "Psycho" is widely regarded as the precursor to the modern slasher film, introducing elements such as the killer's POV shots and the final girl trope that would become staples of the horror genre. Hitchcock's ability to evoke fear from everyday situations and his focus on psychological horror over supernatural elements influenced countless horror films that followed.
- Marketing Genius: Hitchcock's innovative marketing strategies for "Psycho," including the strict no-late-admission policy and his insistence on secrecy surrounding the plot, demonstrated his understanding of the power of suspense and anticipation not just within his films but in the promotion of them as well.

Did you know? Alfred Hitchcock's film 'Rear Window' (1954) was inspired by a real-life incident. Hitchcock based the story on a 1942 short story called 'It Had to Be Murder' by Cornell Woolrich, which was itself inspired by an actual event. Woolrich witnessed a murder from his apartment window but was unable to do anything about it, leading to the idea for the story.

- Legacy and Influence: Hitchcock's legacy extends beyond his filmography; he fundamentally altered how stories are told on screen, how audiences engage with narrative cinema, and how suspense and tension can be crafted through visual storytelling. Directors like Brian De Palma, Martin Scorsese, and David Fincher have cited him as a major influence on their work.
- Pioneering Television Work: Through his television series "Alfred Hitchcock Presents," Hitchcock brought his signature style to the small screen, making high-quality suspense stories accessible to a wider audience and demonstrating the potential of television as a medium for sophisticated storytelling.
- Cameo Appearances: Hitchcock's trademark cameo appearances in his films, including his brief appearance outside Marion Crane's office in "Psycho," added a playful element to his work and became a fun challenge for audiences to spot, contributing to his public persona as a director.

Guess the 60s Movie

A British secret agent embarks on a mission to stop a megalomaniac with a penchant for gold. Starring Sean Connery.
A) Goldfinger
B) Dr. No
C) From Russia with Love

Shipwreck survivors land on a mysterious island where giant creatures roam. Starring Michael Craig.
A) Mysterious Island
B) The Lost World
C) Journey to the Center of the Earth

A family's cross-country road trip in their new car leads to unexpected comedic mishaps. Starring Lucille Ball.
A) The Long, Long Trailer
B) Yours, Mine and Ours
C) It's a Mad, Mad, Mad, Mad World

An advertising executive is mistaken for a government agent by foreign spies and goes on the run. Starring Cary Grant.
A) North by Northwest
B) Charade
C) To Catch a Thief

A young girl's world is turned upside down when she discovers her father's affair. Starring Hayley Mills.
A) The Parent Trap
B) Pollyanna
C) The Trouble with Angels

In this musical, a Cockney flower girl is transformed into a refined lady by a phonetics professor. Starring Audrey Hepburn.
A) My Fair Lady
B) Breakfast at Tiffany's
C) Funny Face

A group of Allied POWs attempts a daring escape from a German camp during World War II. Starring Steve McQueen.
A) The Great Escape
B) The Dirty Dozen
C) Bullitt

A widowed matchmaker seeks to find a match for herself in turn-of-the-century New York. Starring Barbra Streisand.
A) Hello, Dolly!
B) Funny Girl
C) On a Clear Day You Can See Forever

Answers

Answer: A) Goldfinger
- Trivia Tidbit: "Goldfinger" introduced many iconic elements of the James Bond series, including the gadget-laden Aston Martin DB5.

Answer: A) Mysterious Island
- Trivia Tidbit: The film is noted for its special effects by Ray Harryhausen, featuring giant creatures such as bees, crabs, and birds.

Answer: A) The Long, Long Trailer
- Trivia Tidbit: Despite mixed reviews, the film was a box office success, showcasing Lucille Ball's enduring appeal.

Answer: A) North by Northwest
- Trivia Tidbit: The film is famous for its crop duster scene, which has been hailed as one of the most iconic scenes in film history.

Answer: A) The Parent Trap
- Trivia Tidbit: Hayley Mills played dual roles as twin sisters, a technical feat that impressed audiences of the time.

Answer: A) My Fair Lady
- Trivia Tidbit: "My Fair Lady" won eight Academy Awards, including Best Picture, in 1965.

Answer: A) The Great Escape
- Trivia Tidbit: Steve McQueen's motorcycle chase is one of the most memorable escape scenes in film history.

Answer: A) Hello, Dolly!
- Trivia Tidbit: The film's lavish production and memorable musical numbers were a showcase for Barbra Streisand's talents.

To Kill a Mockingbird

"To Kill a Mockingbird," directed by Robert Mulligan and released in 1962, is a monumental film in American cinema, adapted from Harper Lee's 1960 Pulitzer Prize-winning novel of the same name. The film is a profound exploration of racial injustice, morality, and the loss of innocence, set in the Depression-era South. It tells the story of Atticus Finch (Gregory Peck), a widowed lawyer in the fictional town of Maycomb, Alabama, who defends Tom Robinson (Brock Peters), a black man falsely accused of raping a white woman.

Impact and Significance:

- Gregory Peck's Performance: Gregory Peck's portrayal of Atticus Finch is iconic, embodying integrity, compassion, and moral fortitude. Peck's Finch has become a symbol of the ideal lawyer and father figure, earning him an Academy Award for Best Actor.
- Social Commentary: At a time when America was grappling with civil rights issues, "To Kill a Mockingbird" addressed the themes of racial injustice, empathy, and understanding, contributing to the national conversation about race and equality.
- Cinematographic Excellence: The film's black-and-white cinematography, by Russell Harlan, captures the era's essence and accentuates the story's themes of innocence and morality amidst societal prejudice.
- Critical and Commercial Success: The film was both a critical and commercial success, lauded for its faithful adaptation of Lee's novel, powerful performances, and its handling of delicate social issues. It won three Academy Awards, including Best Actor for Peck and Best Adapted Screenplay.

Hidden Things and Interesting Facts:

- Harper Lee's Approval: Harper Lee was highly satisfied with the film adaptation, especially praising Gregory Peck's portrayal of Atticus Finch, which she felt captured the essence of the character her father inspired.
- Mary Badham's Performance: Mary Badham, who played Scout Finch, was nominated for an Academy Award for Best Supporting Actress, making her one of the youngest actresses to be nominated for an Oscar at the time.
- Monroeville, Alabama: The fictional town of Maycomb is closely based on Harper Lee's hometown, Monroeville, Alabama. The film's set design was inspired by Lee's descriptions and her personal photographs of the town.
- Brock Peters' Testimony: The courtroom scene, particularly Brock Peters' testimony as Tom Robinson, is one of the film's most powerful moments. Peters delivered his testimony in one take, leaving the courtroom set in stunned silence before a burst of applause broke out.
- Real-life Inspiration for Atticus: Atticus Finch was inspired by Harper Lee's father, Amasa Coleman Lee, a lawyer who also represented black defendants in a racially charged Alabama.
- Introducing Robert Duvall: The film marked Robert Duvall's screen debut as Boo Radley, a reclusive neighbor. Duvall's portrayal, despite limited screen time, left a lasting impression.
- Universal Themes: Despite its setting in the 1930s South, the film's themes of justice, moral integrity, and the battle against prejudice resonate universally and timelessly.
- Legacy: "To Kill a Mockingbird" remains a staple of educational curricula, used to teach themes of racial injustice, empathy, and ethical integrity.

- AFI Recognition: The American Film Institute named Atticus Finch the greatest movie hero of the 20th century.
- Preservation: In 1995, the film was selected for preservation in the United States National Film Registry by the Library of Congress for being "culturally, historically, or aesthetically significant."
- "To Kill a Mockingbird" stands as a towering achievement in cinema, celebrated for its impact on social issues, storytelling prowess, and memorable performances. Its legacy continues to inspire and challenge viewers to confront societal injustices and to reflect on the human condition.

TV Cult Classics

The 1960s was a decade rich in television innovation, producing several series that, while not always rating juggernauts during their original broadcasts, have since attained "cult classic" status, celebrated for their pioneering concepts, memorable characters, and lasting influence on pop culture. Beyond the widely acknowledged shows like "Star Trek" and "The Twilight Zone," the 1960s birthed a collection of series that have garnered dedicated fan bases over the years, each unique in its appeal and legacy.

The Outer Limits (1963-1965)

An anthology series much like "The Twilight Zone," "The Outer Limits" focused more on science fiction and less on fantasy, featuring a wide range of aliens, monsters, and dystopian futures. Each episode began with the chilling announcement: "There is nothing wrong with your television set. Do not attempt to adjust the picture."

Dark Shadows (1966-1971)

This gothic soap opera broke new ground by integrating supernatural elements, including vampires, witches, werewolves, and ghosts, into its melodramatic storylines. It centered around the wealthy but troubled Collins family of Collinsport, Maine, and is best known for the vampire Barnabas Collins.

The Avengers (1961-1969)

Predating the Marvel superheroes of the same name, "The Avengers" was a British espionage series known for its wit, stylish 60s flair, and the chemistry between its leads, John Steed (Patrick Macnee) and Emma Peel (Diana Rigg). The show combined spy fiction with elements of science fiction and fantasy.

The Prisoner (1967-1968)

This British series starred Patrick McGoohan as a former secret agent who is abducted and held captive in a mysterious coastal village resort, where his captors attempt to find out why he abruptly resigned from his job. Known for its allegorical storytelling, the series tackled themes of individuality, freedom, and surveillance.

Lost in Space (1965-1968)

Focusing on the space-faring adventures of the Robinson family, "Lost in Space" blended science fiction with family drama and campy humor. Their mission to colonize deep space is sabotaged, leading them to navigate strange new worlds and alien civilizations.

Gilligan's Island (1964-1967)

A comedic tale of seven castaways stranded on an uncharted island, "Gilligan's Island" was initially critiqued but grew into a beloved staple of American television. The dynamic between the bumbling first mate Gilligan and the rest of the diverse group fueled the show's humor and heart.

Cult Classics Trivia Tidbits:

Influential Failures: Many cult classics were not hits during their original runs but gained popularity through syndication.

Dedicated Fandoms: These shows have inspired fan conventions, fan fiction, and academic studies, demonstrating their impact.

Innovative for Their Time: Series like "The Outer Limits" and "The Prisoner" were celebrated for pushing the boundaries of genre television, incorporating complex themes and visual effects that were ahead of their time.

Revivals and Remakes: Shows like "Dark Shadows" and "Lost in Space" have seen various adaptations and remakes, attesting to their lasting appeal.

Iconic Characters: Characters like Emma Peel and Barnabas Collins have become iconic figures in pop culture, representing the style and spirit of 60s television.

Genre Pioneers: These shows contributed to the evolution of their respective genres, setting the stage for future developments in science fiction, horror, and adventure television.

Trivia Tidbits

- "The Outer Limits" Control Voice: The iconic opening and closing narrations of "The Outer Limits" were voiced by Vic Perrin, known as the "Control Voice," setting a mysterious and authoritative tone for each episode.
- "Dark Shadows" Midday Phenomenon: Initially airing in the afternoons, "Dark Shadows" unexpectedly drew a large following of teenagers and working adults, leading to its cult status among daytime television.
- "The Avengers" Fashion Icon: Emma Peel (Diana Rigg) became a 1960s fashion icon, with her leather catsuits and mod wardrobe influencing fashion trends and symbolizing female empowerment and sophistication.
- "The Prisoner's" Number 6: Patrick McGoohan not only starred in "The Prisoner" but also created and produced the series. His character, known only as Number 6, is considered one of TV's first antiheroes.
- "Lost in Space" Robot's Line: The Robot's repeated line, "Danger, Will Robinson," became one of the most famous catchphrases in television history, despite being seldom used throughout the series.
- "Gilligan's Island" Theme Song: The show's catchy theme song, detailing the shipwreck story, is instantly recognizable and has been covered and parodied numerous times.
- "The Outer Limits" Monster of the Week: Unlike "The Twilight Zone," "The Outer Limits" often featured a "monster of the week," making groundbreaking use of makeup and special effects for television at the time.
- "Dark Shadows" Innovative Use of Color: When "Dark Shadows" began broadcasting in color in 1967, it used dramatic lighting and color effects to enhance its gothic atmosphere, a novel technique for daytime TV.

- "The Avengers" Role Reversals: The series was progressive for its time, often depicting Emma Peel in the action role while John Steed provided intelligence support, challenging traditional gender roles.
- "The Prisoner's" Rover: The mysterious security device known as "Rover," a giant white balloon, became one of the series' most iconic and enigmatic symbols.
- "Lost in Space" First Humanoid Robot on TV: The show's Robot, B-9, is credited as being one of the first depictions of a humanoid robot with a distinct personality on television.
- "Gilligan's Island" Unseen President: In one episode, the castaways receive a radio message from the President, who was implied to be Lyndon B. Johnson, adding a topical humor layer to the series.
- "The Outer Limits" Famous Directors: Several episodes were directed by future film directors, including Steven Spielberg and Robert Altman, early in their careers.
- "Dark Shadows" Live-to-Tape: The series was shot "live-to-tape," meaning editing was minimal. Mistakes, such as visible boom mics and set wobbles, were often left in, contributing to its cult charm.
- "The Avengers" Changed Leads: The series saw several lead actors before Diana Rigg, including Honor Blackman as Cathy Gale, whose departure led to the casting of Rigg as Emma Peel.
- "The Prisoner's" Final Episode Controversy: The series finale, "Fall Out," was so abstract and unresolved that it led to an uproar among fans, with Patrick McGoohan reportedly receiving death threats.
- "Lost in Space" Dr. Smith's Transformation: Dr. Zachary Smith, played by Jonathan Harris, was initially a sinister saboteur but evolved into a more comedic, cowardly character, providing comic relief.

- "Gilligan's Island" Syndication Success: Despite only three seasons on air, the show's endless syndication runs cemented its status as a cult classic, reaching generations of viewers.
- "The Outer Limits" vs. "The Twilight Zone": While often compared to "The Twilight Zone," "The Outer Limits" distinguished itself with a greater emphasis on science fiction and less on the supernatural or fantasy.
- "Dark Shadows" Barnabas Collins Phenomenon: Jonathan Frid's portrayal of Barnabas Collins, the sympathetic vampire, turned the character into a cultural icon and revitalized the show's ratings.

2001: A Space Odyssey

"2001: A Space Odyssey," directed by Stanley Kubrick and released in 1968, is a landmark in science fiction cinema, renowned for its ambitious storytelling, pioneering special effects, and profound philosophical implications. Co-written by Kubrick and science fiction author Arthur C. Clarke, the film explores themes of evolution, artificial intelligence, and humanity's place in the universe. Its narrative spans from the dawn of man to the space age, following a mysterious monolith that seems to play a key role in human evolution.

The Story:

"2001: A Space Odyssey" unfolds across four distinct yet interconnected segments, each exploring different epochs in the odyssey of human evolution, guided by the enigmatic presence of monoliths, objects of extraterrestrial origin that influence the course of human development.

The film opens with "The Dawn of Man," where a group of early hominids in the African desert encounters a black monolith. This mysterious artifact seems to impart a cognitive awakening, leading one hominid to use a bone as a tool and weapon, marking the first evolutionary leap towards humanity. This segment famously transitions from a thrown bone to a spacecraft, illustrating the leap from primitive tools to advanced technology, signifying humanity's progress.

The narrative then moves to the space age, where humanity has discovered a similar monolith buried on the Moon's surface. The segment, "TMA-1," showcases humanity's scientific achievements and curiosity. When sunlight strikes the unearthed monolith for the first time in millennia, it emits a piercing signal towards Jupiter, suggesting the next phase of humanity's evolution lies beyond Earth.

In the third segment, "Jupiter Mission," we follow the spacecraft Discovery One en route to Jupiter, five years after the lunar discovery. Aboard are two astronauts, Dave Bowman (Keir Dullea) and Frank Poole (Gary Lockwood), and three scientists in cryogenic hibernation, overseen by HAL 9000 (voiced by Douglas Rain), a highly advanced artificial intelligence responsible for operating the spacecraft. HAL is portrayed as a flawless entity, but as the mission progresses, HAL exhibits increasingly erratic and paranoid behavior, leading to a tense confrontation between man and machine. The segment explores themes of artificial intelligence, trust, and the consequences of human reliance on technology.

The final segment, "Jupiter and Beyond the Infinite," sees Bowman journeying alone to Jupiter, where he encounters another monolith orbiting the gas giant. This leads to the film's most visually abstract and interpretive sequence, the "Stargate" experience, a dazzling voyage through time and space, culminating in Bowman's transformation into the Star Child, a new phase of human evolution.

Kubrick's "2001: A Space Odyssey" is a masterpiece of visual and narrative storytelling, blending awe-inspiring visuals with deep philosophical questions about human nature, technology, and the cosmos. Its open-ended narrative and visual metaphors invite endless interpretation, making it a film that transcends its era to speak to the fundamental questions of existence and our place in the universe.

Impact and Significance:

- Visual Effects: Kubrick's use of groundbreaking visual effects set a new standard for realism in the depiction of space. The film's meticulous attention to scientific accuracy and innovative techniques, such as the rotating centrifuge to simulate artificial gravity, have been influential in the genre.
- Narrative Structure: The film's unconventional narrative structure, minimal dialogue, and reliance on visual storytelling challenge traditional cinematic storytelling, encouraging viewers to seek their own interpretations of the film's themes and symbols.
- HAL 9000: The character of HAL 9000, the sentient computer that controls the Discovery One spacecraft, became an iconic symbol of artificial intelligence and its potential dangers. HAL's calm demeanor and malevolent actions have made it one of cinema's most memorable AI characters.
- Musical Score: The use of classical music, including Richard Strauss's "Also sprach Zarathustra" and Johann Strauss II's "The Blue Danube," adds an epic and timeless quality to the film, making the music integral to its atmosphere and impact.

- Philosophical Themes: The film delves into existential and philosophical questions about humanity's origin, evolution, and destiny, using the monolith as a recurring motif that symbolizes a leap in human consciousness and capability.

Hidden Things and Interesting Facts:

Monolith Dimensions: The monolith's dimensions are in the precise ratio of 1:4:9 (the squares of the first three integers), suggesting mathematical perfection and intelligence.

Innovative Filming Techniques: Kubrick employed front projection for the Dawn of Man sequences, allowing for realistic interaction between actors and pre-filmed backgrounds of African landscapes.

No Computer Graphics: All special effects were achieved without computer graphics, using models, practical effects, and pioneering techniques that Kubrick and his team invented.

Dialogue Delay: The first line of dialogue occurs about 30 minutes into the film, and the last line is about 25 minutes before the film ends, emphasizing its visual narrative.

Artificial Gravity: The film's depiction of artificial gravity was among the first to accurately portray how it might function in a spacecraft, influencing future sci-fi media.

Kubrick's Perfectionism: Kubrick's attention to detail extended to consulting with NASA engineers and scientists to ensure the film's portrayal of space travel was as realistic as possible.

The Stargate Sequence: The psychedelic "Stargate" sequence was created using a technique called "slit-scan photography," producing a visual effect that was revolutionary for its time.

Critical Reception: Upon its release, "2001: A Space Odyssey" received mixed reviews, but its reputation grew over time, and it is now considered one of the greatest films ever made.

Cultural Impact: The film has had a profound impact on popular culture, influencing not only cinema but also television, music, and art with its themes, concepts, and visual style.

Academy Award: Kubrick won his only Oscar for the film, in the category of Best Visual Effects, acknowledging the film's groundbreaking achievements in this area.

"2001: A Space Odyssey" remains a seminal work in cinematic history, its exploration of complex themes, combined with Kubrick's visionary direction and groundbreaking effects, continue to inspire and awe audiences and filmmakers alike.

The 1970s: The Decade of Diversification in TV and Cinema

The 1970s stood as a beacon of diversification for television and cinema, breaking new ground with the emergence of genres and formats that had never been explored before. Television saw the evolution of the sitcom, with shows like "All in the Family" and "MASH" tackling social issues with humor and grace, while the birth of the TV miniseries with "Roots" offered a novel way to delve deeper into storytelling. This was also the era of blockbuster cinema, with films like "Jaws" and "Star Wars" redefining what it meant to be a hit movie, while the horror genre began to take a significant place in both the cultural zeitgeist and the industry.

Fantasy and adventure films brought new worlds to life, and the rise of Saturday morning cartoons became a cherished part of childhood for an entire generation. Meanwhile, groundbreaking TV movies brought social issues to the forefront of public consciousness, and cult films like "The Rocky Horror Picture Show" began to form fervent fan communities. The 1970s were a time of experimentation and expansion, setting new standards for what could be achieved in both television and film, and paving the way for the future of entertainment.

The Sitcom Evolution: From "All in the Family" to "MASH"

The 1970s marked a significant evolution in the American sitcom landscape, characterized by a shift towards socially relevant themes and a departure from the idealized family portrayals of previous decades. Two landmark series that epitomized this shift were "All in the Family" and "MASH," both of which challenged audiences with their groundbreaking content, blending humor with commentary on social and political issues.

All in the Family (1971-1979)

Created by Norman Lear, "All in the Family" centered around Archie Bunker (Carroll O'Connor), a working-class, staunchly conservative man with prejudiced views, living with his more understanding and compassionate wife, Edith (Jean Stapleton), in Queens, New York. The show broke new ground by tackling taboo subjects such as racism, homosexuality, women's liberation, and the Vietnam War, often through the lens of Archie's bigoted remarks and the contrasting perspectives of his liberal son-in-law, Mike Stivic (Rob Reiner), and daughter, Gloria (Sally Struthers). "All in the Family" was notable for its use of humor to address and critique social issues, making it a pivotal moment in the evolution of the sitcom genre.

- Pioneering Live Audience: "All in the Family" was one of the first sitcoms to be taped in front of a live audience, enhancing the authenticity of the laughter and reactions.
- Theme Song Sing-Along: The show's theme song, "Those Were the Days," was performed by Carroll O'Connor and Jean Stapleton themselves, setting a cozy, nostalgic tone right from the opening credits.
- Archie Bunker's Chair: Archie's iconic wingback chair became a symbol of his character. It's now housed in the Smithsonian Institution as a piece of American cultural history.
- Spin-offs Galore: The series spawned several spin-offs, including "Maude," "The Jeffersons," and "Archie Bunker's Place," expanding its universe and impact on American television.
- Addressing the Censorship: Norman Lear fought with CBS censors over the show's content, pushing the boundaries of what could be discussed on television.
- First Toilet Flush Sound: "All in the Family" featured the sound of a toilet flushing off-screen, a first for television, breaking yet another taboo.
- Edith's Character Development: Jean Stapleton's character, Edith, evolved from a seemingly naive housewife to a woman with her own opinions and convictions, showcasing Stapleton's range as an actress.
- Real Issues on Screen: The show tackled real-life issues, such as breast cancer and rape, with episodes that are remembered for their sensitive yet candid approach.
- Emmy Awards Milestone: "All in the Family" was the first series to win Emmys for all four lead actors, setting a high bar for television excellence.

- Archie Bunker's Hat: The character's trademark fedora hat was a symbol of his working-class roots and conservative worldview.
- Breaking the Fourth Wall: In several episodes, characters would directly address the audience, a technique not commonly used in sitcoms of that era.
- Viewer Discretion Advised: "All in the Family" was one of the first shows to include a viewer discretion advisory due to its content, underscoring its departure from typical sitcom fare.
- Impact on Norman Lear's Career: The success of "All in the Family" catapulted Norman Lear to fame, establishing him as a force in television who would go on to create other socially conscious programs.
- The Show's Legacy: It consistently ranks high on lists of the greatest TV shows of all time for its groundbreaking approach to comedy and social commentary.
- Preservation for Posterity: Selected episodes of "All in the Family" have been preserved in the United States Library of Congress for being "culturally, historically, or aesthetically significant."

MASH (1972-1983)

Based on the 1970 film of the same name and set during the Korean War, "MASH" followed the lives of the staff of an Army medical unit, using the setting as a backdrop for exploring the absurdities and tragedies of war. The series, created by Larry Gelbart, was distinguished by its adept blend of comedy and drama ("dramedy"), dealing with serious topics such as death, loss, and the moral dilemmas of conflict, while maintaining a sharp wit and humor. Characters like Hawkeye Pierce (Alan Alda), B.J. Hunnicutt (Mike Farrell), and Margaret Houlihan (Loretta Swit) became cultural icons, embodying the complexities of people trying to maintain their humanity in the face of war's horrors.

- Laugh Track Controversy: "MASH" used a laugh track reluctantly, at the insistence of the network. However, creator Larry Gelbart and star Alan Alda negotiated to have it removed for operating room scenes, arguing that laughter was inappropriate in such serious moments.
- Filming Location: The show was filmed at the Fox Ranch in Malibu Creek State Park, California, which stood in for the Korean landscape.
- Alan Alda's Involvement: Beyond acting, Alda directed numerous episodes and became the first person to win Emmy awards for acting, writing, and directing for the same series.
- Real Military Tactics: The show hired technical advisors from the Army to ensure the accuracy of medical procedures and military protocol.
- Character Departures: The departures of characters like Henry Blake and Trapper John were significant TV moments, marking one of the first times a main character was killed off in a series.
- "The Interview" Episode: Presented in a documentary style, this episode featured characters speaking directly to the camera, a novel technique for a sitcom at the time.
- No Traditional Pilot: The series' first episode wasn't a traditional pilot; it was assumed viewers were familiar with the characters from the film.
- Changing Cast Dynamics: The cast underwent several changes throughout its run, reflecting both the realities of war and the actors' desires for character development.
- MASH Finale Viewership: The series finale, "Goodbye, Farewell and Amen," became the most-watched television broadcast in American history at the time, a record it held for many years

- Hawkeye's Mental Health: The show addressed mental health issues head-on, with the character Hawkeye Pierce suffering from a nervous breakdown, highlighting the psychological toll of war.
- Environmental Concerns: The set was eventually demolished and the area restored to its natural state, but the site remains a popular destination for fans.

The Birth of the TV Miniseries: "Roots" and Its Impact

The TV miniseries "Roots," which debuted in 1977 on ABC, represented a transformative moment in television, dramatizing the American history of slavery in a manner never before seen on the small screen. Adapted from Alex Haley's novel "Roots: The Saga of an American Family," it traced Haley's ancestral lineage from Africa to the American South, covering several generations from the capture and enslavement of Kunta Kinte to the liberation of his descendants. Its unflinching portrayal of the brutal realities of slavery and its effects on African American families broke new ground, offering a stark counter-narrative to the sanitized versions of American history often depicted on television.

"Roots" captivated the nation, setting viewership records with its finale and igniting widespread discussions about race, heritage, and the legacy of slavery in the United States. Its historical and cultural impact was profound, driving a deeper, nationwide confrontation with the complexities of American history and racism. The miniseries not only garnered critical acclaim, securing numerous awards including nine Primetime Emmys and a Peabody, but also achieved an enduring legacy as a seminal work in American television.

The casting of "Roots" was particularly notable for its inclusion of both established and then-up-and-coming African American actors such as LeVar Burton, who played the young Kunta Kinte, along with John Amos, Louis Gossett Jr., and Cicely Tyson. This decision brought a significant depth and authenticity to the narrative, highlighting the talents of these actors in a mainstream platform that was often lacking in diversity.

Moreover, "Roots" had an educational impact that extended beyond its initial broadcast. It has been utilized in academic settings as a tool for teaching about the realities of slavery and African American history, attesting to its importance as both a cultural and educational artifact. The series also sparked a renewed interest in genealogy among Americans, inspired by Haley's journey to trace his own family's roots.

The overwhelming success of "Roots" showcased the potential of the miniseries format for telling complex and expansive stories, influencing a wave of similar projects in the years that followed. It demonstrated television's capacity not just to entertain but to enlighten, challenge, and inspire its audience, setting a new benchmark for what could be achieved in the medium. The legacy of "Roots" continues to resonate, underscoring the power of storytelling in shaping our understanding of history and each other.

- Record-Breaking Finale: The final episode of "Roots" was watched by an estimated 100 million people, making it one of the most-watched broadcasts in U.S. television history at the time.
- Pulitzer Prize Connection: Before becoming a groundbreaking TV miniseries, the source material, Alex Haley's "Roots," won the Pulitzer Prize Special Award in 1977, highlighting its significance and impact as a literary work.

- Genealogical Influence: "Roots" played a pivotal role in popularizing genealogy in the United States, inspiring countless individuals to explore and document their own family histories.
- Extensive Research: Alex Haley spent over a decade researching his family's history to write "Roots," traveling to Africa and sifting through records in the U.S. to trace his ancestry back to Kunta Kinte.
- Casting Landmark: LeVar Burton's role as Kunta Kinte was his first professional acting job, catapulting him to fame and setting the stage for a successful career in television, including his long-standing role as the host of "Reading Rainbow."
- Authenticity in Filming Locations: While much of "Roots" was filmed in the United States, significant portions were shot on location in The Gambia, West Africa, adding a layer of authenticity to the depiction of Kunta Kinte's early life.
- Emmy Recognition: With 37 Emmy nominations, "Roots" set a record for the most nominations for a single series at the time, underscoring the television industry's recognition of its quality and impact.
- Cultural Phenomenon: The airing of "Roots" became a cultural event, with schools, churches, and community groups organizing viewings and discussions to better understand the themes of the series.
- Presidential Screening: President Gerald Ford hosted a screening of "Roots" at the White House, illustrating its importance and the widespread attention it garnered.
- Educational Usage: Beyond its broadcast, "Roots" has been used extensively in educational settings to teach about slavery and African American history, often accompanied by study guides and curricula developed specifically for the series.

- **Multi-Generational Cast:** "Roots" featured actors from several generations, creating a rich tapestry of talent that spanned ages and brought depth to the portrayal of the family saga.
- **Impact on Television Formats:** The success of "Roots" proved the viability of the miniseries format as a powerful storytelling medium, leading to an increase in similar epic narrative projects on television.
- **Soundtrack Success:** The "Roots" soundtrack, composed by Quincy Jones, received acclaim for its composition and was integral to setting the emotional tone and historical context of the series.
- **Legacy and Continuation:** The enduring legacy of "Roots" led to a new adaptation in 2016, revisiting the saga for a new generation and reaffirming its relevance in contemporary discussions about race and identity.
- **Viewer Engagement:** The broadcast of "Roots" sparked a nationwide conversation about race, history, and identity, with many viewers for the first time confronting the brutal realities of slavery and its lasting effects on American society.

Did you know? LeVar Burton played the role of Lieutenant Commander Geordi La Forge in the iconic television series 'Star Trek: The Next Generation.' La Forge, who served as the chief engineer aboard the USS Enterprise, was known for his distinctive VISOR (Visual Instrument and Sensory Organ Replacement) eyepiece, which allowed him to see despite being born blind. Burton's portrayal of this character earned him widespread recognition and cemented his place in science fiction history.

Blockbuster Cinema: "Jaws" and "Star Wars"

The 1970s witnessed the birth of the blockbuster era in cinema, fundamentally altering the landscape of film production and consumption. Two films, "Jaws" (1975) directed by Steven Spielberg and "Star Wars" (1977) by George Lucas, stand as monumental pillars that not only defined this new era but also reshaped the entertainment industry. Both movies broke box office records, introduced innovative filmmaking techniques, and captured the imaginations of audiences around the world. Here is a closer look at each film's story, how they were made, and the public's reaction.

Jaws

Story & Making: "Jaws" tells the harrowing tale of a great white shark that terrorizes the small island community of Amity. The story focuses on Chief Martin Brody (Roy Scheider), marine biologist Matt Hooper (Richard Dreyfuss), and shark hunter Quint (Robert Shaw) as they set out to kill the beast. The film's production was notoriously difficult, plagued by technical issues with the mechanical sharks, which frequently malfunctioned. Spielberg's decision to suggest the shark's presence rather than show it directly for much of the film was partly due to these malfunctions. This technique, however, inadvertently heightened the suspense and fear, contributing significantly to the film's success. Shot mostly on location at Martha's Vineyard, "Jaws" faced a troubled shoot that went over budget and schedule but ultimately paid off, creating a palpable sense of realism and tension.

Upon its release, "Jaws" became an instant phenomenon, creating the summer blockbuster trend. It was the first film to surpass $100 million at the box office.

"You're gonna need a bigger boat"

to go into the water. "Jaws" not only terrified viewers but also garnered critical acclaim, winning three Academy Awards and solidifying Spielberg's reputation as a master storyteller.

- Mechanical Sharks: Nicknamed "Bruce" by the crew after Steven Spielberg's lawyer, the mechanical sharks were a source of constant frustration due to their frequent malfunctions.
- First Summer Blockbuster: "Jaws" is often credited with creating the concept of the summer blockbuster, changing how movies are released and marketed.
- Improvised Dialogue: The famous line, "You're gonna need a bigger boat," was improvised by Roy Scheider.
- John Williams' Score: The iconic two-note score by John Williams plays a crucial role in building suspense, even when the shark isn't on screen.
- The USS Indianapolis Monologue: Robert Shaw's chilling monologue about the USS Indianapolis was rewritten by Shaw himself, contributing to one of the film's most memorable scenes.
- Shooting Delays: Originally scheduled for a 55-day shoot, production extended to 159 days due to various challenges.
- Realistic Shark Attacks: Spielberg used real footage of sharks filmed by Australian divers Ron and Valerie Taylor to add realism to the underwater scenes.
- Box Office Milestone: "Jaws" was the first film to earn over $100 million in theatrical rentals, setting a new benchmark for commercial success.
- Spielberg's Absence at the Premiere: Steven Spielberg was so convinced the movie would flop that he didn't attend the premiere.
- Verna Fields' Editing: The film's editor, Verna Fields, played a crucial role in maintaining suspense and pacing, earning her an Academy Award for her work.

- No Oscar for Spielberg: Despite the film's success, Spielberg was not nominated for Best Director at the Oscars, which he found disappointing.
- Martha's Vineyard Locals: Many locals were cast as extras, and their authentic New England accents added to the film's realism.
- Life Magazine Feature: A feature in Life Magazine with photos of the mechanical shark significantly heightened public interest before the release.
- Impact on Beach Attendance: Reports suggest that "Jaws" significantly affected beach attendance in the summer of 1975, as people were afraid to go into the water.
- A Changed Spielberg: The difficulties Spielberg faced during the making of "Jaws" influenced his approach to filmmaking, making him more adaptable and resourceful in future projects.

Star Wars

Story & Making: "Star Wars," later retitled "Star Wars: Episode IV - A New Hope," revolutionized the sci-fi genre with its epic tale of good versus evil set in a galaxy far, far away. The film follows young Luke Skywalker (Mark Hamill) as he joins the Rebel Alliance to defeat the evil Empire and its fearsome leader, Darth Vader. George Lucas drew inspiration from various sources, including Flash Gordon serials and the works of Joseph Campbell. The production faced skepticism from studio executives and numerous challenges, including budget constraints and technical difficulties in creating the groundbreaking special effects. Lucas' persistence and innovation, combined with the talents of Industrial Light & Magic (ILM), led to the creation of never-before-seen visual effects that would change cinema forever.

"Star Wars" was an unprecedented success, quickly becoming a cultural phenomenon and spawning a franchise that remains beloved to this day. It broke box office records, making it the highest-grossing film of its time. The film's imaginative story, engaging characters, and pioneering effects captured the hearts of audiences worldwide, earning it seven Academy Awards. Its impact extended beyond the screen, influencing not only the film industry but also the merchandising business, setting new standards for how movies could engage with audiences and generate revenue.

- The Wampa Scene in "Empire Strikes Back": Introduced to explain Mark Hamill's facial injuries from a car accident, the Wampa attack at the beginning of "The Empire Strikes Back" was a creative solution to a real-world problem.
- Chewbacca's Inspiration: George Lucas' dog, an Alaskan Malamute named Indiana, inspired both Chewbacca's character and the name of another Lucas character, Indiana Jones.
- Budget Overruns: "Star Wars" initially had a budget of $8 million, which ballooned to $11 million by the end of production, a significant risk at the time.
- James Earl Jones' Uncredited Voice Work: James Earl Jones, who provided the iconic voice for Darth Vader, was initially uncredited in "A New Hope."
- R2-D2's Name Origin: The name "R2-D2" allegedly comes from "Reel 2, Dialog 2" during Lucas' work on "American Graffiti."
- The Millennium Falcon's Design: The ship was originally designed to look like a flying saucer, but the design was changed to its iconic shape to avoid similarity with another spacecraft in a TV show.

- Tunisia Challenges: Filming in Tunisia for the Tatooine scenes was fraught with difficulties, including a rare rainstorm that delayed production.
- Leia's Hair Inspiration: Princess Leia's iconic hairstyle was inspired by Mexican revolutionary women.
- Use of Miniatures: The groundbreaking special effects included the extensive use of miniatures and models for space battles, pioneering new techniques in visual effects.
- Alejandro Jodorowsky's Influence: Parts of the crew originally assembled for Alejandro Jodorowsky's unproduced adaptation of "Dune" were recruited for "Star Wars," bringing innovative ideas to the film.
- The Opening Crawl: The opening crawl was inspired by the Flash Gordon serials that Lucas loved as a child.
- Improvised Line: Harrison Ford's famous improvised line, "I know," in response to Leia's "I love you," in "The Empire Strikes Back" became one of the most memorable moments in the series.
- Guinness' Skepticism: Alec Guinness, who played Obi-Wan Kenobi, was skeptical of the film's success, despite his significant role.
- Oscar Wins: "Star Wars" won six competitive Oscars, showcasing its technical achievements and artistic merit.

Luke Skywalker (Mark Hamill) - "Star Wars: Episode IV - A New Hope" (1977)
- Character Representation: Luke Skywalker embodies the archetypal hero's journey, from humble beginnings on Tatooine to becoming a key figure in the fight against the Galactic Empire. He represents hope, courage, and the quest for identity and destiny.

Trivia Tidbits:
- Mark Hamill performed many of his own stunts throughout the filming of the original trilogy.
- The character's last name was originally "Starkiller" but was changed to Skywalker to better fit the character's heroic arc.

Princess Leia (Carrie Fisher) - "Star Wars: Episode IV - A New Hope" (1977)
- Character Representation: Princess Leia Organa is a symbol of leadership, resilience, and defiance against tyranny. She's a diplomat turned rebel leader who isn't afraid to stand up against the Empire.

Trivia Tidbits:
- Carrie Fisher was only 19 years old when she played Princess Leia.
- The hairstyle of Leia, known as the "Leia buns," was inspired by hairstyles worn by women of the Mexican Revolution.

Chief Martin Brody (Roy Scheider) - "Jaws" (1975)
- Character Representation: Chief Brody represents the everyman thrust into extraordinary circumstances. As the new police chief of Amity Island, his battle against the shark is not just about survival but protecting his community.

Trivia Tidbits:
- Roy Scheider was not the first choice for the role; actors including Charlton Heston were considered before him.
- Scheider improvised the famous line, "You're gonna need a bigger boat."

Quint (Robert Shaw) - "Jaws" (1975)
- Character Representation: Quint is the quintessential grizzled sea veteran with a personal vendetta against sharks. His character brings a deep knowledge of the sea and its dangers, symbolizing man's battle against nature.

Trivia Tidbits:
- Robert Shaw and Richard Dreyfuss reportedly did not get along on set, adding tension to their on-screen interactions.
- Shaw's USS Indianapolis monologue, one of the film's most memorable scenes, was largely rewritten by Shaw himself.

Han Solo (Harrison Ford) - "Star Wars: Episode IV - A New Hope" (1977)
- Character Representation: Han Solo, the charismatic smuggler with a heart of gold, represents the skeptical outsider who becomes a crucial ally in the fight for freedom. His character arc from cynicism to heroism underscores the theme of redemption.

Trivia Tidbits:
- Harrison Ford was initially brought in to read lines with other actors during casting and ended up being cast as Han Solo.
- The character's name, "Solo," fittingly reflects his lone wolf persona at the start of the saga.

Darth Vader (Voiced by James Earl Jones, physically portrayed by David Prowse) - "Star Wars: Episode IV - A New Hope" (1977)
- Character Representation: Darth Vader stands as the embodiment of fear and tyranny, the dark side of the Force, and personal downfall due to ambition. Yet, his character also represents the possibility of redemption.

Trivia Tidbits:
- The breathing sound effects of Darth Vader were created by sound designer Ben Burtt with a scuba breathing apparatus.
- James Earl Jones initially requested not to be credited for his voice work as Darth Vader, thinking his contribution was too small to warrant it.

May the Force be with you."

The monumental success of "Jaws" and "Star Wars" in the mid-to-late 1970s not only shattered box office records but also fundamentally altered the cinematic landscape, heralding the advent of the blockbuster era. "Jaws," with its thrilling narrative and innovative use of suspense, captivated audiences worldwide, instilling an enduring fear of the ocean while demonstrating the powerful effect of music and storytelling in filmmaking. Spielberg's ingenious direction and the film's commercial success effectively created the summer blockbuster phenomenon, setting a new standard for movie marketing and release strategies. Similarly, "Star Wars" unleashed a sprawling space saga that went beyond the confines of cinema to become a cultural milestone, inspiring generations with its themes of heroism, adventure, and the battle between good and evil. George Lucas's visionary storytelling and groundbreaking special effects paved the way for the future of the sci-fi genre, establishing a franchise that would become a beloved part of global pop culture.

Together, "Jaws" and "Star Wars" showcased the potential of films to captivate the public imagination, leading to a shift in Hollywood's approach to filmmaking and marketing. These films not only entertained but also created immersive worlds that fans could lose themselves in, evidenced by the enduring franchises, merchandise lines, and fan communities that continue to thrive. The innovations introduced by these movies in visual effects, sound design, and narrative scope have influenced countless filmmakers, pushing the boundaries of what is possible in cinema. Their legacy extends beyond their box office earnings, as they have become integral parts of film history, studied and admired for their contributions to the art of filmmaking. As pioneers of the blockbuster model, "Jaws" and "Star Wars" remain quintessential examples of cinema's power to unite audiences in shared experiences of awe, fear, and wonder, underscoring the timeless appeal of well-crafted storytelling and the universal language of film.

True or False
Steven Spielberg was fully confident in "Jaws" becoming a success and attended the premiere.

True or False
"Star Wars: Episode IV - A New Hope" was the original title George Lucas had for the 1977 release.

True or False
The mechanical sharks used in "Jaws" were nicknamed "Bruce" after Bruce Springsteen.

True or False
Harrison Ford was the original and only choice for the role of Han Solo in "Star Wars."

True or False
"Jaws" was the first film to earn over $100 million in theatrical rentals, setting a new benchmark for commercial success.

True or False
The character of Darth Vader was physically portrayed by James Earl Jones in "Star Wars."

True or False
The famous line, "You're gonna need a bigger boat," from "Jaws" was completely scripted and planned from the beginning.

True or False
"Star Wars" faced no significant challenges or skepticism from studio executives during its production.

True or False
The iconic score of "Jaws" consists of a complex melody that uses a wide range of musical instruments.

Answers

1. True
   The production of "Jaws" was fraught with challenges, particularly with the malfunctioning mechanical sharks, leading to significant delays.

2. False
   Correct Answer: Steven Spielberg was so concerned that "Jaws" would flop that he did not attend the premiere.

3. False
   Correct Answer: The film was simply titled "Star Wars" upon its initial release. The subtitle "Episode IV - A New Hope" was added in a subsequent re-release.

4. False
   - Correct Answer: The mechanical sharks were nicknamed "Bruce" after Spielberg's lawyer, not Bruce Springsteen.

5. False
   Correct Answer: Harrison Ford was not the first choice; he was cast as Han Solo after initially assisting with readings during the casting process.

6. True
   "Jaws" indeed set a new standard for commercial success in the film industry by being the first to surpass $100 million in theatrical rentals.

7. False
   Correct Answer: David Prowse physically portrayed Darth Vader, while James Earl Jones provided the voice.

8. False
   Correct Answer: The line "You're gonna need a bigger boat" was improvised by actor Roy Scheider.

9. False
   Correct Answer: "Star Wars" faced significant skepticism from studio executives and numerous production challenges, including budget overruns and technical difficulties.

10. False
    - Correct Answer: The iconic score of "Jaws," composed by John Williams, is famously simple, primarily using a two-note motif to sig the shark's impending presence.

Did you know? The famous line "Luke, I am your father" from the mo "Star Wars: Episode V - The Empire Strikes Back" is often misquoted actual line spoken by Darth Vader is "No, I am your father." This misquotation has become a classic example of the Mandela Effect

Guess the 70s Movie

A young man with telekinetic powers is pushed to the brink at his high school prom. Starring Sissy Spacek.
- A) Carrie
- B) The Fury
- C) Firestarter

A group of friends face life and death situations in the Vietnam War. Starring Robert De Niro.
- A) Apocalypse Now
- B) Platoon
- C) The Deer Hunter

A shark terrorizes a small island community, prompting the local sheriff to hunt it down. Starring Roy Scheider.
- A) Jaws
- B) Orca
- C) Deep Blue Sea

An archaeologist embarks on a thrilling quest to find a biblical artifact before the Nazis. Starring Harrison Ford.
- A) Raiders of the Lost Ark
- B) The Mummy
- C) King Solomon's Mines

Two musicians on the run disguise themselves as part of an all-female band. Starring Jack Lemmon and Tony Curtis.
- A) Some Like It Hot
- B) The Apartment
- C) Victor/Victoria

A taxi driver becomes disillusioned with the decay around him and plans to clean up the city. Starring Robert De Niro.
- A) Taxi Driver
- B) The French Connection
- C) Serpico

Space travelers embark on a mysterious voyage after a monolith is discovered. Starring Keir Dullea.
- A) 2001: A Space Odyssey
- B) Solaris
- C) Alien

A family moves into a house that's haunted by its previous occupants. Starring James Brolin and Margot Kidder.
- A) The Amityville Horror
- B) Poltergeist
- C) The Shining

Answers

Answer: A) Carrie
- Trivia Tidbit: "Carrie," based on Stephen King's first published novel, became a seminal horror film of the 70s, known for its shocking final scene that has been referenced and parodied in countless other films and shows.

Answer: C) The Deer Hunter
- Trivia Tidbit: "The Deer Hunter" was one of the first major films to tackle the psychological impacts of the Vietnam War on American soldiers and won the Oscar for Best Picture.

Answer: A) Jaws
- Trivia Tidbit: "Jaws" is considered the first summer blockbuster, changing how movies were distributed and marketed, and it established Steven Spielberg as a leading director in Hollywood.

Answer: A) Raiders of the Lost Ark
- Trivia Tidbit: Although "Raiders of the Lost Ark" premiered in 1981, it's heavily influenced by 1930s and 40s serials, capturing the adventurous spirit of the 70s cinema.

Answer: A) Some Like It Hot
- Trivia Tidbit: While actually released in 1959, "Some Like It Hot" carried its groundbreaking humor and social commentary into the 70s, influencing a generation of filmmakers.

Answer: A) Taxi Driver
- Trivia Tidbit: "Taxi Driver's" portrayal of urban alienation and its complex antihero were critical in defining 70s cinema, highlighting the decade's focus on gritty, character-driven narratives.

Answer: A) 2001: A Space Odyssey
- Trivia Tidbit: Stanley Kubrick's "2001: A Space Odyssey" set new standards for special effects and narrative ambition in science fiction, influencing countless future works in the genre.

Answer: A) The Amityville Horror
- Trivia Tidbit: "The Amityville Horror," based on a purportedly true story, became a cornerstone of supernatural horror in cinema, sparking discussions about haunted houses and the paranormal in the mainstream.

Did you know that "Taxi Driver," directed by Martin Scorsese and released in 1976, is a psychological thriller that follows Travis Bickle, a disturbed Vietnam War veteran who becomes a taxi driver in gritty 1970s New York City? The film's exploration of urban alienation, moral ambiguity, and existential angst made it a seminal work in American cinema, delving into themes of loneliness, violence, and the search for meaning in a society marked by decay and corruption.

Inspired by screenwriter Paul Schrader's personal experiences, the case of Arthur Bremer, the gritty backdrop of 1970s New York City, and European art cinema, "Taxi Driver" emerged as a cinematic masterpiece. Its enduring influence can be seen in subsequent works that explore similar themes of isolation, existential crisis, and societal disillusionment, cementing its place in film history as a timeless classic.

The days go on and on... they don't end. All my life needed was a sense of someplace to go. I don't believe that one should devote his life to morbid self-attention, I believe that one should become a person like other people.
- Travis Bickle

Rocky

"Rocky" (1976), directed by John G. Avildsen and written by Sylvester Stallone, who also starred in the titular role, is a quintessential American sports drama that has left an indelible mark on the cinematic world and popular culture. The film follows Rocky Balboa, an unassuming, down-on-his-luck boxer working as a debt collector in Philadelphia, who gets a shot at the world heavyweight championship against the reigning champion, Apollo Creed. Balboa's journey from obscurity to the center stage encapsulates the ultimate underdog story, resonating with themes of perseverance, determination, and the pursuit of the American Dream.

Philadelphia plays a central role in "Rocky," not just as a backdrop but as a character in its own right. The gritty streets, the iconic steps of the Philadelphia Museum of Art that Rocky ascends during his training montage, and the soul of the city itself contribute significantly to the film's atmosphere and Balboa's character development. These elements collectively portray Philadelphia as a city of resilience and hard work, mirroring Rocky's own struggle and journey towards self-realization and dignity. The film's portrayal of Philadelphia has immortalized the city in the hearts of audiences worldwide, making the Art Museum steps a pilgrimage site for fans.

The legacy of "Rocky" extends far beyond its initial release, spawning a successful franchise that includes sequels and spin-offs, such as the "Creed" series, which continues to captivate audiences with its exploration of legacy, family, and fighting spirit. Sylvester Stallone's portrayal of Rocky Balboa has become emblematic of the fighter in all of us, battling against the odds for a chance at glory and self-respect. The series has evolved with the times, introducing new characters and narratives while retaining the core themes that made the original film so impactful.

"Rocky" received critical and commercial acclaim, winning three Academy Awards, including Best Picture, and solidifying Stallone's career as both a writer and actor. The film's success lies not only in its inspirational story but also in its ability to connect with audiences on a personal level, encouraging them to root for the underdog and believe in the power of dreams. The enduring appeal of "Rocky" and its sequels underscores the timeless nature of its message and its significance as a cultural touchstone that continues to inspire generations. The franchise's ability to reinvent itself while staying true to the spirit of the original film is a testament to its lasting legacy, making "Rocky" a symbol of perseverance and the indomitable human spirit.

> "You, me, or nobody is gonna hit as hard as life. But it ain't about how hard you hit. It's about how hard you can get hit and keep moving forward; how much you can take and keep moving forward. That's how winning is done!"

- Sylvester Stallone wrote the initial script for "Rocky" in just three and a half days after being inspired by a championship match between Muhammad Ali and Chuck Wepner, which Wepner nearly won against all odds.
- Before "Rocky" became a success, Stallone was struggling financially and even had to sell his dog, Butkus, who later appeared in the film. After Stallone received his paycheck for the movie, he bought Butkus back.
- The famous training montage, including the iconic run up the Philadelphia Museum of Art steps, was filmed in a single day due to the tight budget.

- The role of Adrian, Rocky's love interest, was turned down by several actresses before Talia Shire accepted it, contributing significantly to her career's success.
- The ice skating date scene between Rocky and Adrian was originally written to have a crowd, but due to budget constraints, it was changed to feature just the couple and the rink attendant, adding to the scene's intimacy.
- The "Rocky Steps" in front of the Philadelphia Museum of Art have become an international tourist attraction, with visitors often replicating Rocky's triumphant run.
- The meatpacking plant where Rocky trains by punching slabs of beef was a real location in Philadelphia, which Stallone discovered while scouting locations.
- Carl Weathers, who played Apollo Creed, and Sylvester Stallone did most of their own stunts during the boxing scenes to make the fight as realistic as possible.
- "Rocky" was made on a modest budget of just over $1 million and went on to gross over $225 million worldwide, making it one of the most profitable films in cinema history.

The Iconic Theme Song

The iconic theme song of "Rocky," known as "Gonna Fly Now," wasn't just a musical piece; it became a symbol of aspiration and perseverance, integral to the film's identity and enduring legacy. Composed by Bill Conti, with lyrics by Carol Connors and Ayn Robbins, the song's creation was a testament to the collaborative spirit that defined the making of "Rocky."

Conti, a relatively unknown composer at the time, was brought on board to score the film due to the tight budget constraints. The filmmakers wanted a song that could encapsulate Rocky Balboa's journey and the emotional highs and lows of his training and personal struggles. "Gonna Fly Now" was crafted to serve as both a training montage and a narrative device, elevating the film's climactic moments and providing an auditory cue to Rocky's indomitable spirit.

The process of composing the song involved balancing the triumphant brass sections with the more tender, motivating moments reflected in the lyrics, which narrate the story of someone striving to rise above their challenges. Once completed, the song was paired with the now-iconic training montage, including the famous scene of Rocky running up the steps of the Philadelphia Museum of Art, cementing its place in cinematic history.

Upon its release, "Gonna Fly Now" soared to the top of the Billboard charts in 1977, becoming a motivational anthem that transcended the film. Its success mirrored that of "Rocky" itself, turning into a cultural phenomenon that continues to inspire those fighting their own battles, proving that with determination, "going the distance" is within everyone's reach. The creation of "Gonna Fly Now" wasn't just about crafting a theme song; it was about embodying the essence of "Rocky" – the belief in the power of the human spirit to overcome adversity.

Did you know? Philadelphia, often referred to as the "City of Brotherly Love," is not only the largest city in Pennsylvania but also played a crucial role in the founding of the United States? Philadelphia served as the temporary capital of the United States from 1790 to 1800, hosting important events such as the signing of the Declaration of Independence in 1776 and the drafting of the United States Constitution in 1787.

The Horror Boom: On Screen and In Culture

The 1970s and early 80s are often hailed as the era of the horror boom in both cinema and broader culture, a period marked by an unprecedented surge in horror's popularity and influence. This boom was characterized by a wave of films that not only pushed the boundaries of on-screen violence and terror but also deeply resonated with the societal anxieties of the time. The emergence of horror as a dominant genre during this period can be attributed to a combination of technological advancements in film-making, changing social norms, and the public's growing fascination with themes of fear, the supernatural, and the macabre.

Horror films of this era, such as "The Exorcist," "Halloween," and "The Texas Chain Saw Massacre," became cultural landmarks, redefining the genre with their innovative storytelling, character development, and use of suspense and special effects. These films explored complex themes such as possession, the nature of evil, and the fragility of human sanity, often reflecting the tumultuous societal climate of the 1970s, marked by political upheaval, economic uncertainty, and a general questioning of traditional values. The horror boom was not confined to the silver screen; it permeated literature, television, and even home entertainment, with novels like Stephen King's "Carrie" and "The Shining" becoming bestsellers and iconic horror-themed TV shows capturing the imagination of viewers.

The impact of the horror boom extended beyond mere entertainment, influencing fashion, music, and visual art, and sparking debates about the psychological effects of horror on audiences, the ethics of screen violence, and the role of horror in confronting or perpetuating societal fears. Horror conventions and fan clubs began to emerge, solidifying the genre's place in popular culture and establishing a dedicated fan base that thrives to this day. The period also saw the rise of horror as a serious subject of academic and critical study, with scholars examining its themes, aesthetics, and cultural significance.

The Exorcist (1973)

"The Exorcist," directed by William Friedkin, broke new ground in horror with its chilling tale of demonic possession and the subsequent exorcism of a young girl. Based on William Peter Blatty's novel, the film was notable for its stark portrayal of good versus evil, sophisticated special effects, and its profound psychological impact on audiences. It became one of the highest-grossing films of its time and sparked widespread discussions about faith, the supernatural, and the power of cinema to evoke deep emotional reactions. "The Exorcist" set a high standard for horror filmmaking and remains a touchstone of the genre, celebrated for its artistic merit and enduring ability to terrify.

> "The demon is a liar. He will lie to confuse us. But he will also mix lies with the truth to attack us."

Halloween (1978)

John Carpenter's "Halloween" introduced audiences to Michael Myers, a masked killer who stalks and murders teenagers, and launched the slasher sub-genre to mainstream success. With its simple yet effective plot, innovative use of first-person camera angles, and a haunting musical score composed by Carpenter himself, "Halloween" achieved critical and commercial success on a modest budget. The film's influence is seen in its numerous sequels, remakes, and imitators, and it is credited with establishing many of the tropes and conventions that would define slasher films. "Halloween" not only showcased the power of suspense over graphic violence but also solidified the concept of the final girl in horror cinema.

The Texas Chain Saw Massacre (1974)

Tobe Hooper's "The Texas Chain Saw Massacre" was a landmark film in horror, known for its visceral intensity and depiction of macabre violence. Drawing inspiration from real-life serial killer Ed Gein, the film tells the story of a group of friends who fall victim to a family of cannibals in rural Texas. Its raw, unflinching portrayal of violence and its ability to instill terror through suggestion rather than explicit gore revolutionized the genre. The film faced controversy and censorship due to its content but has since been recognized as a masterpiece of horror, influencing countless filmmakers and cementing its status as a cult classic.

The horror boom of the 1970s and early 80s forever changed the landscape of popular culture, demonstrating horror's ability to engage with deep-seated fears and societal issues. This era's films remain deeply embedded in the cultural psyche, continuing to inspire and terrify new generations of audiences and filmmakers alike.

Fashion and Aesthetics

The distinctive visual style of horror films from this period, including the iconic costumes and makeup of characters like Michael Myers ("Halloween") and the ghoulish aesthetic of "The

Texas Chain Saw Massacre," found their way into fashion. The punk and gothic subcultures, in particular, drew inspiration from the genre's dark themes and visual motifs, incorporating elements like black clothing, dramatic makeup, and horror-inspired accessories into their style. This blending of horror aesthetics with fashion underscored the genre's influence on personal expression and identity.

Music and Media

The impact of the horror boom was also evident in the music industry, with horror-themed rock and metal bands, such as Alice Cooper and The Misfits, gaining popularity. These artists utilized horror imagery and themes in their lyrics, album art, and stage shows, creating a cross-media synergy that further entrenched horror in the cultural zeitgeist. Additionally, the eerie and memorable scores of films like "The Exorcist" and "Halloween" became iconic in their own right, influencing the soundscapes of future horror films and even crossing over into other music genres.

Literature and Entertainment

Horror literature experienced a renaissance during this period, led by authors like Stephen King, whose novels "Carrie" and "The Shining" became bestsellers and were later adapted into successful films. This synergy between film and literature helped to elevate horror storytelling, making it a staple of mainstream entertainment. Horror also permeated television, with shows like "Dark Shadows" earlier in the decade and later "Tales from the Crypt" in the late 80s, broadening the genre's audience and proving its versatility across different media formats.

Fandom and Subculture

Perhaps one of the most significant impacts of the horror boom was the solidification of a dedicated horror fandom. This community found camaraderie in shared frights and thrills, leading to the creation of horror conventions, fan clubs, and specialized magazines. This subculture celebrated all things horror, from collecting memorabilia to engaging in cosplay, illustrating the genre's ability to create a passionate and engaged community.

Academic and Critical Recognition

Finally, the horror boom prompted a reassessment of the genre's artistic and cultural value. Once dismissed by critics, horror began to be taken seriously as a lens through which to explore societal fears, psychological themes, and philosophical questions. This period saw the emergence of academic studies devoted to horror, analyzing its impact on society and its reflection of human nature.

In sum, the horror boom of the 1970s and early 80s indelibly marked pop culture, shaping fashion, music, literature, and fostering a vibrant community of fans. Its influence persists, proving the enduring power of horror to fascinate, terrify, and provoke thought across generations.

Did you know that the concept of "creepypasta" has spawned numerous horror-themed cosplays? Creepypasta refers to short horror stories or urban legends circulated on the internet, often characterized by their eerie and unsettling themes. Portraying figures such as Slender Man, Jeff the Killer, and the Rake.

The Rise of Saturday Morning Cartoons

The 1970s marked a golden era for Saturday morning cartoons, a period that saw an unprecedented rise in animated programming targeted at children. This era was characterized by a diverse range of shows that not only entertained but also occasionally educated young viewers. The rise of Saturday morning cartoons can be attributed to several factors, including advancements in animation technology, changes in regulatory policies regarding children's programming, and a growing recognition of the lucrative market that children represented.

During this time, networks dedicated specific blocks of their weekend schedules to air cartoons, creating a weekly ritual for children across America. The content ranged from purely comedic and fantastical stories to action-adventure series and even educational programs. This period saw the emergence of iconic shows that remain beloved to this day.

1. "Schoolhouse Rock!" (1973-1985):

This series of educational shorts fused animation with catchy songs to teach children about math, grammar, history, and science. Songs like "Conjunction Junction" and "I'm Just a Bill" became memorable tools for learning, showcasing the potential of cartoons to educate as well as entertain.

2. "Super Friends" (1973-1986):

Bringing comic book heroes to the small screen, "Super Friends" featured the adventures of the Justice League, including Superman, Batman, Wonder Woman, and Aquaman, as they fought against evil forces. The show introduced many children to the world of superheroes, inspiring a love for comic book characters and stories.

3. "Fat Albert and the Cosby Kids" (1972-1985):

Created by Bill Cosby, this show was notable for its predominantly African American cast and its focus on real-life issues and moral lessons. Set in a Philadelphia neighborhood, it followed Fat Albert and his friends as they navigated the challenges of childhood and adolescence.

The success of these and other shows led to the Saturday morning cartoon block becoming a cherished institution in American culture. Networks competed for the attention of young viewers with a mix of original programming and adaptations of popular comics, books, and toys. This era also saw the introduction of stricter regulations regarding the educational content of children's programming, leading to the development of shows that sought to blend entertainment with learning opportunities.

The impact of the rise of Saturday morning cartoons extends beyond nostalgia; it influenced generations of artists, filmmakers, and storytellers who grew up watching these shows. Moreover, it established the viability of the children's television market, leading to the creation of dedicated cable networks for children's programming in the following decades. The legacy of the Saturday morning cartoon era lives on, remembered fondly by those who experienced it and celebrated for its contribution to the landscape of animated entertainment.

- Regulatory Changes: The Children's Television Act of 1990 was a direct response to the rise of Saturday morning cartoons, aimed at increasing the amount of educational programming for children. This act was influenced by the growing trend in the 70s and 80s of using cartoons for both entertainment and education.

- Voice Acting Boom: The popularity of Saturday morning cartoons led to a surge in demand for voice actors, elevating the careers of talents like Mel Blanc (known as "The Man of a Thousand Voices") and June Foray, and establishing voice acting as a key component of animated storytelling.
- First Animated Environmental Advocates: "Captain Planet and the Planeteers" (1990), though slightly after the golden era, was inspired by the eco-consciousness that began in the 70s. It was one of the first cartoons that sought to educate children about environmental issues, reflecting the era's growing concern for the planet.
- Mascot Creation: Many iconic brand mascots, such as Tony the Tiger and Toucan Sam, gained popularity through advertising during Saturday morning cartoon blocks, demonstrating the commercial influence of these programming blocks.
- The Birth of After-School Specials: The success of educational and morally driven content in Saturday morning cartoons paved the way for the creation of "After-School Specials," which tackled more serious topics relevant to young audiences.
- Animation Technology Innovations: The 70s saw significant advancements in animation technology, including the early use of computer-generated imagery (CGI). These advancements were partly driven by the demand for higher quality animations for Saturday morning cartoons.
- Theme Songs as Hit Records: Many theme songs from Saturday morning cartoons became hit records outside of the shows. For instance, the theme song for "Scooby-Doo, Where Are You!" became an iconic piece of music that transcended the show itself.

The Godfather

"The Godfather" (1972), directed by Francis Ford Coppola and based on Mario Puzo's novel of the same name, stands as a monumental film in the gangster genre and cinema at large. Starring Marlon Brando as Vito Corleone, the patriarch of the Corleone crime family, and Al Pacino as his son Michael, the film explores themes of power, family loyalty, and the American Dream corrupted by organized crime. Its narrative spans the 1940s to the 1950s, detailing the Corleone family's attempts to maintain and expand their power in a changing American landscape.

"The Godfather" has left an indelible mark on pop culture and the film industry, redefining the gangster genre with its complex characters, moral ambiguity, and intricate storytelling. The film's impact extends beyond its cinematic achievements, infiltrating various aspects of culture and language with iconic lines such as "I'm gonna make him an offer he can't refuse." It has influenced countless films, television shows, and books, setting a high standard for storytelling in cinema.

The film's portrayal of the Mafia was groundbreaking at its time, offering a nuanced view of organized crime not as a mere backdrop for violence, but as a complex institution with its own codes and loyalties. It humanized its characters, presenting them as multifaceted individuals caught between tradition and ambition, which resonated with audiences worldwide.

This approach contributed to a deeper, more sophisticated understanding of the Mafia in popular culture, moving away from stereotypes to explore the psychological and cultural complexities of the criminal underworld.

"The Godfather" also mirrored contemporary societal tensions, reflecting the struggle between old-world values and modern capitalism, the corruption of the American Dream, and the assimilation challenges faced by immigrants. Its release during a time of significant social change in the United States, amid the Vietnam War and civil rights movement, added layers of meaning to its narrative, resonating with audiences grappling with issues of power, loyalty, and morality.

"I'm gonna make him an offer he can't refuse."

The film's influence on the gangster genre and broader filmmaking is profound. It inspired a surge in crime family dramas, both in film and television, such as "Goodfellas," "The Sopranos," and even elements of "Breaking Bad." Its narrative techniques, character development, and thematic depth have become benchmarks for storytelling, influencing generations of filmmakers and writers. "The Godfather" trilogy itself, particularly the first two films, is often cited among the greatest films in world cinema, celebrated for their artistry, depth, and influence.

"The Godfather's" legacy is a testament to its enduring appeal and significance in film history. Its exploration of power, family, and the complexities of the human condition continues to captivate and provoke thought among audiences, securing its place as a cultural cornerstone and a masterclass in cinematic storytelling.

Did You Know? Francis Ford Coppola's heritage is a fascinating blend of Italian and Irish ancestry. On his paternal side, Coppola's grandfather, Francesco Pennino, immigrated to the United States from Italy, representing the Italian branch of his family tree. Meanwhile, on his paternal grandmother's side, Italia Pennino, who bore the maiden name Whalen, hailed from an Irish background.

"The Godfather" masterfully interweaves key themes of power, family loyalty, and the tarnished American Dream through its rich narrative and complex character dynamics, embedding itself in the cultural consciousness as a profound exploration of the human condition within the framework of organized crime.

Power and Authority: At the heart of "The Godfather" is the theme of power—its acquisition, exercise, and consequences. The film delves into the mechanisms of power within the Corleone family and the broader Mafia world, showcasing how authority is negotiated and maintained. Vito Corleone's reign is marked by a strategic blend of benevolence and ruthlessness, an approach that earns him respect and loyalty but also engenders conflict. His son Michael's transformation from a reluctant outsider to a commanding don illustrates the seductive and corrupting nature of power, highlighting the moral compromises required to wield it effectively. This transition is symbolized in the film's iconic closing scene, where the door closes on Kay Adams (Diane Keaton), Michael's wife, physically and metaphorically shutting her out from the machinations of power that now define Michael's existence.

Family and Loyalty: The Corleone family saga foregrounds the theme of loyalty, with familial bonds serving both as a source of strength and a cause of turmoil. The film portrays the Mafia not merely as a criminal enterprise but as a complex social system where personal and familial loyalties intersect with business interests. The tension between personal desires and family obligations is a recurrent motif, exemplified by Michael's initial resistance to and eventual acceptance of his role within the family business. The dichotomy between the public and private faces of the Corleone family exposes the challenges of navigating loyalty in a world where personal and professional spheres are inextricably linked.

The American Dream: "The Godfather" presents a nuanced critique of the American Dream, exploring how the pursuit of success and prosperity can be tainted by ambition and moral decay. The Corleones, like many immigrant families, seek to secure their piece of the American Dream, albeit through illicit means. Their story reflects the dark underbelly of the pursuit of happiness, suggesting that the dream is often built on exploitation and violence. The film's portrayal of the Corleone family's rise to power serves as a metaphor for the complexities of American capitalism, where success is frequently intertwined with corruption.

Trivia Tidbits

- Marlon Brando's Makeup Test: For his role as Vito Corleone, Marlon Brando stuffed cotton balls in his cheeks during his audition to achieve the character's distinctive jowly appearance. This makeshift approach was refined by the makeup team for the final film.
- The Horse Head Was Real: The infamous horse head scene used a real horse's head obtained from a dog food company. This shocking choice added to the scene's realism and horror.
- Coppola's Directorial Struggle: Francis Ford Coppola faced significant pressure and was nearly fired multiple times during production due to disagreements with the studio over casting and the film's direction.
- Nino Rota's Score Controversy: Nino Rota's original score for "The Godfather" was disqualified from an Oscar nomination after it was revealed that he reused his own composition from a previous film.

- Improvised Orange Prophecy: The use of oranges in scenes preceding acts of violence was not originally scripted. Coppola added this motif during filming as an ominous sign of impending danger.
- Al Pacino's Casting Battles: Studio executives were opposed to casting Al Pacino as Michael Corleone, preferring more established actors. Coppola fought hard for Pacino, believing he embodied the character's quiet intensity.
- The Godfather's Cat: The cat held by Marlon Brando in the opening scene was a stray that Coppola found on the studio lot. Its purring was so loud that some of Brando's lines had to be overdubbed.
- Multiple Languages: To maintain authenticity, parts of "The Godfather" were filmed in Sicilian and Italian. This choice added depth to the film's portrayal of its characters' cultural backgrounds.
- The Godfather Effect on Mafia Terminology: Terms like "consigliere," "caporegime," and "the Don" entered popular usage in part due to the film's influence, shaping the public's perception of the Mafia.
- Talia Shire's Casting: Francis Ford Coppola's sister, Talia Shire, who played Connie Corleone, initially auditioned for the role of Michael Corleone's wife, Kay Adams, but was cast as the Corleone sister instead. Her performance earned her an Academy Award nomination for Best Supporting Actress.

Did you know? that the word "Mafia" originated from Sicilian slang? The term "Mafia" is believed to derive from the Sicilian adjective "mafiusu," which means "bold" or "swaggering." Over time, "Mafia" evolved to denote a secret criminal organization involved in various illegal activities, particularly in Sicily and later in the United States and other parts of the world. This linguistic connection highlights the historical roots of the Mafia and its significance in Sicilian culture and beyond.

Grease

"Grease" (1978) is a beloved musical romantic comedy that captures the essence of the 1950s American high school experience through the lens of song, dance, and teenage romance. Directed by Randal Kleiser and based on the 1971 musical of the same name by Jim Jacobs and Warren Casey, the film stars John Travolta as Danny Zuko and Olivia Newton-John as Sandy Olsson.

The story revolves around the summer romance between Danny, a leather-jacket-clad leader of the T-Birds gang, and Sandy, the sweet and innocent new girl in town. Their love is tested when they unexpectedly reunite at Rydell High School, where peer pressure and social norms challenge their relationship.

The film is renowned for its catchy and iconic soundtrack, which played a significant role in its success, blending rock 'n' roll with doo-wop and pop to create memorable musical numbers that have stood the test of time. Here is a list of some of the standout songs from "Grease":

"Grease" (Theme) – Performed by Frankie Valli
"Summer Nights" – Performed by John Travolta, Olivia Newton-John, and Cast
"Hopelessly Devoted to You" – Performed by Olivia Newton-John
"You're the One That I Want" – Performed by John Travolta and Olivia Newton-John
"Sandy" – Performed by John Travolta
"Beauty School Dropout" – Performed by Frankie Avalon
"Look at Me, I'm Sandra Dee" – Performed by Stockard Channing
"Greased Lightnin'" – Performed by John Travolta and Cast
"It's Raining on Prom Night" – Performed by Cindy Bullens

"Born to Hand Jive" – Performed by Sha-Na-Na
"There Are Worse Things I Could Do" – Performed by Stockard Channing
"We Go Together" – Performed by John Travolta, Olivia Newton-John, and Cast

"Summer Nights" – Performed by John Travolta, Olivia Newton-John, and Cast
- Scene: This song is performed when Danny and Sandy, along with their friends, recount their summer romance from their own perspectives. The number is set in the schoolyard and cafeteria of Rydell High, showcasing the contrasting worlds of the T-Birds and Pink Ladies, as well as the innocent love between Danny and Sandy. It's a lively and engaging scene that introduces the central conflict of their relationship: the difference between their summer selves and school-year identities.

"You're the One That I Want" – Performed by John Travolta and Olivia Newton-John
- Scene: This iconic song marks the climax of the film, set at the carnival that celebrates the end of the school year. Sandy undergoes a transformation, adopting a more rebellious look to win Danny's heart, while Danny reveals he has lettered in track to impress her. The song and dance number, full of energy and flirtation, symbolizes their mutual acceptance and the resolution of their differences, culminating in a joyous reunion.

Did you know? Actor John Travolta is a prominent member of the Church of Scientology, a religion founded by L. Ron Hubbard in the 1950s. Travolta has been open about his beliefs in Scientology and has credited the religion with helping him in his personal and professional life.

"Greased Lightnin'" – Performed by John Travolta and Cast
- Scene: Set in the auto shop at Rydell High, this song features Danny and the T-Birds fantasizing about restoring an old car (the Greased Lightnin') into a dream racing machine. The scene is known for its dynamic choreography, energetic performance by Travolta, and the transformation of the mundane into the magical. It reflects the themes of aspiration and camaraderie that run through the film, highlighting the youthful optimism and the culture surrounding American cars and teenage dreams in the 1950s.

Which song does Sandy sing to express her feelings for Danny?
- A) "Hopelessly Devoted to You"
- B) "Summer Nights"
- C) "You're the One That I Want"

What event brings Danny and Sandy back together towards the end of "Grease"?
- A) A basketball game
- B) A school dance
- C) A carnival

What is the name of the gang that Danny is a part of?
- A) The T-Birds
- B) The Scorpions
- C) The Pink Ladies

Who performs the song "Beauty School Dropout"?
- A) John Travolta
- B) Frankie Avalon
- C) Stockard Channing

What does Danny try to win to impress Sandy?
- A) A dance contest
- B) A car race
- C) A track and field medal

Where does the iconic "You're the One That I Want" scene take place?
- A) At the beach
- B) In the gym
- C) At the carnival

A) "Hopelessly Devoted to You"
- Sandy sings "Hopelessly Devoted to You" as she ponders her feelings for Danny, showcasing her emotional struggle and deep affection for him despite their differences.

C) A carnival
- The carnival at the end of the school year serves as the backdrop for Danny and Sandy's reunion, where they both make significant gestures to show their commitment to each other.

A) The T-Birds
- Danny is the leader of the T-Birds, a group of leather-jacket-wearing, car-loving boys at Rydell High, representing the quintessential high school clique of the era.

B) Frankie Avalon
- Frankie Avalon appears in a dream sequence to perform "Beauty School Dropout," offering advice to Frenchy about her future after dropping out of beauty school.

C) A track and field medal
- In an effort to impress Sandy and prove he can be more than just a gang leader, Danny earns a letterman's sweater by competing in track and field.

C) At the carnival
- The "You're the One That I Want" scene, symbolizing the resolution of Danny and Sandy's love story, is memorably set at the school carnival, highlighting their newfound understanding and acceptance of each other.

The 1980s: The Explosion of Pop Culture in TV and Cinema

The 1980s were characterized by an explosion of pop culture that resonated through television and cinema, making it a decade of iconic characters, unforgettable narratives, and technological advancements.

The era witnessed a sitcom renaissance with classics such as "Cheers" and "The Cosby Show" dominating the small screen, while MTV revolutionized the music industry and how music was consumed, intertwining with TV like never before. The teen movie explosion, led by John Hughes and the Brat Pack, captured the essence of adolescence, and the golden age of action heroes brought larger-than-life characters to the forefront.

Sci-fi and fantasy genres saw significant milestones with films like "E.T." and "Back to the Future," captivating audiences with their imaginative storytelling and special effects. Meanwhile, the landscape of television drama evolved with soap operas and prime-time dramas like "Dallas" and "Dynasty" captivating millions of viewers with their intricate plots and memorable characters. The 1980s were not just about entertainment; they were about setting new cultural trends, pushing the boundaries of technology in filmmaking, and laying the groundwork for the future of digital effects in cinema.

Cheers (1982-1993)

Set in a Boston bar where "everybody knows your name," "Cheers" was initially met with poor ratings and faced early cancellation. However, its focus on the lives of the bar's staff and patrons, each with their unique backstories and personalities, soon captured the hearts of viewers. The show became a staple of American television, celebrated for its witty dialogue, warm humor, and the chemistry among its ensemble cast. "Cheers" explored themes of friendship, love, and the everyday struggles of its characters, making it relatable to a broad audience.

The reaction to "Cheers" was overwhelmingly positive as it grew in popularity, securing its place as one of the most beloved sitcoms in television history. The series garnered numerous awards, including multiple Emmys, and is credited with redefining the sitcom landscape of the 1980s. Its success paved the way for numerous other character-driven comedies and proved the viability of shows centered around a close-knit community.

- Original Concept Evolution: Initially, "Cheers" creators Glen and Les Charles and James Burrows envisioned the show set in a hotel, but they eventually settled on a bar in Boston to create a more intimate, communal atmosphere.
- The Theme Song's Popularity: The show's theme song, "Where Everybody Knows Your Name," performed by Gary Portnoy, became almost as beloved as the show itself, embodying the sense of belonging and community that defined "Cheers."
- Ted Danson's Bartending Training: Ted Danson, who played Sam Malone, underwent training as a bartender to lend authenticity to his role, despite his character being a recovering alcoholic and former baseball player.

- Live Studio Audience: "Cheers" was filmed in front of a live studio audience, contributing to the genuine reactions and timing of the comedy. The laughter and energy of the audience played a key role in the show's dynamic.
- Norm's Ever-Changing Job: George Wendt's character, Norm Peterson, was known for frequently changing jobs throughout the series, a running joke that mirrored the character's lack of direction but beloved status in the bar.
- Celebrity Guest Appearances: Over its run, "Cheers" featured numerous guest appearances by celebrities playing themselves, including sports figures like Kevin McHale of the Boston Celtics, showcasing the bar as a nexus of Boston's social life.

The Cosby Show (1984-1992)

"The Cosby Show" portrayed the life of the Huxtables, an upper-middle-class African American family living in Brooklyn, New York. Breaking away from the stereotypes typically portrayed in television at the time, the show focused on the family's everyday experiences, emphasizing education, parenting, and love. Bill Cosby's portrayal of Cliff Huxtable, alongside an exceptional cast, resonated with audiences, offering both humor and heartfelt moments.

The show's reception was phenomenal, quickly becoming the number one show in America for several years and revitalizing the sitcom genre.

It played a crucial role in addressing and changing racial perceptions in the United States, showcasing an African American family that was both successful and relatable. "The Cosby Show" was praised for its positive representation of African American culture and its impact on family-oriented television programming.

- Based on Cosby's Stand-Up: Many of the show's themes and episodes were inspired by Bill Cosby's own life and stand-up comedy routines, particularly those related to family life and parenting.
- Impact on Fashion: The show had a notable impact on fashion, particularly with Bill Cosby's iconic sweaters, known as "Cosby sweaters," which became a fashion trend in their own right.
- Introduction of a Future Star: Raven-Symoné, who played Olivia Kendall, started her career on "The Cosby Show," showcasing her talent at a very young age and setting the stage for her future success in the entertainment industry.
- Educational Storylines: "The Cosby Show" often incorporated educational storylines, including episodes about the importance of attending college, which was emphasized through the Huxtable children's aspirations and achievements.
- Historic Musical Guests: The series featured several musical guests and references to jazz and classical music, reflecting Cosby's personal interest in music and its role in African American culture.

Legacy

Bill Cosby's legacy, particularly through "The Cosby Show," is complex and deeply marred by his criminal activities and subsequent convictions related to sexual assault. Initially celebrated as a pioneer who transformed the television landscape and challenged racial stereotypes, Cosby's public persona as a beloved father figure and moral educator has been irrevocably tarnished. While "The Cosby Show" remains an important part of television history for its cultural impact and the barriers it broke down, the revelations about Cosby's personal misconduct have prompted a reevaluation of his legacy and contributions. Discussions around the show and Cosby's place in entertainment history now navigate the challenging waters of separating the artist's contributions from their personal actions.

This dichotomy represents a broader conversation within the entertainment industry and society about accountability, the legacy of influential figures, and how to reconcile an individual's creative output with their personal failings.

Music Television: MTV Changes the Game

Launched on August 1, 1981, Music Television, better known as MTV, revolutionized not only the music industry but also television broadcasting, setting a new paradigm for music consumption and entertainment. Its inception marked the beginning of a new era where music was not just to be listened to but watched, giving rise to the music video as a crucial element of an artist's promotional toolkit and creative expression.

MTV's impact was immediate and far-reaching. By offering a platform for continuous music video broadcasts, it provided artists with a powerful new medium to reach audiences, transforming the way music was marketed and significantly influencing popular culture.

MTV became synonymous with youth culture, shaping fashion trends, dance moves, and even vernacular. It was instrumental in catapulting artists like Madonna, Michael Jackson, and Duran Duran into global superstardom, with their innovative videos defining the visual language of music in the 1980s.

The channel also played a pivotal role in the crossover success of genres such as rap and heavy metal, which had previously received limited exposure on mainstream radio. Acts like Run-D.M.C. and Metallica found a vast audience through MTV, underscoring the channel's ability to diversify musical tastes and break new ground in music appreciation.

However, MTV's journey was not without controversy. Criticism over the lack of diversity in the artists featured during its early years led to significant changes in programming, ultimately embracing a broader spectrum of musical genres and artists. The introduction of shows like "Yo! MTV Raps" and "MTV Unplugged" highlighted the channel's adaptability and its commitment to showcasing a wide array of musical talents and styles.

As MTV evolved, it expanded its programming beyond music videos to include reality TV shows, documentaries, and other content, but its legacy as the pioneer of music television remains undisputed. MTV not only changed the game for the music industry but also left an indelible mark on television production and pop culture, establishing the music video as an art form in its own right.

MTV Trivia Tidbits

- The first music video aired on MTV was "Video Killed the Radio Star" by The Buggles.
- MTV's original five VJs (Video Jockeys) were Nina Blackwood, Mark Goodman, Alan Hunter, J.J. Jackson, and Martha Quinn.
- Michael Jackson's "Thriller" was the first world premiere video aired on MTV in December 1983.

- Madonna's performance of "Like a Virgin" at the first MTV Video Music Awards in 1984 became one of the most iconic moments in the channel's history.
- MTV launched the "I Want My MTV" ad campaign, featuring famous musicians demanding their MTV, which significantly boosted the network's popularity and subscription rates.
- "Yo! MTV Raps" premiered in 1988, dramatically increasing the visibility of hip-hop music and culture.
- "MTV Unplugged," showcasing artists performing acoustic sets, debuted in 1989, offering a new way to experience live music.
- MTV introduced the world to reality television with "The Real World" in 1992.
- "Beavis and Butt-head," which premiered in 1993, became one of MTV's most popular and controversial shows.
- In 1998, MTV launched "Total Request Live" (TRL), a daily live music video countdown show that became a cultural phenomenon.
- The MTV Moonman trophy was awarded to winners at the MTV Video Music Awards, becoming an iconic symbol of the channel.
- MTV was initially available to just 2 million subscribers in parts of New Jersey.
- The network faced criticism for not playing enough videos by African American artists in its early years, leading to more inclusive programming.
- In 2005, MTV was broadcasted for the first time in Africa, highlighting its expansion as a global network.

True or False Questions

1. MTV was originally conceived as a channel exclusively for classical music videos before pivoting.
True or False

2. "Thriller" by Michael Jackson was the first music video ever aired on MTV.
- True or False

3. "Yo! MTV Raps" was instrumental in bringing hip-hop music into mainstream American homes and is credited with helping to launch the careers of artists like Tupac Shakur and Notorious B.I.G.
- True or False

4. MTV's first reality TV show, "The Real World," was initially intended to be a documentary series about the music industry.
- True or False

5. The MTV Video Music Awards (VMAs) were first held in the 1990s, introducing the iconic Moonman trophy.
- True or False

Did you know? Michael Jackson's "Thriller" music video, released in 1983, is widely regarded as one of the most iconic and influential music videos in history. Directed by John Landis, the 14-minute video is renowned for its groundbreaking special effects, elaborate choreography, and cinematic storytelling.

Featuring a memorable narrative that combines horror elements with Jackson's signature dance moves, "Thriller" became a cultural phenomenon upon its release. It revolutionized the music video industry, setting new standards for creativity and production value. Michael Jackson's portrayal as a dancing zombie alongside the iconic "Thriller" dance sequence solidified his status as the "King of Pop" and cemented the song's legacy as one of the greatest pop music achievements of all time.

Answers

1. MTV was originally conceived as a channel exclusively for classical music videos before pivoting to a broader range of genres.
   - False
   - Trivia Tidbit: MTV was always intended to focus on pop and rock music to attract a young audience.

2. "Thriller" by Michael Jackson was the first music video ever aired on MTV.
   - False
   - Correct Answer: The first music video aired on MTV was "Video Killed the Radio Star" by The Buggles.

3. "Yo! MTV Raps" was instrumental in bringing hip-hop music into mainstream American homes and is credited with helping to launch the careers of artists like Tupac Shakur and Notorious B.I.G.
   - True
   - Trivia Tidbit: "Yo! MTV Raps" played a crucial role in the global spread of hip-hop culture, featuring interviews and performances that highlighted emerging and established hip-hop artists.

4. MTV's first reality TV show, "The Real World," was initially intended to be a documentary series about the music industry.
   - False
   - Correct Answer: "The Real World" was designed as an innovative reality show that put diverse strangers together in a house, focusing on their interactions and the resulting dynamics, rather than on the music industry.

5. The MTV Video Music Awards (VMAs) were first held in the 1990s, introducing the iconic Moonman trophy.
   - False
   - Correct Answer: The first MTV Video Music Awards were held in 1984, becoming an annual celebration of the best in music videos and introducing the Moonman trophy from the start.

The Teen Movie Explosion: John Hughes and the Brat Pack

The 1980s heralded a seismic shift in the landscape of teen cinema, largely due to the seminal work of John Hughes and the iconic ensemble known colloquially as the Brat Pack. This era witnessed the teen movie explosion, a period where films about the adolescent experience resonated deeply with audiences, blending humor, angst, and a candid exploration of youth. John Hughes, in particular, became synonymous with this movement, crafting narratives that spoke directly to teenagers' hearts and minds, while the Brat Pack—a group of young actors who frequently appeared together in these films—became the defining faces of a generation.

John Hughes' films, such as "The Breakfast Club," "Sixteen Candles," and "Ferris Bueller's Day Off," delved into the complexities of teenage life with a rare authenticity and sensitivity. His characters were multifaceted individuals navigating the trials and tribulations of high school, family dynamics, and self-discovery.

Hughes had an unparalleled ability to mix comedy with poignant moments, creating films that were as thought-provoking as they were entertaining. He painted a portrait of teenage life that was both specific in its '80s context and timeless in its emotional truths.

The Brat Pack, including actors like Molly Ringwald, Emilio Estevez, Anthony Michael Hall, Judd Nelson, Ally Sheedy, and Rob Lowe, among others, became emblematic of '80s youth culture. Their performances in Hughes' films and other teen movies of the time, such as "St. Elmo's Fire," showcased a wide range of teenage experiences and emotions, from the angst of feeling misunderstood to the joy of finding one's identity and community. The chemistry and dynamic between these actors lent an authenticity to their portrayals, making the films they starred in resonate with audiences both during the 1980s and in the decades since.

The impact of John Hughes and the Brat Pack on the teen movie genre cannot be overstated. They shifted the cultural perception of teen movies from being mere entertainment to being seen as significant narratives that could artfully address the complexities of growing up. This period also saw the emergence of the soundtrack as an essential element of the teen movie experience, with music often playing a pivotal role in conveying the film's themes and emotions.

The legacy of the teen movie explosion of the 1980s, led by Hughes and the Brat Pack, continues to influence filmmakers and audiences. These films remain a beloved part of popular culture, celebrated for their heartfelt storytelling, character development, and depiction of the universal journey of adolescence. They paved the way for future generations of teen films and solidified the teen movie as a crucial and respected genre in cinema.

The Breakfast Club (1985)

Directed by John Hughes, "The Breakfast Club" is a seminal teen drama that brings together five high school students from different social circles to serve detention on a Saturday. Throughout the day, the group, which includes the brain (Anthony Michael Hall), the athlete (Emilio Estevez), the basket case (Ally Sheedy), the princess (Molly Ringwald), and the criminal (Judd Nelson), share their stories and discover they have more in common than they thought.

Casting What-Ifs: Originally, John Hughes considered casting other actors for the roles, including John Cusack for Bender and Robin Wright for Claire.

Improvised Scenes: Much of the dialogue was improvised, including the scene where the characters sit in a circle, revealing their deepest secrets.

Iconic Soundtrack: The film's theme song, "Don't You (Forget About Me)" by Simple Minds, wasn't the band's first choice to perform but ended up becoming a defining anthem of the '80s.

Single Setting: Almost the entire film takes place in the Shermer High School library, emphasizing the characters' interactions and dialogues.

Sixteen Candles (1984)

"Sixteen Candles" is a coming-of-age comedy that follows high school sophomore Samantha "Sam" Baker, played by Molly Ringwald, as she navigates the chaos surrounding her sixteenth birthday. The film opens with Sam's family forgetting her birthday amidst the preparations for her older sister's wedding the next day. This oversight leaves Sam feeling overlooked and insignificant, especially as she harbors a crush on the popular senior, Jake Ryan, portrayed by Michael Schoeffling.

As Sam navigates the ups and downs of her day, she encounters a series of mishaps and misadventures, from embarrassing encounters with her eccentric grandparents to enduring the relentless teasing of her family. Meanwhile, she pines for Jake, hoping he'll notice her amidst the chaos of the wedding festivities. Along the way, Sam finds unexpected companionship with the quirky and endearing freshman, Ted, played by Anthony Michael Hall.

The film beautifully captures the angst and awkwardness of teenage life, portraying Sam's journey of self-discovery and longing for acceptance.

Viggo Mortensen Auditioned: Viggo Mortensen auditioned for the role of Jake Ryan, and Molly Ringwald preferred him, but Michael Schoeffling got the part.
Molly Ringwald's Breakout: "Sixteen Candles" was Molly Ringwald's breakout role, establishing her as a muse for John Hughes and an '80s teen icon.
Real-Life Inspiration: Hughes wrote the script in just one weekend, inspired by a headshot of Molly Ringwald he had on his desk.
Cultural Impact: The film's portrayal of Asian character Long Duk Dong has been criticized for perpetuating stereotypes, sparking discussions on racial representation in media.
Improvised Moments: The scene where Anthony Michael Hall's character is drunk and talking to Jake was largely improvised.
The Cake Scene: The iconic birthday cake scene at the end of the film was shot in the middle of the night, adding to the intimacy and spontaneity of the moment.

Ferris Bueller's Day Off (1986)

In "Ferris Bueller's Day Off," charismatic high schooler Ferris Bueller (Matthew Broderick) decides to take a day off from school and embark on an adventure through Chicago with his girlfriend Sloane (Mia Sara) and best friend Cameron (Alan Ruck), all while avoiding his suspicious principal and unsympathetic sister.

> "Life moves pretty fast. You don't stop and look around once in a while, you could miss it."

Save Ferris: The "Save Ferris" campaign seen in the film sparked real-life imitations, becoming a cultural phenomenon.
Cameron's House: The modernist house belonging to Cameron's family is a real house located in Highland Park, Illinois, known as the Ben Rose House.
Broderick and Hughes Collaboration: Matthew Broderick was John Hughes' first and only choice for the role of Ferris Bueller.
Improvised Parade Scene: Matthew Broderick improvised some of his dance moves during the parade scene, including the famous twist and shout performance.
Ferrari Replica: The Ferrari used in the film was a replica, as using a real Ferrari for the stunts would have been too expensive.
The Museum Scene: The Art Institute of Chicago scene was Hughes' personal favorite, showcasing his appreciation for art and its impact on the characters.

> *"You're still here? It's over. Go home."*

This direct address to the audience adds to the film's playful and irreverent tone, as Ferris acknowledges that the movie has come to an end while cheekily urging viewers to move on with their lives.

The Golden Age of Action Heroes

The 1980s are often celebrated as the Golden Age of Action Heroes, a time when cinema was dominated by larger-than-life characters and the actors who portrayed them became icons of the genre. This era saw the rise of films that were characterized by high-octane action sequences, straightforward narratives of good versus evil, and a clear focus on the physical prowess and charisma of their leads. The period was marked by a surge in blockbuster hits that brought audiences flocking to theaters for their fix of adrenaline-pumping entertainment.

Key Figures and Films

Sylvester Stallone emerged as one of the quintessential action stars of the decade, particularly through his roles in the "Rocky" and "Rambo" series. These characters—Rocky Balboa, the underdog boxer, and John Rambo, the troubled Vietnam War veteran—became cultural symbols of resilience and American heroism. Stallone's physical dedication to the roles and the emotional depth he brought to these characters elevated them beyond mere action heroes.

- Rocky Script: Sylvester Stallone wrote the script for "Rocky" in just three and a half days, inspired after watching the Chuck Wepner vs. Muhammad Ali fight.
- Personal Investment: Stallone insisted on playing Rocky himself, despite offers to buy the script without him. This decision was a gamble that ultimately paid off, catapulting him to fame.
- Rambo's Bandana: The red bandana worn by John Rambo became an iconic symbol of the character and has been part of military and pop culture ever since.
- Physical Transformation: For "Rocky III," Stallone underwent a rigorous training regimen with former Mr. Olympia, Franco Columbu, dramatically altering his physique.
- "Rocky" Steps: The sequence of Rocky running up the steps of the Philadelphia Museum of Art has become one of the most iconic scenes in film history, inspiring countless recreations.
- On-Set Injury: While filming "Rocky IV," Stallone was hospitalized after a punch from Dolph Lundgren (Ivan Drago) caused his heart to swell.
- Voice of an Era: Stallone's portrayal of Rambo and Rocky has made him a symbol of American resilience, with both characters being cited in political speeches and cultural discussions.

- Cameo in "Staying Alive": Stallone directed "Staying Alive," the sequel to "Saturday Night Fever," and made a brief cameo appearance in it.
- Real Boxer Inspiration: Rocky Balboa was partially inspired by real-life boxer Rocky Marciano, known for his relentless fighting style.
- Alternative Ending for "Rambo: First Blood": The original ending had Rambo dying, which was changed to allow for future sequels.

Arnold Schwarzenegger's rise to fame was meteoric, with roles in "The Terminator," "Predator," and "Commando" cementing his status as an action superstar. Schwarzenegger's imposing physique, combined with his ability to deliver memorable one-liners amidst explosive action scenes, made his films must-see cinema.
"The Terminator" franchise, in particular, showcased Schwarzenegger's unique presence, blending science fiction with action in a way that was innovative for its time.

- Bodybuilding to Acting: Before his acting career, Schwarzenegger was a world-renowned bodybuilder, winning Mr. Olympia seven times.
- "I'll Be Back": Schwarzenegger's famous line from "The Terminator" was initially scripted as "I'll come back." Arnold suggested the change, which became one of the most iconic lines in cinema.
- Training for "Predator": The cast of "Predator" underwent rigorous military training to prepare for their roles, adding authenticity to their performances.
- Voice Dubbing: Due to his thick Austrian accent, Schwarzenegger's voice was initially dubbed in his first leading role in "Hercules in New York."
- "Terminator" Makeup: The Terminator's iconic metal skeleton required hours of makeup and prosthetics, showcasing early advancements in movie makeup and special effects.

- Governor of California: Schwarzenegger took a hiatus from acting to serve as the Governor of California from 2003 to 2011, earning the nickname "The Governator."
- "Commando" One-Liners: "Commando" is renowned for its memorable one-liners, many of which were improvised by Schwarzenegger on set.
- Cameo in "The Expendables": Schwarzenegger made a cameo appearance in "The Expendables," alongside Stallone, uniting two of the biggest action stars of the era.
- Physical Comedy in "Twins": Schwarzenegger showcased his versatility as an actor in "Twins," successfully venturing into comedy alongside Danny DeVito.
- "Terminator 2" Motorcycle: Schwarzenegger performed many of his own motorcycle stunts in "Terminator 2: Judgment Day," despite having limited prior experience.

Bruce Willis brought a different kind of action hero to the forefront with "Die Hard." His portrayal of John McClane, a New York cop caught in a terrorist takeover of a Los Angeles skyscraper, was lauded for its everyman appeal. Willis's performance balanced vulnerability with toughness, humor with heroism, redefining what it meant to be an action star.

- Harmonica Player: Willis showcased his harmonica skills in "Die Hard with a Vengeance," a talent he has in real life and has performed publicly.
- Barefoot Challenge: Willis spent much of "Die Hard" barefoot, a detail that added a unique vulnerability to his character, John McClane.
- Improvised Line: The famous "Yippee-ki-yay" line was improvised by Willis, becoming a signature catchphrase for John McClane.

- "Die Hard" Christmas Debate: Willis has weighed in on the debate over whether "Die Hard" is a Christmas movie, declaring at his Comedy Central Roast that it is not.
- "Moonlighting" Schedule: While filming "Die Hard," Willis was also starring in the TV show "Moonlighting," juggling both commitments.
- Stunt Work: Willis performed many of his own stunts in the "Die Hard" series, contributing to the authenticity and intensity of the action sequences.

The Influence of Directors like James Cameron, John McTiernan, and George Miller was instrumental in shaping the action genre. They pushed the boundaries of special effects, stunt work, and cinematic storytelling, creating immersive worlds where their action heroes could thrive.

James Cameron

James Cameron's influence in the '80s action genre is most notably marked by "The Terminator" (1984) and its profound impact on science fiction and action cinema. Cameron's vision for a post-apocalyptic future, where a cyborg assassin is sent back in time to kill the mother of the future resistance leader, introduced audiences to a new kind of action narrative that was both intellectually stimulating and viscerally thrilling.

- Pioneering Special Effects: Cameron pushed the boundaries of what was possible with special effects, using a combination of practical effects, miniatures, and the early stages of CGI to bring the Terminator to life.
- Storytelling Depth: Beyond the action, Cameron infused "The Terminator" with themes of fate, love, and human resilience, adding depth to the film that transcended its genre.

- Innovative Action Sequences: Cameron's direction in the action sequences set new standards for the genre, combining relentless pace with technical precision.

John McTiernan

John McTiernan became a defining figure in action cinema with the release of "Predator" (1987) and "Die Hard" (1988). His ability to create tension-filled narratives, coupled with groundbreaking action sequences, made these films genre-defining classics.

- "Predator": With its mix of sci-fi and action, McTiernan presented a thrilling hunt between an alien creature and a team of commandos, leading to a new sub-genre of action.
- "Die Hard": Revolutionizing the action genre, McTiernan's "Die Hard" introduced the concept of the everyman hero, balancing explosive set-pieces with character-driven storytelling.
- Technical Mastery: McTiernan's films are noted for their innovative use of camera work and editing, enhancing the immersive experience of the action sequences.

George Miller

George Miller's contribution to the action genre in the '80s is epitomized by "Mad Max 2: The Road Warrior" (1981). Miller's post-apocalyptic vision and kinetic action sequences not only advanced the action genre but also set a benchmark for world-building in cinema.

- Miller's depiction of a post-apocalyptic wasteland set the standard for future films in the genre, blending stark visuals with a compelling narrative.
- "The Road Warrior" is celebrated for its high-speed chase scenes and practical effects

Sci-Fi and Fantasy: "E.T." to "Back to the Future"

The realms of science fiction and fantasy have long captivated audiences with their ability to transport viewers to other worlds, present alternative realities, and explore the human condition through the lens of the fantastical and the futuristic. Historically, these genres have evolved alongside technological advancements and shifting cultural landscapes, reflecting society's hopes, fears, and imaginative spirit. From the speculative visions of early sci-fi cinema to the epic quests of fantasy literature, these genres have undergone significant transformation, culminating in a period of unprecedented innovation and popularity in the 1980s.

The 1980s marked a watershed moment for sci-fi and fantasy, driven by a combination of advancing film technology, rising interest in space exploration, and a growing appetite for escapism amidst the backdrop of the Cold War. This era introduced audiences to some of the most enduring and beloved works in both genres, with films like "E.T. the Extra-Terrestrial" and "Back to the Future" not only achieving commercial success but also redefining what was possible in storytelling.

During the Cold War era, marked by geopolitical tensions and fears of nuclear conflict, people sought solace in escapist entertainment like sci-fi and fantasy. These genres offered imaginative visions of the future and alternate realities, providing a welcome distraction from the grim realities of the time. In essence, sci-fi and fantasy provided a comforting narrative that allowed people to imagine a world where heroism and resilience triumphed over adversity, offering a respite from the uncertainties of the present and a glimpse of a brighter future.

E.T. the Extra-Terrestrial (1982)

"E.T., phone home."

Directed by Steven Spielberg and featuring a young Henry Thomas as Elliott, "E.T. the Extra-Terrestrial" tells the heartwarming story of a young boy who befriends an alien left behind on Earth and his subsequent efforts to help his new friend return home. The film explores themes of friendship, innocence, and the wonders of discovery through the eyes of Elliott, his siblings (played by Drew Barrymore and Robert MacNaughton), and the titular character, E.T., a creature from another world with special powers. Spielberg's direction, coupled with John Williams' iconic score, crafted a cinematic experience that was both a touching portrayal of childhood and an exciting adventure.

The film was a monumental success, becoming the highest-grossing film of its time and solidifying Spielberg's status as a master storyteller. The practical effects used to bring E.T. to life, designed by Carlo Rambaldi, were groundbreaking, enhancing the film's realism and emotional impact. "E.T." also popularized the phrase "E.T. phone home," reflecting the film's cultural penetration. Beyond its box office success, "E.T." received numerous accolades, including four Academy Awards, and is revered for its significant contributions to the sci-fi genre, particularly in how it presents extraterrestrial life in a sympathetic and relatable light.

Did you know? Steven Spielberg, often hailed as the "Master of Blockbusters," co-founded the film studio DreamWorks SKG in 1994 alongside Jeffrey Katzenberg and David Geffen. This studio has produced numerous critically acclaimed and commercially successful films

Directed by Steven Spielberg and featuring a young Henry Thomas as Elliott, "E.T. the Extra-Terrestrial" tells the heartwarming story of a young boy who befriends an alien left behind on Earth and his subsequent efforts to help his new friend return home. The film explores themes of friendship, innocence, and the wonders of discovery through the eyes of Elliott, his siblings (played by Drew Barrymore and Robert MacNaughton), and the titular character, E.T., a creature from another world with special powers. Spielberg's direction, coupled with John Williams' iconic score, crafted a cinematic experience that was both a touching portrayal of childhood and an exciting adventure.

The film was a monumental success, becoming the highest-grossing film of its time and solidifying Spielberg's status as a master storyteller. The practical effects used to bring E.T. to life, designed by Carlo Rambaldi, were groundbreaking, enhancing the film's realism and emotional impact. "E.T." also popularized the phrase "E.T. phone home," reflecting the film's cultural penetration. Beyond its box office success, "E.T." received numerous accolades, including four Academy Awards, and is revered for its significant contributions to the sci-fi genre, particularly in how it presents extraterrestrial life in a sympathetic and relatable light.

> **"You could be happy here, I could take care of you. I wouldn't let anybody hurt you. We could grow up together, E.T.."**

- The Concept Originated from an Imaginary Friend: Director Steven Spielberg conceived the idea for E.T. from an imaginary alien friend he created after his parents' divorce.

- Improvisation of the Famous Line: The line "E.T. phone home," which became one of the most iconic in film history, was improvised by the young actor who played Elliot, Henry Thomas.
- Debut of Drew Barrymore: Playing Gertie, Drew Barrymore's role in E.T. was her breakout role, launching her into child stardom.
- E.T.'s Voice: The voice of E.T. was provided by Pat Welsh, an elderly woman who smoked two packs of cigarettes a day, which gave her voice the gravelly texture that the filmmakers were looking for.
- The Halloween Scene: In the Halloween scene, E.T. is disguised in a ghost costume, which is a nod to the classic ghost costumes of traditional Halloween, and he encounters a child dressed as Yoda from "Star Wars," showcasing Spielberg's friendship with George Lucas.
- Reese's Pieces: The use of Reese's Pieces in the film significantly boosted the candy's sales. M&M's had turned down the product placement opportunity.
- Puppetry and Animatronics: E.T. was brought to life through a combination of puppetry and animatronics, with a team of operators controlling his movements.
- The Bike Flight: The iconic scene of bicycles flying in front of the moon became so emblematic that it was incorporated into the logo of Spielberg's production company, Amblin Entertainment.
- John Williams' Score: The film's emotional depth is heightened by John Williams' memorable score, which won the Academy Award for Best Original Score.
- Real Tears: The tears in the scene where E.T. is dying were real, as Spielberg shot the scene in chronological order to elicit genuine emotional responses from the young cast.

True or False

Steven Spielberg decided to voice E.T. himself, using a synthesizer to alter his voice for the final film.
True or False

"E.T. the Extra-Terrestrial" was originally intended to be a horror film about aliens terrorizing a family.
True or False

The concept for E.T.'s appearance was inspired by poet Carl Sandburg, Albert Einstein, and a pug dog.
True or False

To maintain secrecy during filming, "E.T. the Extra-Terrestrial" was shot under the fake working title "A Boy's Life."
True or False

A sequel to "E.T. the Extra-Terrestrial," titled "E.T. 2: Nocturnal Fears," was written but ultimately shelved by Spielberg.
True or False

The iconic flying bicycle scene was filmed in a single take without any visual effects.
True or False

E.T. was able to speak English fluently by the end of the film.
True or False

The original script for "E.T. the Extra-Terrestrial" was written in just two weeks.
True or False

Answers

False - E.T.'s voice was provided by Pat Welsh, an elderly woman, and not voiced by Steven Spielberg.

True - Spielberg initially explored a darker concept titled "Night Skies" about malevolent aliens, before deciding on the more heartwarming tale of E.T.

True - The design of E.T. was indeed inspired by a mix of Carl Sandburg, Albert Einstein to create his wise look, and a pug dog for the wrinkled texture of his skin.

True - "E.T. the Extra-Terrestrial" was filmed under the fake working title "A Boy's Life" to keep the project secret and avoid leaks during production.

True - A sequel titled "E.T. 2: Nocturnal Fears" was indeed conceptualized and had a written treatment by Spielberg and Mathison, but Spielberg decided against it, feeling it would only take away from the original's purity.

False - The flying bicycle scene used a combination of practical effects and early computer-generated imagery (CGI) to achieve the final result; it was not filmed in a single take without visual effects.

False - While E.T. does learn a few words in English, including the iconic "E.T. phone home," he never becomes fluent in the language by the end of the film.

True - The original script for "E.T. the Extra-Terrestrial" was indeed written by Melissa Mathison in just two weeks. Spielberg was so impressed with the first draft that it underwent minimal changes afterwards.

"Back to the Future" (1985)

"Roads? Where we're going, we don't need roads."

"Back to the Future," directed by Robert Zemeckis and starring Michael J. Fox as Marty McFly and Christopher Lloyd as Dr. Emmett "Doc" Brown, is a seminal sci-fi adventure comedy that blends time travel with the exploration of familial and societal dynamics. The film follows Marty as he accidentally travels back in time to the 1950s in a DeLorean car modified to be a time machine by Doc Brown. There, he must ensure his teenage parents-to-be meet and fall in love, or he will cease to exist.

The film cleverly navigates the intricacies of time travel, cause and effect, and the impact of small changes in the past on the future, all while delivering humor, action, and heart.

The chemistry between Fox and Lloyd, alongside the innovative special effects and Alan Silvestri's memorable score, contributed to its massive success. "Back to the Future" spawned two sequels, creating a beloved trilogy that has stood the test of time.

"Back to the Future" was not only a box office hit but also a critical darling, praised for its imaginative premise, sharp writing, and engaging performances. The film's impact on popular culture is extensive, with references to the film appearing in various media, and its portrayal of time travel influencing subsequent sci-fi works. Its enduring appeal is evidenced by its continued popularity, including various re-releases, merchandise, and an animated series. The DeLorean time machine, in particular, has become an iconic symbol of the film and 1980s cinema.

Both "E.T. the Extra-Terrestrial" and "Back to the Future" stand as towering achievements in the sci-fi and fantasy genres, showcasing the 1980s as a time of significant creativity and innovation in film. These works not only pushed the boundaries of storytelling and special effects but also captured the hearts of audiences around the world, leaving a lasting legacy that continues to inspire filmmakers and captivate viewers.

> *"If you're gonna build a time machine into a car, why not do it with some style?"*

- The Original Time Machine: The time machine was initially conceived to be a refrigerator before being changed to the iconic DeLorean to avoid children accidentally locking themselves in refrigerators.
- Casting Marty McFly: Michael J. Fox was always the first choice for Marty McFly, but due to scheduling conflicts with his TV show "Family Ties," Eric Stoltz was initially cast before Fox ultimately took over.
- The Clock Tower: The Hill Valley clock tower is one of the film's central locations, and its design was inspired by the real-life courthouse in Pasadena, California.
- Einstein the Dog: Doc Brown's dog, Einstein, was the first character to time travel in the DeLorean, making him the "world's first time traveler" in the film's universe.
- Hoverboard Hoax: The hoverboard used by Marty in the sequel caused a stir among fans, many of whom believed it was a real product, leading to a public statement from the filmmakers that it was a fictional device.
- The Johnny B. Goode Scene: Michael J. Fox actually played the guitar for the "Johnny B. Goode" scene, although the singing was dubbed.

- President Ronald Reagan was so amused by Doc Brown's disbelief that an actor like him could become president that he quoted the film in a State of the Union address.
- The theme song "The Power of Love" by Huey Lewis and the News not only became a hit on its own but also perfectly captured the film's spirit.
- The mall changes its name from Twin Pines to Lone Pine, a subtle detail that reflects Marty's impact on the past.
- Actor Crispin Glover, who played George McFly, sued the producers for using his likeness in the sequel without his permission, leading to changes in how actors' images are used in film.

True or False Questions

1. In "Back to the Future," Marty McFly plays "Johnny B. Goode" at his parents' high school prom in the 1950s.
True or False

2. The original script for "Back to the Future" involved Marty traveling back in time using a microwave instead of a DeLorean.
True or False

3. The film "Back to the Future" was almost titled "Time Man."
True or False

4. "Back to the Future" was filmed entirely in and around the city of New York.
True or False

5. The "Back to the Future" trilogy includes a visit to the future year of 2015, where Marty and Doc Brown encounter flying cars and hoverboards.
True or False

Answers

1. In "Back to the Future," Marty McFly plays "Johnny B. Goode" at his parents' high school prom in the 1950s.
True
This scene is iconic for showcasing Michael J. Fox's musical talent and the cultural impact of rock and roll.

2. The original script for "Back to the Future" involved Marty traveling back in time using a microwave instead of a DeLorean.
False
The initial concept involved a refrigerator as the time travel device, not a microwave.

3. The film "Back to the Future" was almost titled "Time Man."
False
One of the alternate titles considered was "Spaceman From Pluto," suggested by a studio executive, but Steven Spielberg tactfully dismissed the suggestion.

4. "Back to the Future" was filmed entirely in and around the city of New York.
False
The majority of the film was shot in California, including locations like the Universal Studios lot and the town of Pasadena.

5. The "Back to the Future" trilogy includes a visit to the future year of 2015, where Marty and Doc Brown encounter flying cars and hoverboards.
True
The portrayal of 2015 included many imaginative technologies, some of which, like hoverboards.

Other Notable Sci-Fi and Fantasy 80s Classics:

Blade Runner (1982)

Ridley Scott's Vision: Directed by Ridley Scott, "Blade Runner" is renowned for its innovative visual style and complex narrative, blending science fiction with noir elements.

The Voight-Kampff Test: This fictional test used to identify replicants is a central element in the film, symbolizing the theme of humanity and identity.

Multiple Versions: There are several versions of "Blade Runner," including the Director's Cut and the Final Cut, each offering different perspectives on the film's ambiguous storyline.

Vangelis' Score: The haunting and atmospheric score by Vangelis has become as iconic as the film itself, setting the tone for its futuristic and dystopian setting.

Influence on Cyberpunk: "Blade Runner" is credited with shaping the cyberpunk genre, influencing countless works in film, literature, and video games with its depiction of a high-tech, low-life future.

The NeverEnding Story (1984)

A German Production: Directed by Wolfgang Petersen, this was one of the most expensive films produced outside the United States or the Soviet Union at the time.

Falkor the Luckdragon: Falkor became an iconic character, beloved for his wisdom and friendly nature, symbolizing hope and luck.

Practical Effects: The film utilized groundbreaking practical effects and puppetry to bring its fantastical creatures to life, contributing to its magical appeal.

The Theme Song: The theme song, performed by Limahl, became a hit of the '80s, capturing the film's sense of adventure.

Symbolism: The story is rich in symbolism, exploring themes of bravery, loss, and the power of imagination and storytelling.

Ghostbusters (1984)

Combination of Genres: "Ghostbusters" masterfully combined comedy, action, and supernatural elements, creating a new genre hybrid that became wildly popular.
Iconic Catchphrase: The line "Who you gonna call? Ghostbusters!" became an instantly recognizable catchphrase, epitomizing the film's blend of humor and paranormal action.
The Stay Puft Marshmallow Man: This character's appearance as a giant monster made of marshmallows is one of the film's most memorable and visually striking moments.
Improvised Lines: Much of the film's dialogue was improvised, contributing to its natural humor and the chemistry between the cast members.
Cultural Impact: "Ghostbusters" spawned sequels, animated series, and merchandise, becoming a defining pop culture phenomenon of the '80s.

Tron (1982)

Pioneering Use of CGI: "Tron" was one of the first films to make extensive use of computer-generated imagery (CGI), opening new avenues for visual storytelling in cinema.
Video Game Aesthetic: The film's aesthetic was heavily influenced by video games, reflecting the growing interest in computer and arcade games at the time.
Cult Following: Despite a mixed initial reception, "Tron" has gained a cult following, appreciated for its innovative visuals and exploration of digital worlds.
Soundtrack: Wendy Carlos composed the film's electronic score, which perfectly complemented its futuristic themes and visuals.

Legacy: "Tron" has been recognized for its groundbreaking contributions to special effects and digital animation, influencing the development of CGI in film.

The Dark Crystal (1982)

Jim Henson's Vision: Directed by Jim Henson and Frank Oz, "The Dark Crystal" was a departure from Henson's previous work, showcasing his ability to create a complex fantasy world.
Puppet Mastery: The film is notable for its exclusive use of puppets, brought to life by skilled puppeteers, without any human actors on screen.
Thra's Ecology: The world of Thra was meticulously designed, with a rich backstory and ecology that added depth to its fantasy setting.
Soundtrack: Trevor Jones composed the film's ethereal score, enhancing the mystical and epic qualities of the narrative.
Cult Classic: While it had a mixed reception upon release, "The Dark Crystal" has since been celebrated for its imaginative storytelling and unique visual style.

Labyrinth (1986)

David Bowie as Jareth: Rock legend David Bowie played the Goblin King, Jareth, contributing iconic songs like "Magic Dance" to the film's soundtrack.
Jennifer Connelly's Early Role: A young Jennifer Connelly played Sarah, marking one of her first leading roles in a film.
Henson's Puppetry: Like "The Dark Crystal," "Labyrinth" featured complex puppet characters, showcasing the height of Jim Henson's creativity and craftsmanship in puppetry.
Escher-Inspired Set: The film's climax in the Goblin King's castle was inspired by the works of M.C. Escher, featuring impossible architecture and optical illusions.

Cult Status: "Labyrinth" has achieved a lasting legacy as a cult classic, beloved for its imaginative story, memorable characters, and the blend of music, fantasy, and adventure.

The 1980s marked a golden age for soap operas and prime-time dramas, with "Dallas" and "Dynasty" standing as towering examples of the genre's success during this era. These shows captivated millions of viewers with their complex narratives, opulent settings, and larger-than-life characters, all while exploring themes of power, greed, family, and romance. Their influence extended beyond the television screen, impacting fashion, pop culture, and even international diplomacy, as they were broadcast worldwide.

Dallas

"Dallas," a prime-time soap opera that defined an era, invites viewers into the tumultuous and opulent world of the Ewing family, entrenched in the oil-rich fields of Texas. At the heart of the series is the intense rivalry between two brothers: J.R. Ewing (Larry Hagman), the cunning, power-hungry magnate of Ewing Oil, whose manipulations and schemes know no bounds, and Bobby Ewing (Patrick Duffy), the younger brother whose integrity and moral compass often put him at odds with J.R.'s ruthless tactics. This central conflict, set against the backdrop of the sprawling Southfork Ranch, serves as the nexus for a web of intrigue, betrayal, and familial drama that unfolds over the show's 14 seasons.

The narrative complexity of "Dallas" extends beyond the brothers' rivalry, exploring themes such as loyalty, greed, ambition, and redemption through a cast of richly developed characters, including Sue Ellen Ewing (Linda Gray), J.R.'s long-suffering wife, and Pamela Barnes Ewing (Victoria Principal),

Bobby's wife, who comes from the Barnes family, Ewing Oil's longtime rivals. The show's ability to intertwine personal and professional stakes with the larger-than-life setting of the Texas oil industry captured the imagination of viewers worldwide, making it a staple of 1980s television.

"Dallas" was pioneering in its use of cliffhangers, most notably the "Shot J.R.?" storyline at the end of the third season, which became a cultural phenomenon. The mystery surrounding the shooting of the show's primary antagonist captured global attention, demonstrating show's immense popularity and the power of television narrative to engage audiences on a massive scale. Over its run, "Dallas" didn't ju entertain; it became a mirror reflecting the excesses, ambitions, anc complexities of American life, leaving an indelible mark on the lands of television drama.

Trivia Tidbits:

- "Who Shot J.R.?": This storyline from the end of the third season resulted in one of the most-watched television episodes in history at the time and sparked international speculation and betting.
- Impact on Fashion: The characters' extravagant lifestyles and fashion choices influenced 1980s style, with viewers emulating the looks of their favorite characters.
- Cultural Phenomenon: "Dallas" was broadcast in over 90 countries, making it one of the most internationally successful television shows of its time.
- Longevity: Running for 14 seasons, "Dallas" is one of the longest-running prime-time dramas in American TV history.
- Revival and Continuation: In 2012, a revival of "Dallas" aired, featuring original cast members and new characters, continuing the Ewing family saga.

Dynasty

Set against the glittering backdrop of Denver, Colorado's high society, "Dynasty" is a lavish exploration of the trials and tribulations of the Carrington family, led by the oil tycoon Blake Carrington (John Forsythe). The show, known for its sumptuous portrayal of wealth and the intricate dynamics of power and family, dives deep into the life of Blake, his new wife Krystle (Linda Evans), and his scheming ex-wife Alexis (Joan Collins), whose entrance in the second season adds fuel to the already blazing fires of drama and rivalry.

At its core, "Dynasty" is a narrative battlefield where love, loyalty, and ambition clash against the backdrop of the corporate boardroom and the luxury of the Carrington mansion. Krystle, with her integrity and kindness, often finds herself navigating the complex waters of her new family and their opulent world, while Alexis embodies the quintessence of a soap opera villain—ruthless, cunning, and fabulously dressed, thanks to the iconic costume designs by Nolan Miller. The show's flair for the dramatic is matched by its willingness to tackle social issues, including homosexuality, through the character of Steven Carrington (Al Corley and later Jack Coleman), Blake's son, in a time when such topics were rarely addressed on prime-time television.

"Dynasty" didn't just captivate audiences with its storylines; it set trends in fashion with its extravagant gowns and power suits, becoming a defining aesthetic of the 1980s. The show's influence extended beyond the screen, shaping viewers' perceptions of luxury and power in the decade of excess. Its blend of melodrama, memorable characters, and opulent settings ensured that "Dynasty" remains a landmark series in the annals of television history, epitomizing the allure and fantasy of the 1980s prime-time soap opera.

Trivia Tidbits:

- Joan Collins' Arrival: The show saw a significant boost in ratings with the introduction of Joan Collins as Alexis in the second season, becoming an iconic TV villain.
- Fashion Icon: The show's extravagant costumes, designed by Nolan Miller, set fashion trends and epitomized the luxurious style of the 1980s.
- The Moldavian Massacre: The cliffhanger ending of the fifth season, involving a fictional coup in the European country of Moldavia, is one of the show's most memorable (and criticized) moments.
- Spin-offs and Reboots: "Dynasty" spawned a successful spin-off, "The Colbys," and a modern reboot in 2017, introducing the Carringtons to a new generation.
- Impact on Soap Operas: "Dynasty" elevated the prime-time soap opera genre, incorporating elaborate sets and costumes, thereby setting a new standard for drama and luxury on television.

"Dallas" and "Dynasty" not only dominated the airwaves throughout the 1980s but also left a lasting legacy on television storytelling, influencing countless dramas that followed. Their blend of high stakes, familial conflict, and opulence continues to be a template for success in television drama, cementing their place as cultural landmarks of the 1980s.

"The Colbys" sought to capitalize on the immense success of "Dynasty" by extending the family drama and opulent lifestyles to another branch of the Carrington family, it didn't achieve the same level of critical or commercial success as its predecessor. The show struggled in the ratings and faced criticism for its outlandish plot twists and character developments. After two seasons and 49 episodes, "The Colbys" was cancelled due to low viewership.

Guess the 80s Movie: Synopsis and Star Challenge

A high school student. Basketball team. Starring Michael J. Fox.
A) Teen Wolf
B) Back to the Future
C) The Secret of My Success

A group of kids from the Goon Docks neighborhood set off on an adventure to find a pirate's treasure. Starring Sean Astin.
A) The Goonies
B) Stand By Me
C) Explorers

An unconventional detective must navigate a dystopian Los Angeles to retire four rogue replicants. Starring Harrison Ford.
A) Blade Runner
B) The Fugitive
C) Witness

A young girl is transported to a magical world by a tornado, where she must confront an evil emperor. Starring Fairuza Balk.
A) Labyrinth
B) The NeverEnding Story
C) Return to Oz

A Chicago teenager. Starring Matthew Broderick.
A) Ferris Bueller's Day Off
B) WarGames
C) The Breakfast Club

A New York cop battles terrorists in a Los Angeles skyscraper. Starring Bruce Willis.
A) Die Hard
B) Lethal Weapon
C) The Last Boy Scout

Two high school nerds use a computer program to literally create the perfect woman, but chaos ensues. Starring Anthony Michael Hall.
A) Sixteen Candles
B) Weird Science
C) The Breakfast Club

A freelance exorcist cleanses spirits from a possessed house, uncovering a deeper evil. Starring Craig T. Nelson.
A) Poltergeist
B) The Amityville Horror
C) Ghostbusters

A talented fighter pilot is sent to an elite naval flying school where he struggles with a personal loss.
A) Top Gun
B) Iron Eagle
C) The Right Stuff

A teenager discovers his neighbor is a vampire, leading to a desperate fight for survival. Starring Chris Sarandon.
A) Fright Night
B) The Lost Boys
C) Near Dark

A man with no memory is trapped in a dystopian city where he discovers he's wanted for a series of brutal murders.
A) Blade Runner
B) The Hitcher
C) Split Second

"I've seen things you people wouldn't believe"

Answers

Answer: A) Teen Wolf
- Trivia Tidbit: "Teen Wolf" was one of two major films released in 1985 that starred Michael J. Fox, the other being "Back to the Future," making it a banner year for the actor.

Answer: A) The Goonies
- Trivia Tidbit: "The Goonies" was written by Chris Columbus from a story by Steven Spielberg. The film's iconic pirate ship was a real set that the cast saw for the first time during filming to capture their genuine reactions.

Answer: A) Blade Runner
- Trivia Tidbit: "Blade Runner" is based on Philip K. Dick's novel "Do Androids Dream of Electric Sheep?" The film's visual style has influenced many science fiction movies and TV shows that followed.

Answer: C) Return to Oz
- Trivia Tidbit: "Return to Oz" is a much darker sequel to "The Wizard of Oz," not featuring songs and significantly deviating from the original's tone. It has since gained a cult following for its unique take on the Oz lore.

Answer: A) Ferris Bueller's Day Off
- Trivia Tidbit: The parade scene in "Ferris Bueller's Day Off" was filmed during an actual parade in Chicago. Matthew Broderick had limited time to perfect the choreography for his dance sequence.

Answer: A) Die Hard
- Trivia Tidbit: "Die Hard" was Alan Rickman's feature film debut, where he played the memorable villain Hans Gruber. The film is often cited as one of the greatest action movies of all time.

Answer: B) Weird Science
- Trivia Tidbit: "Weird Science" was written and directed by John Hughes, known for his impactful teen movies. The story was inspired by a pre-Comics Code Authority 1950s EC Comics magazine of the same name.

Answer: A) Poltergeist
- Trivia Tidbit: "Poltergeist" was directed by Tobe Hooper, with Steven Spielberg serving as a writer and producer. The film's production was rumored to be cursed, with several cast members experiencing tragic events.

Answer: A) Top Gun
- Trivia Tidbit: "Top Gun" was instrumental in popularizing the U.S. Navy's Fighter Weapons School, known as Top Gun. The film's success led to a significant increase in young men enlisting to become naval aviators.

Answer: A) Fright Night
- Trivia Tidbit: "Fright Night" combines horror and humor in a suburban setting, making it a beloved 80s classic. The special effects and makeup for the vampires were groundbreaking at the time, contributing to the film's enduring popularity.

Answer: B) The Hitcher
- Trivia Tidbit: Rutger Hauer's chilling performance as the hitchhiker in "The Hitcher" is often cited as one of the most memorable villain roles in horror cinema.

Animation Breakthroughs: From "The Simpsons" to "Who Framed Roger Rabbit"

The late 1980s marked a pivotal moment in the history of animation, characterized by significant breakthroughs that expanded the medium's creative and commercial possibilities. This period saw the emergence of "The Simpsons," a groundbreaking animated TV show that redefined prime-time television, and "Who Framed Roger Rabbit," a film that blended live-action and animation in unprecedented ways. Both works not only pushed technical and narrative boundaries but also shifted public perception of animation from being solely for children to a form
of entertainment with broad appeal across all ages.

The Simpsons (1989-Present)

"D'oh"

Debuting in 1989, "The Simpsons" began as a series of shorts on "The Tracey Ullman Show" before becoming a half-hour prime-time show on FOX. Created by cartoonist Matt Groening, "The Simpsons" centered around the Simpson family, living in the fictional town of Springfield. The family consists of the bumbling but well-meaning Homer, his patient wife Marge, troublemaker son Bart, overachieving daughter Lisa, and baby Maggie. The show's satirical depiction of American culture, society, and television itself quickly resonated with audiences, making it an instant hit.

"Thank You, Come Again"

"The Simpsons" was groundbreaking for several reasons. It was the first successful animated series in prime-time television since "The Flintstones," challenging the notion that animated shows were only for Saturday mornings or children. Its sophisticated humor, cultural references, and clever writing attracted adult viewers, while its colorful animation and lively characters appealed to children. The show's ability to tackle a wide range of topics—from politics and religion to pop culture and family dynamics—allowed it to remain relevant and poignant for decades.

Beyond its content, "The Simpsons" also pioneered in terms of animation technology. The transition to digital ink and paint in the late '90s allowed for a more vibrant and consistent visual quality, setting a new standard for animated television. With over 30 seasons and counting, "The Simpsons" has become the longest-running American sitcom and animated series, earning numerous awards, including 34 Primetime Emmy Awards. Its influence extends beyond television, impacting film, music, and even politics, solidifying its place in the pantheon of American pop culture.

Homer Simpson

Paragraph: Homer Simpson, voiced by Dan Castellaneta, is the lovably inept patriarch of the Simpson family. His character is defined by his love for donuts, Duff beer, and his often misguided but well-intentioned attempts to be a good father and husband. Homer's antics and simple wisdom often lead to humorous yet insightful reflections on the complexities of life, work, and family.
Iconic Catchphrase: Homer's frustrated grunt, "D'oh!", has become one of the most recognizable catchphrases in television history. Occupation: Despite his lack of competence, Homer has held over 188 different jobs throughout the series, reflecting the show's playful exploration of American work culture.

Did You Know? Dan Castellaneta, Born on October 29, 1957, in Chicago, Illinois, he has voiced Homer since the show's debut in 1989, along with numerous other characters on the series, including Abraham Simpson, Barney Gumble, Krusty the Clown, and Groundskeeper Willie, among others.

Marge Simpson

Marge Simpson, voiced by Julie Kavner, is the steadying force in the Simpson household. With her trademark blue beehive hairdo and nurturing nature, Marge embodies the quintessential American mother. She balances the chaos of her family's antics with grace, offering a voice of reason and a deep well of patience.

- Artistic Talent: Marge has a hidden talent for painting, which is explored in various episodes, highlighting her depth beyond her role as a homemaker.
- Moral Compass: Marge often serves as the moral compass of the family, guiding them through ethical dilemmas with her strong sense of right and wrong.

Bart Simpson

Bart Simpson, voiced by Nancy Cartwright, is the mischievous eldest child of the Simpson family. Known for his rebellious attitude, love for skateboarding, and clever pranks, Bart embodies the spirit of youthful defiance. Despite his troublemaker persona, Bart's moments of vulnerability and loyalty to his family reveal a complex character.

"Eat My Shorts"

Bart's prank calls to Moe's Tavern are a recurring gag

Lisa Simpson

Lisa Simpson, voiced by Yeardley Smith, is the middle child and the intellectual and moral center of the family. An ardent saxophone player, environmental activist, and feminist, Lisa's intelligence and ethical convictions often put her at odds with her environment but underscore her role as a voice for social justice and change.

- Vegetarianism: Lisa's decision to become a vegetarian in the episode "Lisa the Vegetarian" is a significant aspect of her character development, reflecting her compassion and ethical convictions.
- Achievements: Despite being only eight years old, Lisa has demonstrated a remarkably high IQ of 159, has mastered the saxophone, and has been involved in various social causes throughout the series.

Maggie Simpson

Maggie Simpson, the baby of the family, communicates solely through expressive pacifier sucks and the occasional giggle or cry, yet her silent observations offer a unique perspective on the world around her. Despite her age, Maggie has had moments of heroism and insight, contributing significantly to the family's adventures.

- First Word: Maggie's first word, "Daddy," spoken in the episode "Lisa's First Word," reveals her deep bond with Homer.
- Resourcefulness: Maggie has displayed surprising resourcefulness, such as when she saved Homer from drowning or when she cleverly escapes from her crib.

Mr. Burns

Charles Montgomery Burns, voiced by Harry Shearer, stands as the quintessential antagonist of Springfield. As the wealthy, power-hungry owner of the Springfield Nuclear Power Plant, where Homer works, Mr. Burns' schemes and disregard for others highlight themes of corporate greed and environmental neglect.

- Age: Mr. Burns is often humorously depicted as being extraordinarily old, to the point where his exact age is a running gag within the series.
- "Excellent": His signature catchphrase, accompanied by steepled fingers, perfectly encapsulates his nefarious personality and delight in others' misfortunes.

Ned Flanders

Ned Flanders, voiced by Harry Shearer, is the Simpsons' overly optimistic and devoutly Christian next-door neighbor. His unwavering faith, boundless enthusiasm, and penchant for saying "diddly" and "doodly" in his speech contrast sharply with Homer's cynicism, creating a dynamic that's both comedic and reflective of broader religious and cultural conversations.

- Left-Handedness: Ned owns the Leftorium, a store specializing in products for left-handed people, highlighting his entrepreneurial spirit and the show's attention to character detail.
- Resilience: Despite facing numerous personal tragedies, including the loss of his wife Maude, Ned's resilience and unshakeable faith provide a complex look at coping and character strength.

Krusty the Clown

Paragraph: Krusty the Clown, voiced by Dan Castellaneta, is Springfield's celebrity TV clown with a less-than-glamorous off-screen life marked by gambling debts and heartache. Krusty's role as both a children's entertainer and a deeply flawed individual explores the dichotomy between public personas and private lives.

- Jewish Heritage: Krusty's Jewish heritage and estranged relationship with his rabbi father are central to his character development, offering depth beyond his clown persona.
- Real Name: His real name, Herschel Shmoikel Pinchas Yerucham Krustofsky, reflects his complex identity and cultural background, adding layers to his comedic character.

Apu Nahasapeemapetilon

Paragraph: Apu Nahasapeemapetilon, voiced by Hank Azaria, is the hardworking proprietor of the Kwik-E-Mart. His character has sparked discussions about representation and stereotypes, leading to a reevaluation of how the show depicts cultural diversity.

- Education: Apu holds a Ph.D. in computer science, demonstrating the character's intelligence and work ethic, despite often being depicted in the context of his convenience store.
- Cultural Reassessment: The documentary "The Problem with Apu" prompted discussions about Apu's portrayal and its impact on societal perceptions of South Asians, leading to ongoing conversations about diversity and representation in animation.

Who Framed Roger Rabbit (1988)

"Who Framed Roger Rabbit," directed by Robert Zemeckis and produced by Steven Spielberg, was a landmark film released in 1988 that seamlessly blended live-action and animated characters. Set in a 1947 version of Hollywood where humans and animated characters (Toons
) coexist, the film follows private detective Eddie Valiant (Bob Hoskins) as he becomes entangled in a murder mystery involving Roger Rabbit, a Toon framed for the murder of a wealthy businessman. The film explores themes of prejudice and unity through its noir-inspired narrative, presenting a groundbreaking technical achievement in the integration of live-action and animation.

The film was a technical marvel for its time, employing then-state-of-the-art computer graphics, traditional animation techniques, and intricate practical effects to create interactions between the live-action and animated characters. This required innovative filmmaking techniques, including the use of robotic arms to mimic the actions of animated characters and complex compositing to blend animation with live-action footage seamlessly. The result was a visually stunning film that felt cohesive and immersive, setting a new benchmark for what could be achieved in cinema.

"Who Framed Roger Rabbit" also stood out for its unprecedented collaboration between competing studios, featuring characters from Disney, Warner Bros., and other animation studios sharing the screen for the first time. This crossover was a monumental feat of licensing and negotiation, contributing to the film's unique and eclectic cast of characters, including appearances by icons like Mickey Mouse and Bugs Bunny.

Critical and commercial success, "Who Framed Roger Rabbit" won four Academy Awards, including a Special Achievement Award for Animation Direction. The film's impact on the industry was profound, revitalizing interest in classic American animation and paving the way for the Disney Renaissance of the 1990s.

It demonstrated the potential of animation as a medium that could appeal to both adults and children, blending genres and storytelling modes to create something entirely new. "Who Framed Roger Rabbit" remains a beloved classic, celebrated for its innovation, creativity, and the way it pushed the boundaries of animated storytelling.

Eddie Valiant

Eddie Valiant, portrayed by Bob Hoskins, is the grizzled private detective at the heart of "Who Framed Roger Rabbit." Haunted by the death of his brother at the hands of a Toon, Eddie's journey from Toon-hating cynic to a defender of their rights is central to the film's narrative. His character serves as the audience's entry point into the film's unique world, where humans and Toons coexist. Eddie's transformation is not just a personal redemption arc but also a commentary on prejudice and the power of empathy.

- Method Acting: Bob Hoskins studied his young daughter's interactions with imaginary friends to realistically portray interacting with characters that wouldn't be animated until post-production.
- Physical Comedy: Hoskins' performance required extensive physical comedy and mime skills, as he often interacted with "invisible" characters, showcasing his versatile acting chops.

Roger Rabbit

Paragraph: Roger Rabbit, voiced by Charles Fleischer, is the zany, lovable Toon at the center of the film's murder mystery. His character combines the physical comedy of classic cartoons with a genuine heart and innocence, making him immediately endearing. Roger's unwavering love for his wife, Jessica, and his desperate quest to clear his name drive much of the film's plot, blending humor with moments of real tension and emotion.

- Voice Consistency: Charles Fleischer insisted on wearing a Roger Rabbit costume during recordings to maintain the energy and consistency of his performance.
- Animation Technique: Roger's animation was revolutionary, with artists ensuring he interacted seamlessly with the live-action environment, including realistic shading and movement.

Jessica Rabbit

Paragraph: Jessica Rabbit, Roger's wife, voiced by Kathleen Turner (uncredited) and performed by Amy Irving for her singing voice, is a sultry nightclub singer and a significant departure from traditional animated female characters. Her famous line, "I'm not bad; I'm just drawn that way," encapsulates her role as a femme fatale with a twist. Jessica is a complex character who defies expectations, proving to be loyal and fiercely intelligent, challenging stereotypes about beauty and superficiality.

- Visual Inspiration: Jessica's design was inspired by classic Hollywood glamour, blending the looks of Veronica Lake and Rita Hayworth with the impossible proportions of a Toon.

- Character Depth: Despite her overtly sexualized appearance, Jessica's character is developed with care, showcasing strength, depth, and a genuine love for Roger, contributing to the film's themes of acceptance and breaking down prejudices.

Judge Doom

Paragraph: Judge Doom, portrayed by Christopher Lloyd, is the film's chilling antagonist, whose true identity and nefarious plans are central to the plot's mystery. His character embodies the noir genre's dark, menacing figures, with a twist unique to the film's blended world. Doom's frightening demeanor and the revelation of his Toon nature beneath his human facade create a compelling commentary on the duality of characters and the nature of evil.

- No Blinking: Christopher Lloyd chose not to blink while on screen as Judge Doom to enhance the character's unsettling presence.
- Physical Transformation: Lloyd's performance, combined with groundbreaking special effects, made Judge Doom one of the most memorable and terrifying villains in animation history, particularly in his Toon form during the film's climax.

The Simpsons Legacy

Since its debut in 1989, "The Simpsons" has not only remained a fixture of American pop culture but has also garnered attention for its uncanny ability to predict future events. This long-running animated series, while primarily a satirical depiction of a typical American family and society, has shown a remarkable knack for forecasting technological advancements, political shifts, and various significant occurrences with eerie accuracy. Here's a look at how "The Simpsons" has peered into the future and a brief overview of the show's enduring legacy.

Predictions That Came True

- Smartwatches: In a 1995 episode, "Lisa's Wedding," a future world showcased characters communicating through watches, predating the smartwatch technology by decades.
- Donald Trump's Presidency: Perhaps one of the most talked-about predictions, the show depicted Donald Trump as the President of the United States in the 2000 episode "Bart to the Future," a full 16 years before he was elected.
- Disney's Acquisition of Fox: The 1998 episode "When You Dish Upon a Star" featured a sign reading "20th Century Fox, a Division of Walt Disney Co.," predicting the 2019 acquisition nearly two decades in advance.
- FaceTime and Video Calls: Episodes like "Lisa's Wedding" again showed characters communicating via video calls, a commonplace technology today that was far from widespread at the time of airing.
- The FIFA Corruption Scandal: In 2014, "The Simpsons" episode "You Don't Have to Live Like a Referee" depicted a FIFA official being arrested for corruption, a year before real-world arrests were made in the FIFA corruption scandal.
- Ebola Virus Outbreak: In the 1997 episode "Lisa's Sax," Marge offers a sick Bart a book titled "Curious George and the Ebola Virus," eerily predating the 2014-2016 West Africa Ebola outbreak.
- Greece's Economic Crisis: A 2013 episode titled "Politically Inept, with Homer Simpson" featured a news ticker that mentioned Europe putting Greece on eBay, hinting at the country's financial troubles that escalated in the following years.

- The Higgs Boson Particle Prediction: In the 1998 episode "The Wizard of Evergreen Terrace," Homer is seen standing in front of a blackboard with an equation that, years later, physicists stated was nearly correct for predicting the mass of the Higgs Boson particle.
- Autocorrect Frustrations: The 1994 episode "Lisa on Ice" features a school bullies' memo device that auto-corrects "Beat up Martin" to "Eat up Martha," humorously foreseeing the frustrations of early autocorrect technology.
- The Siegfried and Roy Tiger Attack: In 1993, an episode titled "$pringfield" depicted a tiger attacking its trainers, a scenario that mirrored the real-life attack on Roy Horn of Siegfried & Roy during a Las Vegas show in 2003.
- U.S. Winning Olympic Curling Gold: The 2010 episode "Boy Meets Curl" depicted Homer and Marge winning an Olympic gold medal for the USA in mixed doubles curling, which unexpectedly came true when the U.S. men's curling team won gold at the 2018 Winter Olympics.

The Show's Legacy

"The Simpsons" has transcended the realm of television to become a cultural phenomenon, impacting not just entertainment but also language, politics, and societal norms. Its legacy is multifaceted:

As the longest-running American sitcom and scripted prime-time series, "The Simpsons" has adapted to changing times while maintaining its relevance and humor, a testament to its creative storytelling and character development.

The series has left an indelible mark on pop culture, with phrases like "D'oh!" entering the Oxford English Dictionary and influencing countless other shows and films.

Beyond its predictive prowess, "The Simpsons" has been lauded for its sharp social and political commentary, tackling everything from environmental issues to cultural trends with intelligence and wit.

"The Simpsons" continues to entertain, provoke thought, and, at times, predict the future, solidifying its place as a cornerstone of television history. Its blend of humor, cultural critique, and foresight will likely ensure its relevance and popularity for years to come.

1980s Pop Culture Quiz

Which 1980s TV show featured a car that could talk and had advanced artificial intelligence?
A) Knight Rider
B) The A-Team
C) Miami Vice

In the film "E.T. the Extra-Terrestrial," what type of candy does Elliott use to lure E.T.?
A) M&M's
B) Skittles
C) Reese's Pieces

Which iconic 1980s movie is known for the quote, "Nobody puts Baby in a corner"?
A) Dirty Dancing
B) Flashdance
C) Footloose

What is the name of the fictional high school in the TV series "Saved by the Bell"?
A) Bayside High
B) West Beverly High
C) Ridgemont High

Who performed the theme song for the 1980s TV show "Cheers"?
A) Gary Portnoy
B) Billy Joel
C) Elton John

In "Back to the Future," what makes time travel possible?
A) A black hole
B) A flux capacitor
C) Quantum mechanics

Which 1980s movie featured a group of kids searching for pirate treasure to save their homes from foreclosure?
A) The Goonies
B) Stand By Me
C) The Lost Boys

What was the profession of Tom Selleck's character in the TV show "Magnum, P.I."?
A) Police Detective
B) Private Investigator
C) Army Officer

Answers

Answer: A) Knight Rider
- Trivia Tidbit: The car, named KITT (Knight Industries Two Thousand), was a modified Pontiac Trans Am with a fully sentient AI capable of conversation, analysis, and autonomous action to assist its owner, Michael Knight.

Answer: C) Reese's Pieces
- Trivia Tidbit: The use of Reese's Pieces in "E.T." is often credited with significantly boosting the candy's sales. Spielberg originally approached M&M's, but they declined, leading to one of the most successful instances of product placement in film history.

Answer: A) Dirty Dancing
- Trivia Tidbit: This line is delivered by Patrick Swayze's character, Johnny Castle, in one of the film's climactic scenes. "Dirty Dancing" became a cultural phenomenon, noted for its music, dance sequences, and memorable quotes.

Answer: A) Bayside High
- Trivia Tidbit: "Saved by the Bell" focused on the lives of several high school students, navigating the trials and tribulations of adolescence. The show became iconic for its portrayal of '90s youth culture and school life.

Answer: A) Gary Portnoy
- Trivia Tidbit: Gary Portnoy co-wrote and performed "Where Everybody Knows Your Name," the theme song for "Cheers." The song's reflective lyrics about finding a place where you're always welcome resonated with viewers.

Answer: B) A flux capacitor
- Trivia Tidbit: The flux capacitor is the key component that allows the DeLorean to time travel when it reaches 88 miles per hour. This fictional device became one of the most memorable elements of the "Back to the Future" trilogy.

Answer: A) The Goonies
- Trivia Tidbit: Directed by Richard Donner and produced by Steven Spielberg, "The Goonies" adventure is driven by a map leading to pirate "One-Eyed" Willy's treasure. The film is celebrated for its spirit of adventure, camaraderie, and the phrase "Goonies never say die!"

Answer: B) Private Investigator
- Trivia Tidbit: Tom Selleck's character, Thomas Magnum, is a private investigator living in Hawaii. "Magnum, P.I." was notable for its mix of action, humor, and drama.

The 1990s: The Broadening Horizons of TV and Cinema

The 1990s marked a period of broadening horizons in television and cinema, characterized by the rise of reality TV, the animation renaissance, and the era of must-see TV with shows like "Friends" and "Seinfeld" defining a generation. This decade also saw the indie film movement rise from Sundance to mainstream success, challenging the conventions of storytelling and filmmaking.

The advent of blockbusters and CGI ushered in a new era of cinema, making the impossible seem possible on the big screen, while cult classics like "The X-Files" and "Buffy the Vampire Slayer" garnered massive followings, redefining genre television.

The rise of premium cable channels like HBO marked the beginning of what would be known as the golden age of television, offering content that pushed the boundaries of what could be shown on TV.

Teen dramas and sitcoms captured the complexities of youth, resonating with audiences across the globe. The 1990s were a time of innovation and expansion, where the boundaries of television and cinema were pushed further than ever before, setting the stage for the incredible growth and diversification that would follow in the new millennium.

The Reality TV Revolution: "The Real World" and Beyond

The 1990s marked a significant shift in television programming, heralding the dawn of the reality TV revolution with the debut of MTV's "The Real World" in 1992. This pioneering show broke away from traditional scripted entertainment, offering viewers a glimpse into the lives of seven strangers picked to live in a house and have their lives taped. "The Real World" was not just a television program; it was a cultural phenomenon that reshaped the landscape of TV by introducing the concept of real people, rather than actors, as the main characters of their own narratives.

"The Real World" set the template for reality TV by showcasing real-life interactions, conflicts, and relationships, providing an unfiltered look at issues such as race, sexuality, and substance abuse. It was groundbreaking in its ability to discuss social issues candidly, making it both controversial and compelling. The success of "The Real World" spawned numerous imitators and successors, each taking the concept of reality television in new directions.

Following "The Real World," the 1990s and early 2000s saw an explosion of reality TV programming, with shows like "Survivor," "Big Brother," and "The Amazing Race" offering viewers different formats and experiences. These shows turned ordinary people into household names and demonstrated the public's voracious appetite for reality-based entertainment. The competition-based format of "Survivor," which premiered in 2000, introduced the concept of contestants participating in challenges for a grand prize, adding a game show element to the reality TV formula.

The reality TV revolution also extended into talent shows, with "American Idol" debuting in 2002. It provided a platform for aspiring singers to showcase their talents to a national audience, further blurring the lines between ordinary people and celebrities. "American Idol" not only revolutionized the talent show format but also had a significant impact on the music industry, launching the careers of many successful artists.

The impact of the reality TV revolution of the 1990s is still felt today, with the genre continuing to evolve and expand into various sub-genres, including reality competition, reality documentary, and reality-drama hybrid shows. Reality TV has become a staple of television programming, offering viewers a diverse array of content that ranges from the mundane to the extraordinary. It has challenged traditional notions of storytelling and entertainment, proving that real life, with all its unpredictability and drama, can be as captivating as any scripted show.

This shift towards reality-based content in the 1990s not only changed television but also had a broader impact on popular culture, influencing everything from social media to celebrity culture. Reality TV stars have become influencers and trendsetters, and the lines between reality and entertainment have increasingly blurred. The legacy of shows like "The Real World" and the reality TV boom of the 1990s continues to shape the television landscape, reflecting and shaping societal norms and values in the process.

- Innovative Casting: "The Real World" was one of the first shows to use an open casting process to select its cast members from thousands of applicants, a practice now standard in reality TV.
- Social Impact: "The Real World: San Francisco" (1994) is credited with bringing awareness to HIV/AIDS through cast member Pedro Zamora's struggle with the disease.

- "Survivor" Origins: The concept for "Survivor" was initially rejected by every major network before CBS took a chance on it, leading to its massive success and the proliferation of the reality competition genre.
- The First "Reality" Show: Although "The Real World" is often cited as the first reality show, the PBS series "An American Family," which aired in 1973, is considered by many as the genre's true pioneer.
- "Big Brother" Concept: The name "Big Brother" is derived from George Orwell's dystopian novel "1984," reflecting the show's concept of constant surveillance.
- "American Idol" Influence: Kelly Clarkson, the winner of the first season of "American Idol," went on to win multiple Grammy Awards, proving the show's ability to launch successful music careers.
- Reality TV and Social Media: The rise of reality TV in the 1990s coincided with the advent of the internet, allowing fans to interact with shows and cast members in unprecedented ways, laying the groundwork for modern social media culture.
- International Formats: Many reality TV shows, including "Survivor," "Big Brother," and "The Amazing Race," are based on formats that were originally developed in other countries and then adapted for the American audience.
- Crossover Stars: Several reality TV stars from the 1990s and early 2000s, such as Elisabeth Hasselbeck from "Survivor" and Jamie Chung from "The Real World," transitioned into mainstream media and entertainment careers.

The Animation Renaissance: Nickelodeon and Cartoon Network

The 1990s marked a transformative period in the animation industry, often referred to as the Animation Renaissance, with the emergence of Nickelodeon and Cartoon Network as pivotal platforms for innovative and diverse animated content. These networks redefined children's television, blending entertainment with thoughtful storytelling, and introduced a new era of animated shows that appealed to both kids and adults.

Nickelodeon, already known for its child-centric programming, launched a series of original animated shows, or "Nicktoons," starting with "Doug," "Rugrats," and "The Ren & Stimpy Show" in 1991. These shows, with their unique animation styles and wide range of themes, from everyday childhood dilemmas to absurdist comedy, set the stage for the network's future successes and established Nickelodeon as a leader in children's entertainment. "Rugrats," in particular, became a cultural phenomenon, exploring the world from a baby's perspective and winning multiple awards during its run.

Cartoon Network, established in 1992 by Turner Broadcasting, became the first U.S. channel dedicated entirely to cartoons. It initially aired classic animation but soon ventured into original programming with "Cartoon Cartoons," which included iconic shows like "Dexter's Laboratory," "The Powerpuff Girls," "Johnny Bravo," and "Cow and Chicken." These series were notable for their creative storytelling, humor, and distinct animation styles, contributing to the network's reputation for pushing the boundaries of children's animation.

The Animation Renaissance was characterized by its creativity, innovation, and willingness to explore complex characters and narratives that challenged the conventions of children's television. Shows from this era tackled a variety of themes, including family dynamics, personal identity, and social issues, making them relevant to a broader audience and paving the way for the acceptance of animated series as a legitimate form of storytelling for all ages.

The impact of Nickelodeon and Cartoon Network during the 1990s extended beyond their programming. They fostered a generation of animators and writers who would continue to influence the industry for years to come. The networks also contributed to the rise of merchandise, movies, and even theme park attractions based on their popular shows, highlighting the commercial potential of animated content.

Today, the legacy of the Animation Renaissance lives on, with many shows from the era enjoying continued popularity through reruns, streaming platforms, and cultural references in other media. The period also set the groundwork for subsequent innovations in animation, including the advent of adult-oriented animated series and the widespread use of digital animation techniques. Nickelodeon and Cartoon Network's contributions to the Animation Renaissance have cemented their status as iconic channels that changed the face of television animation.

"Rugrats" (Nickelodeon)

"Rugrats" offered a unique perspective on the world through the eyes of a group of toddlers and babies, led by the adventurous Tommy Pickles. The show explored their imaginative adventures as they navigated the mysteries of the adult world, which often ed to humorous and heartwarming misinterpretations of everyday life.

"Rugrats" was groundbreaking for its ability to appeal to both children and adults, weaving in sophisticated humor and themes that resonated across age groups.

The series also stood out for its depiction of diverse family structures and dynamics, including the representation of Jewish culture and holidays in several episodes, which was rare in children's programming at the time. "Rugrats" became one of Nickelodeon's longest-running shows, spawning multiple movies and a spin-off series, "All Grown Up!" which followed the characters into their pre-teen and teenage years.

- "Rugrats" was the first Nicktoon to receive a star on the Hollywood Walk of Fame.
- The character of Chuckie Finster was originally voiced by Christine Cavanaugh, who also voiced characters like Dexter from "Dexter's Laboratory."
- In the show, Tommy's father, Stu, is often seen inventing toys. His profession was inspired by one of the show's creators, Gabor Csupo, who had aspirations of becoming an inventor.

"Dexter's Laboratory" (Cartoon Network)

"Dexter's Laboratory" centered on Dexter, a boy-genius with a secret laboratory filled with his inventions. The show humorously juxtaposed Dexter's scientific ambitions with the chaos of everyday family life, especially the interference of his bubbly older sister, Dee Dee, who often unwittingly ruins Dexter's experiments. The series was celebrated for its clever writing, distinct visual style, and the way it balanced Dexter's extraordinary intellect with his very ordinary problems as a child.

Created by Genndy Tartakovsky, "Dexter's Laboratory" was one of the original "Cartoon Cartoons" and helped establish Cartoon Network as a prime destination for innovative animated content. The show's mix of science fiction, comedy, and family dynamics, along with memorable side characters and segments, made it a staple of 1990s animation.

- Genndy Tartakovsky got the inspiration for Dexter from one of his university projects.
- Dexter's last name is never revealed in the show.
- The episode "Dial M for Monkey: Barbequor" was banned after its initial airing due to concerns over its content, making it a sought-after episode for fans of the series.

"Hey Arnold!" (Nickelodeon)

"Hey Arnold!" stood out for its urban setting and a diverse cast of characters, centered around the thoughtful and football-headed Arnold. Living with his eccentric grandparents in a boarding house, the show delved into the lives of Arnold and his friends as they navigated the challenges of childhood and adolescence in the city. The series was praised for addressing complex themes such as poverty, parental absence, and the value of community, all while maintaining a sense of humor and optimism.

"Hey Arnold!" was notable for its emotional depth, with episodes that often ended on reflective and sometimes bittersweet notes, setting it apart from other children's programming of the time. Its depiction of a multicultural urban environment was also groundbreaking, providing a relatable and enriching perspective for many viewers.

- The character of Helga Pataki was based on a girl who used to bully creator Craig Bartlett in elementary school.
- Arnold's last name was revealed to be "Shortman," hinted at throughout the series by his grandpa calling him "short man."
- The show was originally conceived as a claymation short for "Sesame Street."

"The Powerpuff Girls" (Cartoon Network)

"The Powerpuff Girls" combined superhero action with a unique brand of humor to tell the story of three kindergarten-aged sisters with superpowers. Created by Professor Utonium in an attempt to make the "perfect little girl," Blossom, Bubbles, and Buttercup instead became crime-fighting heroes dedicated to protecting their city of Townsville from villains and monsters. The show was celebrated for its empowering female protagonists, vibrant animation style, and its clever blend of action and comedy.

The series broke stereotypes by presenting its young female leads as powerful and independent heroes, making it a significant cultural icon for promoting positive female role models in animation. "The Powerpuff Girls" became a merchandising powerhouse and was instrumental in defining Cartoon Network's identity as a leader in original animated content.

- The show was originally titled "Whoopass Stew!" during its development.
- Creator Craig McCracken was only 25 years old when the show premiered.
- The Powerpuff Girls' hotline number is the actual number for Cartoon Network's Atlanta headquarters.

The Era of Must-See TV: "Friends" and "Seinfeld"

The 1990s heralded the era of "Must-See TV," a period dominated by groundbreaking sitcoms that redefined the landscape of television comedy. Among the titans of this era were "Friends" and "Seinfeld," two shows that, despite their comedic foundations, offered distinctly different styles and approaches to storytelling and humor, capturing vast audiences and leaving a lasting impact on popular culture.

"Friends," premiering in 1994, quickly became a cultural phenomenon, drawing viewers into the lives of six friends navigating the complexities of adulthood, relationships, and careers in New York City. Its widespread appeal lay in its relatable characters, witty dialogue, and the chemistry among the cast. The show's portrayal of friendship and the transition into adult life struck a chord with a generation, making it a staple of '90s television and a fixture in living rooms around the world. "Friends" was celebrated for its ability to blend humor with touching moments, creating a feel-good experience that resonated with a broad audience. Its popularity was unmatched, consistently ranking in the top ten of the final television season ratings, and it concluded its run in 2004 with one of the most-watched TV finales of all time, drawing 52.5 million American viewers.

In contrast, "Seinfeld," debuting in 1989, carved its niche as a "show about nothing," focusing on the minutiae of everyday life and the peculiarities of social norms. Created by Larry David and Jerry Seinfeld, the show was revolutionary for its observational humor, complex storytelling, and a refusal to adhere to the traditional sitcom formula. "Seinfeld" was characterized by its unique brand of humor, often highlighting the absurdity in the mundane and eschewing the typical sentimental moments found in other sitcoms of its time. This distinct approach garnered a dedicated fanbase, making it one of the most beloved and critically acclaimed shows of the decade. It enjoyed immense popularity and ratings success, famously ending on a high note in 1998 with over 76 million viewers tuning in for its finale.

Both "Friends" and "Seinfeld" not only dominated the ratings and captivated millions of viewers throughout the 1990s but also contributed significantly to the evolution of television comedy. Their different styles—"Friends" with its warmth and relatability, and "Seinfeld" with its innovative, cynical take on life—offered something for everyone, cementing their status as cornerstones of '90s pop culture. Their enduring popularity, decades after their respective finales, underscores the lasting appeal of quality storytelling and humor, as new generations continue to discover and embrace these iconic shows.

Friends

"WE WERE ON A BREAK!"

"Friends" masterfully created a world that, while perhaps idealized, felt immensely relatable and inviting to its audience. The show's setting, primarily the iconic Central Perk coffee shop and the apartments of Monica and Joey, became as much a part of the show's identity as the characters themselves. Central Perk, with its oversized coffee mugs, plush sofas, and intimate stage for impromptu performances, became a symbol of '90s culture—a place where friends could gather, share their lives, and find comfort amidst the chaos of city living. This welcoming environment, coupled with the aspirational yet attainable lifestyle it depicted, allowed viewers to imagine themselves within the cozy confines of the "Friends" universe.

The New York City of "Friends" was a sanitized, almost utopian version of the actual city, where the challenges of urban life were present but never insurmountable. The characters navigated careers, relationships, and personal growth against the backdrop of a city that was vibrant and full of opportunities. The show's portrayal of New York played into the fantasies many held about life in the big city during the '90s, filled with chance encounters, lasting friendships, and the pursuit of dreams. This portrayal contributed significantly to the show's charm and appeal, offering an escape to a world where the right coffee shop, apartment, or group of friends could turn the mundane into the extraordinary.

Moreover, "Friends" tapped into the zeitgeist of its time, reflecting the evolving dynamics of young adulthood. The show's setting—the apartments and coffee shop—served as safe havens where the characters could retreat from the pressures of the outside world, symbolizing the changing concept of family and community.

Unlike the traditional nuclear family setup prevalent in earlier sitcoms, "Friends" presented a new kind of family, one chosen through friendship rather than blood, resonating with viewers who saw their own lives and relationships reflected in the show.

Through its ten seasons, "Friends" didn't just entertain; it created a comforting, familiar world that millions tuned into weekly, eager to spend time with their favorite characters. The show's success lay not only in its humor but in its ability to craft a world that felt like home, a world where, despite the ups and downs of life, you were never alone. This sense of belonging and the universal desire for connection are key to understanding the world of "Friends" and its enduring legacy in the landscape of television.

"You're My Lobster"

Ross Geller (David Schwimmer)

Ross, the ever-nerdy paleontologist, navigates through the series with his intelligent yet often socially awkward demeanor. Known for his three divorces and on-again, off-again relationship with Rachel, Ross's character adds depth with his blend of loyalty, jealousy, and passion for science. David Schwimmer, before "Friends," had a budding career in theater and television. Post-"Friends," Schwimmer directed several episodes of the series and went on to direct films and plays, proving his versatility in the entertainment industry. He also voiced Melman in the "Madagascar" film series, showcasing his ability to connect with a younger audience.

- Schwimmer directed 10 episodes of "Friends," showcasing his skills behind the camera.
- He's an accomplished stage actor and co-founded the Lookingglass Theatre Company in Chicago.
- Schwimmer voiced Melman in all of the "Madagascar" animated films.
- He received critical acclaim for his role as Robert Kardashian in "The People v. O.J. Simpson: American Crime Story."

Rachel Green (Jennifer Aniston)

Rachel's journey from a spoiled runaway bride to a successful fashion executive in New York City is a key storyline. Her evolving relationship with Ross is central to the series. Jennifer Aniston became an international star during and after "Friends," known for her role in numerous films and as a style icon, particularly her hairstyle, known as "The Rachel." Aniston's post-"Friends" career includes award-winning performances in both film and television, solidifying her as one of the most successful actresses of her generation.

- Aniston won an Emmy for Outstanding Lead Actress in a Comedy Series for her role as Rachel in 2002.
- "The Rachel" haircut became one of the most requested hairstyles of the 1990s.
- Aniston's film career post-"Friends" includes hits like "Marley & Me" and "Horrible Bosses."
- She returned to TV with the Apple TV+ series "The Morning Show," earning critical praise and awards nominations.

Monica Geller (Courteney Cox)

Monica, Ross's sister, is the group's mother hen, known for her competitiveness and obsessive cleanliness. Her relationship with Chandler blossoms from friendship to marriage, highlighting her desire for family and stability. Courteney Cox had already made a name for herself in the industry before "Friends," most notably in music videos and the "Scream" film series. After "Friends," she continued her success with "Cougar Town," earning critical acclaim and a dedicated fanbase.

- Cox was the only "Friends" cast member not to receive an Emmy nomination for her work on the show.
- Before "Friends," she appeared in Bruce Springsteen's music video for "Dancing in the Dark."
- "Cougar Town," her post-"Friends" series, earned her a Golden Globe nomination.
- Cox has ventured into directing, with projects including episodes of "Cougar Town" and the film "Just Before I Go."

"Not just health-department clean, "Monica" clean."

Chandler Bing (Matthew Perry)

Chandler's sarcastic humor and struggle with an odd family background make him a beloved character. His relationship with Monica showcases his growth from a commitment-phobe to a loving husband. Matthew Perry's performance is marked by his comedic timing, although he struggled with personal issues during and after the show. Despite these struggles, Perry has been involved in various film and television projects, using his platform to discuss addiction and recovery.

- Perry's own struggles with addiction mirrored Chandler's storyline of quitting smoking in the series.
- He wrote an episode of "Friends" in Season 6: "The One Where Chandler Can't Cry."
- He received critical acclaim for his role in "The West Wing" as Joe Quincy.

Joey Tribbiani (Matt LeBlanc)

Joey, the charming but dim-witted actor, is known for his catchphrase "How you doin'?" and his unyielding loyalty to his friends. His acting career, filled with ups and downs, provides comic relief and heartfelt moments. Matt LeBlanc's portrayal of Joey earned him a spin-off series, "Joey," though it did not achieve the same success. LeBlanc later found success with the Showtime series "Episodes," earning critical acclaim and awards for playing a fictionalized version of himself.

- LeBlanc received three Emmy nominations for his role as Joey Tribbiani.
- "Joey," his "Friends" spin-off, lasted for two seasons.
- For his role in "Episodes," LeBlanc won a Golden Globe for Best Actor in a TV Series Comedy.
- LeBlanc became a presenter on "Top Gear," showcasing his passion for cars.

Phoebe Buffay (Lisa Kudrow)

Phoebe, the eccentric masseuse and musician, is known for her quirky outlook on life and her hit song "Smelly Cat." Her backstory, involving a troubled childhood, adds layers to her character, making her both hilarious and empathetic. Lisa Kudrow, already an established comedian before "Friends," leveraged her role to explore more dramatic roles in film and television. Kudrow also produced and starred in the acclaimed series "The Comeback" and "Web Therapy," showcasing her range and innovation as an actress and producer.

- Kudrow won an Emmy for Outstanding Supporting Actress in a Comedy Series in 1998 for her role as Phoebe.
- She's a producer and writer, with credits including "Web Therapy" and "The Comeback."
- Kudrow has a Bachelor's degree in Biology from Vassar College.
- She conducted extensive genealogy research for the show "Who Do You Think You Are?"

Greatest Episodes

To binge-watch all 236 episodes of "Friends," it would take approximately 5,192 minutes, which is about 86.5 hours or roughly 3.6 days of continuous viewing without any breaks. This calculation assumes you're watching back-to-back with each episode lasting an average of 22 minutes. Remember, this doesn't account for any extended specials or breaks you might take! So, What are the greatest episodes!

"The One Where Ross Finds Out" (Season 2, Episode 7)
This pivotal episode features the moment Rachel realizes she still has feelings for Ross, leading to her drunkenly leaving him a voicemail confessing her love. Ross's subsequent confrontation with Rachel results in their passionate first kiss at Central Perk, marking the beginning of their iconic on-again, off-again relationship.

- The scene where Ross and Rachel kiss for the first time was met with one of the longest studio audience applause in the show's history.
- David Schwimmer and Jennifer Aniston both acknowledged feeling real emotional tension during the filming of the kiss scene.
- This episode solidified Ross and Rachel's relationship as a central storyline of the series.
- The subplot involving Monica becoming obsessed with becoming the best at a new video game provides comic relief and showcases her competitive nature.

"The One with the Prom Video" (Season 2, Episode 14)

A throwback to Monica and Rachel's high school prom night revealed through an old video tape, this episode is most memorable for Ross's sweet gesture from the past and the group's reactions to their younger selves. It ends with Rachel forgiving Ross, leading to another significant moment in their relationship.

- The phrase "See? He's her lobster!" spoken by Phoebe is one of the show's most quoted lines, referring to Ross and Rachel's meant-to-be relationship.
- The old prom video was a significant prop, taking considerable effort to create a believable teenage past for Monica, Rachel, and Ross.
- This episode won the Primetime Emmy Award for Outstanding Directing in a Comedy Series.

"The One Where Everybody Finds Out" (Season 5, Episode 14)

When Phoebe discovers Monica and Chandler's secret relationship, it leads to a comedic game of who-knows-what. The episode is famous for Phoebe and Chandler's fake seduction scene, ending with Monica and Chandler admitting they love each other.

- Lisa Kudrow's performance in this episode, particularly her fake seduction scene with Matthew Perry, is often highlighted as one of her best.
- The chemistry between the cast during the revelation scene is noted as a testament to their off-screen friendship.
- This episode showcases the series' ability to balance humor with emotional depth, a hallmark of "Friends."

"The One with Ross's Wedding" (Season 4, Episodes 23 and 24)
Set in London, this two-part episode features Ross's wedding to Emily and the group's adventures in England. It includes memorable moments like Joey's sightseeing tour, Monica and Chandler beginning their relationship, and Ross accidentally saying Rachel's name at the altar.
- The filming in London was a significant event for the show, marking one of the few times "Friends" filmed significant scenes outside the studio.
- The iconic moment when Ross says Rachel's name instead of Emily's at the altar was ranked as one of the most shocking season finales in television history.
- The episodes featured cameo appearances by British actors, including Hugh Laurie and Jennifer Saunders, adding to the special nature of the London episodes.
- The London setting provided an opportunity for the show to explore cultural differences and humor, including the characters' interactions with the British locals, which added a fresh dynamic to the familiar group dynamic. Notably, Joey's attempts to blend in and understand British culture were a source of comedic relief.
- The decision to film in London was partly to capitalize on the show's growing international popularity at the time. It served as a celebration of the global fan base "Friends" had cultivated, making the episodes a landmark moment in the show's history.

"The One with the Embryos" (Season 4, Episode 12)
Though titled for Phoebe's storyline of getting implanted with embryos, this episode is best known for the trivia game that leads to Monica and Rachel swapping their apartment with Joey and Chandler. It's a fan favorite for showcasing the characters' deep knowledge (and ignorance) of each other.

- The trivia contest in this episode was inspired by the producers' realization of how well the audience knew the characters after four seasons.

- The swapping of the apartments led to a fresh dynamic and new comedic situations for several episodes.

- The episode is a fan favorite for its balance of humor and the emotional moment when Phoebe agrees to carry her brother's children.

"The One Where No One's Ready" (Season 3, Episode 2)
Set in real-time, this episode takes place entirely in Monica's apartment as Ross struggles to get everyone ready for a museum benefit. The episode is a showcase of the ensemble's comedic talent and the characters' quirky personalities clashing under time pressure.

- This episode was filmed entirely on one set to save costs, which inadvertently led to a tightly scripted and highly praised episode.

- The scene where Joey wears all of Chandler's clothes was an improvised moment that became iconic.

- The episode highlighted the show's ability to create compelling, character-driven comedy within the confines of a single location.

Trivia Tidbits

- "Friends" originally had the working title "Insomnia Café" before it was changed to "Friends Like Us" and finally shortened to "Friends."
- The iconic orange couch in Central Perk was found in the Warner Bros. studio's basement.
- The show was shot in front of a live audience, except for cliffhangers to prevent plot leaks.
- Courteney Cox initially auditioned for the role of Rachel, but she requested to play Monica instead.
- The frame around the peephole on Monica's apartment door was originally a mirror that got broken, so the crew decided to use it as a frame.
- The show's creators, Marta Kauffman and David Crane, also co-wrote the theme song "I'll Be There for You" with The Rembrandts.
- "Friends" is known for its Thanksgiving episodes, but the very first season did not include one.
- The exterior shots of the "Friends" apartment building are actually located in Greenwich Village, at the corner of Grove and Bedford Streets.
- Joey's character was not originally written to be dim, but Matt LeBlanc suggested it during his audition, and it was incorporated into the role.
- The artwork in Central Perk and in the apartments changed every few episodes to keep the background interesting.
- Lisa Kudrow was actually afraid of the duck that appeared in later seasons.
- The show made a deal with Warner Bros. to move production to Los Angeles if any of the cast members became pregnant. This was utilized when Lisa Kudrow was pregnant with her son.

- Jennifer Aniston and Courteney Cox are godmothers to David Schwimmer's daughter.
- The white dog statue in Joey and Chandler's apartment actually belonged to Jennifer Aniston, a gift from a friend.

True or False

The coffee shop in "Friends" was originally supposed to be a diner.
True or False
Every season of "Friends" has a Thanksgiving episode.
True or False
The refrigerator in Monica's apartment was fully functional and stocked with real food.
True or False
"Friends" was filmed in New York City.
True or False
The role of Ross Geller was written specifically for David Schwimmer.
True or False
The duck and the chick were real animals that lived on the set during filming.
True or False
Central Perk is based on a real coffee shop in Greenwich Village.
True or False
The "Friends" theme song was almost a completely different song by R.E.M.
True or False
Before settling on "Friends," the show was nearly titled "Across the Hall."
True or False
Lisa Kudrow improvised the song "Smelly Cat."
True or False

Answers

False. Central Perk was always intended to be a coffee shop. The idea was to create a relaxed, coffeehouse setting where the characters could hang out outside their apartments.

False. While "Friends" is known for its iconic Thanksgiving episodes, there was no Thanksgiving episode in the first season.

True. The fridge in Monica's apartment was indeed functional and often stocked with beverages and snacks for the cast and crew.

False. Although set in New York City, "Friends" was filmed in Los Angeles at Warner Bros. Studios.

True. The producers had David Schwimmer in mind for the role of Ross when they were writing the character.

True. The duck and the chick were real animals introduced in the show, adding to the quirky household of Joey and Chandler.

False. While Central Perk feels like it could belong in Greenwich Village, it is a fictional coffee shop created for the show.

True. The producers considered various songs for the theme, but "I'll Be There for You" by The Rembrandts was chosen to reflect the show's themes of friendship and support.

True. One of the early titles considered for the show was "Across the Hall," emphasizing the living arrangements of the characters.

False. "Smelly Cat" was written by the show's writers, though Lisa Kudrow's portrayal of Phoebe's performance added to its charm and memorability.

Seinfeld

"Seinfeld," often hailed as "a show about nothing," revolutionized the television landscape with its unique approach to comedy. Created by Larry David and Jerry Seinfeld, the series debuted in 1989 and ran for nine seasons, cementing its place as one of the most iconic and influential sitcoms in TV history. Starring Jerry Seinfeld as a fictionalized version of himself, the show explored the minutiae of everyday life, focusing on the trivialities and absurdities that other sitcoms often overlooked. Set in New York City, "Seinfeld" revolved around the neurotic comedian Jerry, his ex-girlfriend Elaine Benes (Julia Louis-Dreyfus), his neurotic best friend George Costanza (Jason Alexander), and his eccentric neighbor Cosmo Kramer (Michael Richards).

Unlike "Friends," which depicted a warm, idealized version of New York City life through the lens of friendship and romance, "Seinfeld" adopted a more cynical and observational tone. The series was groundbreaking in its refusal to adhere to traditional sitcom formulas, often eschewing common tropes like learning moments or moral conclusions. Instead, "Seinfeld" found humor in the mundane, turning everyday scenarios—waiting for a table at a Chinese restaurant, losing a car in a parking garage, or dealing with the minutiae of social etiquette—into the basis of entire episodes.

"Seinfeld's" impact on pop culture is immense, introducing phrases and concepts into the American lexicon such as "yada yada yada," "master of your domain," and "the Soup Nazi." The show's distinct brand of humor, characterized by its emphasis on sharp wit, irony, and the peculiarities of social conventions, has inspired a generation of comedians and television writers. Its influence can be seen in countless shows that followed, from

"Curb Your Enthusiasm" to "Arrested Development" and "The Office," all of which owe a debt to "Seinfeld's" innovative approach to comedy.

The show's success was not immediate, but it grew in popularity, becoming a cornerstone of NBC's "Must-See TV" lineup in the 1990s. By its final season, "Seinfeld" was among the top-rated shows on American television, concluding with a highly anticipated finale that drew over 76 million viewers.

Despite some viewers' mixed reactions to the finale, the episode was a cultural event, demonstrating the show's significant impact on its audience.

The legacy of "Seinfeld" endures, with the series continuing to attract new fans through syndication and streaming platforms. Its approach to comedy—focusing on the characters' selfishness, their interactions with the eccentricities of New York City, and their often morally ambiguous choices—has cemented its status as a timeless classic. "Seinfeld" remains a masterclass in comedy writing and performance, celebrated for its unique voice, memorable characters, and its unparalleled ability to find humor in the trivial aspects of daily life.

"Hello, Newman"

Jerry Seinfeld

Jerry, playing a semi-fictional version of himself, stands at the center of "Seinfeld's" universe. As a stand-up comedian living in New York, his observations on everyday absurdities provide much of the show's comedic fodder. Jerry's character is marked by his quick wit, skepticism, and a certain level of emotional detachment, often acting as the voice of reason amid the chaos created by his friends. Off-screen, Jerry Seinfeld's career took off following the success of "Seinfeld." He returned to stand-up comedy, where he remains a significant figure, and ventured into web series with "Comedians in Cars Getting Coffee," showcasing his enduring love for comedy and conversation.

- Jerry's apartment, a frequent setting for the show, was designed to reflect his character's simple and unpretentious lifestyle.
- Seinfeld's real-life passion for cars, especially Porsches, is mirrored in his character's interests.

Elaine Benes (Julia Louis-Dreyfus)

Elaine, Jerry's ex-girlfriend and friend, is known for her assertive personality, sharp wit, and sometimes chaotic dating life. Her relationships with Jerry, George, and Kramer provide some of the show's most memorable dynamics.

Julia Louis-Dreyfus's portrayal of Elaine broke new ground for female characters in comedy, making Elaine a role model for her independence and complexity. After "Seinfeld," Louis-Dreyfus continued to find success on television, particularly with "Veep," for which she won multiple Emmy Awards, solidifying her status as one of the most talented comedic actresses of her generation.

- Elaine's dance moves in "The Little Kicks" episode are famously awkward and have become an iconic moment in TV history.
- Louis-Dreyfus has won more Emmy Awards for acting than any other performer in history.

George Costanza (Jason Alexander)

George, loosely based on co-creator Larry David, is characterized by his neuroticism, constant scheming, and often self-destructive behavior. His struggles with relationships, work, and his parents are a source of endless comedy and relatability. Jason Alexander's portrayal of George is critically acclaimed, making the character a quintessential example of a loveable loser. Post-"Seinfeld," Alexander has had a successful career in theater, film, and television, including directing and participating in various philanthropic efforts.

- The infamous "George is getting upset!" line became one of the character's catchphrases, highlighting his often comical overreactions to life's frustrations.
- Alexander's theatrical background greatly influenced his expressive performance style on the show.

Cosmo Kramer (Michael Richards)

Kramer, Jerry's eccentric neighbor, is known for his wild hair, quirky mannerisms, and mysterious sources of income. His entrances into Jerry's apartment are legendary, often accompanied by applause from the studio audience. Kramer's bizarre ideas and ventures add a unique flavor to the show's comedy. After "Seinfeld," Michael Richards faced controversy but also took roles in series and films, though none matched the success of his role as Kramer.

- Kramer's character was based on Larry David's real-life neighbor, Kenny Kramer.
- Richards performed many of his own stunts, contributing to Kramer's physical comedy.

Newman (Wayne Knight)

Newman, the scheming nemesis of Jerry and somewhat of an ally to Kramer, is a postal worker who revels in petty grievances and small-scale conspiracies. His character is often shrouded in mystery regarding his full range of activities and motivations.

Wayne Knight's portrayal of Newman provided "Seinfeld" with a delightfully wicked character, whose catchphrase, "Hello, Jerry," became synonymous with impending trouble or annoyance. After "Seinfeld," Knight continued to work in television, film, and voice acting, showcasing his versatile talent in various genres.

- Despite Newman's antagonistic role, he became a beloved character for his cunning plans and deep-seated rivalry with Jerry.
- Knight's performance was so memorable that Newman is often ranked as one of the best TV characters of all time, despite being a supporting role.

Frank Costanza (Jerry Stiller)

Frank Costanza, George's father, is known for his explosive temper, eccentricities, and the invention of the holiday "Festivus." Stiller's portrayal of Frank added a layer of comedic genius to the show, with his outbursts and peculiar logic becoming a highlight of the series. Before joining "Seinfeld," Jerry Stiller was already an established comedian, part of the comedy duo Stiller and Meara. His role on "Seinfeld" introduced him to a new generation of fans, and he continued to entertain as Arthur Spooner on "The King of Queens" following his time on "Seinfeld."

- Stiller's casting as Frank Costanza came after another actor had originally filmed the role, but the producers felt Stiller's interpretation brought something uniquely hilarious to the character.
- The character's creation of Festivus has led to the pseudo-holiday being celebrated by fans in real life every December 23rd.

Susan Ross (Heidi Swedberg)

Susan Ross, George's on-again, off-again girlfriend and later fiancée, is a character whose relationships with the main cast, particularly George, are central to many of the show's plots. Her untimely death by licking toxic wedding envelope glue is one of "Seinfeld's" most shocking moments. Heidi Swedberg's portrayal of Susan provided a counterbalance to George's antics, and her interactions with the rest of the cast highlighted the sometimes-absurd consequences of their actions. After "Seinfeld," Swedberg focused on her music, particularly playing the ukulele, and occasionally acted in television and theatre.

- The decision to kill off Susan's character was controversial but ultimately added to the show's legacy of pushing comedic boundaries.
- Swedberg's musical talents have been showcased in her post-"Seinfeld" career, leading ukulele workshops and performances.

Estelle Costanza (Estelle Harris)

Estelle Costanza, George's loud, overbearing mother, is a character whose dramatic flair and constant nagging provide a comedic look into George's family life. Harris's portrayal of Estelle is unforgettable, contributing to the show's exploration of neurotic family dynamics. Estelle is unforgettable, contributing to the show's exploration of neurotic family dynamics. Her chemistry with Jerry Stiller created one of television's most hilariously dysfunctional marriages. Following "Seinfeld," Harris became known to a new generation as the voice of Mrs. Potato Head in the "Toy Story" series, among other roles.

- Harris's unique voice and delivery made Estelle Costanza a standout character, often imitated by fans.
- Her role in "Seinfeld" helped solidify the show's depiction of eccentric yet endearing family relationships.

Trivia Tidbits

- The iconic bass music in "Seinfeld" was different in every episode. Composer Jonathan Wolff would slightly alter the theme to match the pacing and tone of Jerry's opening and closing stand-up bits.
- Larry David, co-creator of "Seinfeld," made several cameo appearances throughout the series, most notably as the voice of George Steinbrenner, the owner of the New York Yankees.
- "Seinfeld" was almost named "The Seinfeld Chronicles." NBC aired the pilot under this title before it was shortened to just "Seinfeld."
- The show's finale was so highly anticipated that TV Land aired a message during its broadcast time that simply read, "Gone watching 'Seinfeld'! Back in 60 minutes."
- The character of Elaine Benes was not in the pilot episode. The network suggested adding a female character after the pilot, leading to Julia Louis-Dreyfus's casting.
- Kramer's character was based on Larry David's real-life neighbor across the hall, Kenny Kramer, who later ran for Mayor of New York City on the Libertarian Party ticket.

- "No hugging, no learning" was an unofficial rule for the show, emphasizing that characters would not have sentimental growth or moral lessons by the end of each episode.
- The coffee shop where the characters frequently hang out, Monk's Café, is based on a real-life diner in New York City called Tom's Restaurant, which is located near Columbia University.
- Jerry's apartment number changes from 411 to 5A during the series.
- A real contest inspired the "contest" episode in which the main characters bet on who can go the longest without masturbating. Larry David later said it was based on a real contest he participated in.

Before the inception of "Seinfeld," Jerry was already established in the comedy circuit, known for his unique ability to find humor in everyday situations. His stand-up career, characterized by an acute observation of life's trivialities, laid the groundwork for what would become the show's signature style. Together with Larry David, Seinfeld developed a sitcom that was essentially about "nothing" — focusing on the minutiae of daily life that most people overlook. This concept, combined with the fictionalized version of Jerry as a stand-up comedian living in New York, allowed the show to explore various social norms and personal idiosyncrasies in a manner that was both hilarious and relatable.

Jerry's stand-up routines bookend many of the episodes, providing not just a narrative frame but also emphasizing the comedy inherent in the ordinariness of life. This innovative integration of stand-up comedy into a television series format was instrumental in making "Seinfeld" a groundbreaking show that reshaped the sitcom genre.

Questions

Before "Seinfeld" became a hit, Jerry Seinfeld was known for:
A) Being a sitcom actor
B) His stand-up comedy
C) Writing children's books

Jerry's stand-up comedy is prominently featured in "Seinfeld" as:
A) The opening scene of every episode
B) The closing scene of every episode
C) Both the opening and closing scenes of every episode

Jerry Seinfeld's character in the show has a particular obsession with:
A) Vintage cars
B) Superman
C) Breakfast cereal

In the series, Jerry lives in:
A) Brooklyn
B) Manhattan's Upper West Side
C) Queens

Jerry's approach to comedy in "Seinfeld" is often described as:
A) Observational humor
B) Slapstick comedy
C) Political satire

Answers

B) His stand-up comedy
- Trivia Tidbit: Jerry Seinfeld's return to stand-up after "Seinfeld" concluded was highly anticipated, leading to sold-out shows and a Netflix special titled "Jerry Before Seinfeld," where he revisits the comedy clubs where he started his career.

C) Both the opening and closing scenes of every episode
- Trivia Tidbit: Many of Jerry's stand-up bits in the show were adapted from his real-life routines, providing insights into his thought process and creating a seamless transition between his on-stage persona and his character on the show.

B) Superman
- Trivia Tidbit: Superman references are scattered throughout "Seinfeld," reflecting Jerry Seinfeld's admiration for the superhero. This includes posters in Jerry's apartment and numerous verbal references to Superman and his universe.

B) Manhattan's Upper West Side
- Trivia Tidbit: The exterior shot of Jerry's apartment building is actually located in Los Angeles, not New York City, a common practice in television production to use different locations for filming.

A) Observational humor
- Trivia Tidbit: Jerry Seinfeld's focus on observational humor influenced a generation of comedians, emphasizing the comedy inherent in everyday life and situations, rather than relying on setups and punchlines alone.

The Indie Film Movement: Sundance to Mainstream

The Indie Film Movement marked a significant shift in the cinematic landscape, challenging the dominance of major studios and showcasing the creativity and vision of independent filmmakers. This movement gained momentum in the late 1980s and flourished throughout the 1990s, with the Sundance Film Festival emerging as a pivotal platform for indie films. Founded by Robert Redford in 1981, Sundance became synonymous with independent cinema, offering a space for filmmakers to present their work without the creative constraints often imposed by studio systems.

Indie films distinguished themselves through their storytelling, exploring themes and narratives that were often considered too niche, controversial, or avant-garde for mainstream cinema. These films were characterized by their low budgets, innovative narrative structures, and a focus on character-driven stories, providing a stark contrast to the blockbuster mentality of high budgets and spectacle over substance. The movement was not just about the films themselves but also about challenging the status quo and democratizing the filmmaking process, making it more accessible to those outside the traditional Hollywood system.

The impact of the Indie Film Movement extended beyond the festivals and art houses, gradually influencing mainstream cinema as well. Major studios took notice of the commercial success and critical acclaim garnered by many indie films, leading to the establishment of independent divisions within larger studios, such as Fox Searchlight and Sony Pictures Classics. This blurred the lines between indie and mainstream, allowing independent filmmakers to reach wider audiences without compromising their artistic integrity.

Notable films of the Indie Film Movement include "Sex, Lies, and Videotape" by Steven Soderbergh, "Pulp Fiction" by Quentin Tarantino, and "Clerks" by Kevin Smith. These films, among others, not only achieved critical and commercial success but also inspired a new generation of filmmakers. They demonstrated that compelling storytelling and innovative filmmaking could captivate audiences and critics alike, regardless of budget size.

Today, the legacy of the Indie Film Movement continues to influence the film industry. The spirit of independence, innovation, and the willingness to tackle complex, nuanced subjects have become integral to the fabric of modern cinema. Festivals like Sundance remain vital for discovering and nurturing new talent, ensuring that the indie ethos—a commitment to artistic freedom and storytelling—lives on.

"Sex, Lies, and Videotape" (1989)

Steven Soderbergh's "Sex, Lies, and Videotape" is often heralded as the film that ignited the Indie Film Movement. Premiering at Sundance in 1989, where it won the Audience Award, the film's success on the festival circuit led to widespread acclaim and a Palme d'Or at Cannes. "Sex, Lies, and Videotape" delves into the intimate lives of four characters in Baton Rouge, Louisiana, exploring themes of voyeurism, intimacy, and personal truth. Its minimalist approach, focusing on dialogue and character interaction over action, showcased the potential for low-budget films to make a significant impact. The film's success opened the door for independent films in the mainstream market, proving that there was an audience for thoughtful, character-driven stories.

- Steven Soderbergh was only 26 years old when he wrote the screenplay for "Sex, Lies, and Videotape," making him one of the youngest directors to win the Palme d'Or at Cannes.
- The film was shot in only five weeks, largely due to the tight budget and Soderbergh's efficient planning.
- "Sex, Lies, and Videotape" cost under $1.2 million to produce but grossed over $24 million at the box office, exemplifying the financial potential of indie films.
- The movie's success is credited with boosting the careers of its stars, including Andie MacDowell and James Spader, who received critical acclaim for their performances.
- Soderbergh used natural lighting throughout much of the film to keep production costs down, adding to its authentic, intimate feel.
- The film's title sparked controversy and debate, drawing attention to its themes before viewers even saw the movie.
- "Sex, Lies, and Videotape" was added to the United States Library of Congress' National Film Registry in 2006, being recognized as "culturally, historically, or aesthetically significant."

"Clerks" (1994)

Kevin Smith's "Clerks" is a prime example of the DIY ethic at the heart of the Indie Film Movement. Shot on a shoestring budget in a convenience store where Smith worked, "Clerks" featured non-professional actors and a script based on Smith's own experiences. The film's raw, unpolished aesthetic, coupled with its sharp, witty dialogue, resonated with audiences and critics alike, turning it into a cult classic. "Clerks" showcased the potential for minimal resources and sheer creativity to result in a compelling and relatable film, inspiring countless aspiring filmmakers to pursue their visions despite financial constraints.

- Kevin Smith financed "Clerks" by selling his comic book collection and using credit cards, accumulating a debt of about $27,000.
- The film was shot in black and white because it was cheaper than shooting in color, which inadvertently contributed to its unique look.
- "Clerks" introduced audiences to the characters Jay and Silent Bob, who would become recurring characters in Smith's View Askewniverse.
- The original ending of "Clerks" was much darker, involving the death of one of the main characters, but it was changed after feedback from early screenings.
- Much of the dialogue was based on actual conversations and experiences Kevin Smith had while working at the Quick Stop and video store.
- "Clerks" premiered at the Sundance Film Festival and was picked up by Miramax for distribution, making it one of the indie success stories of the early '90s.
- The film's soundtrack, featuring alternative rock bands, was more expensive than the cost of filming, highlighting the importance of music in creating the film's atmosphere.

Following the success of "Clerks," Kevin Smith became a prominent figure in the independent film movement, continuously pushing the boundaries of indie filmmaking. He further explored the lives of his characters through a series of interconnected films known as the "View Askewniverse," which includes "Mallrats" (1995), "Chasing Amy" (1997), "Dogma" (1999), "Jay and Silent Bob Strike Back" (2001), and "Clerks II" (2006). Each film varied in commercial and critical reception, but collectively, they solidified Smith's reputation for his unique narrative style, blending humor, philosophy, and commentary on pop culture and societal norms. "Chasing Amy," in particular, was praised for its mature handling of complex themes such as sexuality, identity, and friendship, earning Smith a wider recognition for his directorial prowess beyond the slacker comedy genre.

Outside of directing, Smith made significant contributions to other areas of entertainment. He wrote comics for major publishers like Marvel and DC, bringing his storytelling skills to beloved characters like Daredevil and Green Arrow. Smith also became an influential voice in the podcasting world, hosting shows like "SModcast" and "Fatman on Batman," where he shares his insights on filmmaking, comics, and pop culture. His engagement with fans through social media and public speaking engagements further exemplified his commitment to the indie ethos, leveraging his platform to support up-and-coming filmmakers and to advocate for creative freedom within the industry. Despite facing challenges and evolving trends in cinema, Kevin Smith's legacy as a pioneer of independent film and a multifaceted storyteller remains unassailable, inspiring a new generation of filmmakers to follow their creative instincts.

"Pulp Fiction" (1994)

"English, motherfucker, do you speak it?"

"Pulp Fiction," directed by Quentin Tarantino, is an epochal film that reshaped the landscape of modern cinema with its nonlinear narrative, sharp dialogue, and stylized violence. Released in 1994, it weaves together multiple stories of crime and redemption in Los Angeles, featuring a sprawling cast including John Travolta, Uma Thurman, Samuel L. Jackson, Bruce Willis, and Ving Rhames. The film's structure, inspired by pulp magazines and hardboiled crime novels, breaks away from traditional storytelling by intertwining seemingly unrelated narratives into a cohesive mosaic that explores themes of chance, redemption, and the impact of violence. Its iconic dance scenes, memorable lines, and unique characters have left an indelible mark on pop culture.

The decision to create "Pulp Fiction" as an independent film was partly a result of the unconventional narrative and content that major studios might have shied away from.

Tarantino's vision required creative freedom that only the indie film scene could provide at the time. Funded by Miramax, then a leading company in independent cinema, "Pulp Fiction" was made for approximately $8 million—a modest budget by Hollywood standards. This financial and creative independence allowed Tarantino to craft a film that defied genre conventions, mixing comedy, drama, and suspense in a way that had seldom been seen before.

"Pulp Fiction's" success at Cannes, where it won the Palme d'Or, and its subsequent critical and commercial triumph underscored the viability and importance of independent cinema in the 1990s. The film grossed over $200 million worldwide, proving that indie films could compete with major studio releases both financially and artistically. It played a pivotal role in bringing indie cinema to a broader audience, demonstrating that films outside the mainstream could achieve significant cultural and commercial impact.

- The "Pulp Fiction" screenplay was written by Quentin Tarantino and Roger Avary, who initially conceived their stories as part of a single, larger narrative. Avary's contributions primarily became the "Gold Watch" segment of the film.
- The famous dance scene between Uma Thurman and John Travolta at Jack Rabbit Slim's was inspired by the dance sequence in the film "Band of Outsiders" (1964) by Jean-Luc Godard, a director whom Tarantino greatly admires.

- The role of Vincent Vega was originally intended for Michael Madsen, who played Vic Vega in "Reservoir Dogs." Scheduling conflicts led to Travolta getting the part, which revitalized his then-waning career.
- The briefcase's glowing contents are never revealed, leading to widespread speculation and theories among fans. Tarantino has described it as a "MacGuffin," a plot device that motivates the characters but is insignificant to the audience.
- Jules Winnfield's (Samuel L. Jackson) Ezekiel 25:17 speech was mostly fabricated by Tarantino and not a direct Bible quote, blending various passages with original dialogue to create one of the film's most memorable monologues.
- The "Kangaroo" watch mentioned in the "Gold Watch" segment is not a real brand. This detail adds to the film's blending of reality with fictional elements.
- Bruce Willis's character, Butch Coolidge, was named after Burt Coolidge, a character in Tarantino's unproduced screenplay, "Pandemonium Reigns," part of which evolved into the "Gold Watch" story.
- The "Pulp Fiction" title refers to the pulp magazines and hardboiled crime novels popular during the mid-20th century, known for their graphic violence and punchy dialogue, which inspired the film's style.
- Tarantino makes a cameo in the film as Jimmie Dimmick, whose house is used by Jules and Vincent to clean up after a particularly messy hit goes wrong.
- The film's nonlinear structure was influenced by such works as Stanley Kubrick's "The Killing" (1956) and Jean-Luc Godard's "Week End" (1967), showcasing Tarantino's penchant for drawing inspiration from film history.

Tarantino

Quentin Tarantino's journey to creating "Pulp Fiction" began in the video stores and independent film scene of the late 1980s and early 1990s. His debut film, "Reservoir Dogs" (1992), introduced his talent for sharp dialogue and nonlinear storytelling, earning him critical acclaim and a cult following. Tarantino's deep appreciation for cinema, especially genre films and the work of international directors, influenced his filmmaking style, characterized by references to film history, homage to his influences, and a unique blend of humor and violence.

Following "Pulp Fiction," Tarantino continued to explore and deconstruct genres with films like "Jackie Brown" (1997), "Kill Bill" (2003-2004), "Inglourious Basterds" (2009), and "Django Unchained" (2012). Each project reflected his signature style while also pushing the boundaries of narrative and character development. Tarantino's films are known for their eclectic soundtracks, ensemble casts, and intricate plots, making him one of the most distinctive and influential voices in contemporary cinema. His work not only pays tribute to the past but also innovates, challenging both filmmakers and audiences to reconsider their perceptions of cinema.

Tarantino's origin story is almost as legendary as his films. Born in Knoxville, Tennessee, and raised in Los Angeles, he dropped out of high school to pursue acting, eventually finding his way behind the camera. His early work included writing, directing, and acting in the uncompleted film "My Best Friend's Birthday," the screenplay of which formed the basis for "True Romance." Tarantino's encyclopedic knowledge of film, honed during his years working at a video rental store, along with his unique vision for storytelling, set the stage for his breakout success with "Reservoir Dogs." This film, along with "Pulp Fiction," solidified his reputation as a filmmaker capable of blending high art with popular culture, forever changing the landscape of American cinema.

Pop Culture

"Pulp Fiction" not only marked a significant moment in film history but also permeated pop culture, influencing fashion, dialogue, and attitudes towards cinema. The film's unique blend of sharp wit, stylistic violence, and memorable characters created a cultural phenomenon that extended beyond the indie film scene into mainstream consciousness. Its impact is evident in the numerous references and homages found in other movies, television shows, music videos, and even comic books. The dialogue, particularly catchphrases like "English, motherfucker, do you speak it?" and "Say 'what' again," has been quoted, parodied, and celebrated in various forms of media, embedding itself in the lexicon of popular culture.

One of the most striking aspects of "Pulp Fiction's" cultural footprint is its influence on fashion. Uma Thurman's character, Mia Wallace, with her bob haircut, white button-down shirt, and black pants, became an iconic look that inspired Halloween costumes and fashion editorials alike. Similarly, John Travolta and Samuel L. Jackson's suited appearances as Vincent Vega and Jules Winnfield brought back the cool allure of the classic black suit, making it a symbol of sleek, timeless style.

The film's structure, characterized by its non-linear narrative, became a blueprint for storytelling in cinema and television, inspiring filmmakers and writers to experiment with time and perspective in their work. "Pulp Fiction" demonstrated that audiences were ready for complex narratives that challenged conventional storytelling methods, leading to a wave of films and series that adopted similar techniques to tell their stories.

> *"Blessed is he who, in the name of charity and good will, shepherds the weak through the valley of the darkness, for he is truly his brother's keeper and the finder of lost children. And I will strike down upon thee with great vengeance and furious anger those who attempt to poison and destroy My brothers."*

Moreover, Jules Winnfield's (Samuel L. Jackson) misquoted Ezekiel 25:17 speech is a prime example of how "Pulp Fiction" creatively borrowed and reinterpreted elements from various sources. The passage, as recited by Jackson in the film, combines phrases from the actual Bible verse with Tarantino's own additions, creating a compelling monologue that has been celebrated, analyzed, and memorized by fans.

This reinterpretation of biblical text for dramatic effect underscores Tarantino's skill in blending the sacred with the profane, further embedding the film into the fabric of pop culture.

"Pulp Fiction's" legacy in pop culture is a testament to its innovative approach to filmmaking and storytelling. The film not only challenged and expanded the boundaries of cinema but also captured the imagination of a generation, leaving an enduring impact on pop culture. Its characters, dialogue, and aesthetic continue to be celebrated and referenced, solidifying "Pulp Fiction" as a seminal work that resonates with audiences even decades after its release.

- Music Influence: The song "Scooby Snacks" by Fun Lovin' Criminals directly references dialogues from "Pulp Fiction," incorporating samples of Samuel L. Jackson's lines into the track, highlighting the film's influence on '90s music culture.
- Fashion Trends: Uma Thurman's Mia Wallace has inspired countless Halloween costumes and fashion looks, particularly her black bob haircut, white shirt, and black trousers ensemble, which has become an iconic fashion statement.
- Cultural Sayings: The phrase "Pulp Fiction" itself has become synonymous with a certain style of storytelling—non-linear, sharp, and filled with dark humor, influencing writers and directors across mediums.

- Parodies and Homages: "Pulp Fiction" has been parodied and referenced in numerous TV shows, including "The Simpsons," "Family Guy," and "Community," showcasing its pervasive influence on television.
- Cafe Theme: In some cities, themed cafes have emerged that recreate the aesthetic of Jack Rabbit Slim's, the diner from "Pulp Fiction," offering fans a taste of the film's world.
- Video Games: Video games like "Grand Theft Auto" have drawn inspiration from "Pulp Fiction's" narrative style and character archetypes, incorporating similar themes and storytelling techniques.
- Literature: The film has inspired a range of literary works, from graphic novels to academic analyses, exploring its themes, style, and cultural significance.
- Social Media Memes: "Pulp Fiction" remains a popular source for memes, especially images of Vincent and Jules with their guns drawn, which have been used to comment on everything from mundane annoyances to political issues.

- Dance Competitions: The dance scene between Mia Wallace and Vincent Vega has been replicated in dance competitions and school performances, becoming a popular routine for its style and ease of recognition.
- Language: Terms like "Tarantinoesque" have entered the film critique lexicon, used to describe movies that embody the director's distinctive style of sharp dialogue, non-linear storytelling, and graphic violence, all hallmarks of "Pulp Fiction."

Blockbusters and CGI: A New Era of Filmmaking

The 1990s marked a transformative era in the world of cinema, characterized by the rise of blockbuster films and the revolutionary use of computer-generated imagery (CGI). This period saw filmmakers push the boundaries of what was technically possible, leveraging emerging technologies to create visual spectacles that captivated audiences worldwide. Blockbusters became synonymous with summer hits, drawing in massive crowds with their mix of high-stakes narratives, charismatic leads, and groundbreaking special effects. The integration of CGI allowed for the creation of scenes and characters that would have been impossible or prohibitively expensive to realize with practical effects alone, opening up new realms of creativity and storytelling.

The use of CGI was not merely a technical advancement; it was a storytelling revolution. Films began to explore fantastical worlds with unprecedented realism, from distant planets and prehistoric earth to imaginary creatures and futuristic cities. This era's blockbusters often combined compelling narratives with awe-inspiring visuals, setting new standards for production value and box office success. Movies like "Jurassic Park" demonstrated the potential of CGI to bring dinosaurs to life with a realism that had never been seen before, thrilling audiences and setting a new benchmark for visual effects.

These advancements were not without their challenges. The high costs associated with CGI and blockbuster productions raised the stakes for studios, which now had to manage ballooning budgets and the pressure to deliver commercially successful films. Despite these pressures, the 1990s saw some of the most iconic and financially successful films in cinema history, many of which remain cultural touchstones today.

The influence of 90s blockbusters and the use of CGI can still be felt in contemporary cinema. They paved the way for the visual and narrative ambition of modern films, from superhero franchises to science fiction epics. The era's technological innovations also democratized filmmaking tools, eventually allowing independent filmmakers to access CGI and special effects resources that were once the exclusive domain of major studios.

The legacy of the 90s blockbuster and CGI era is a testament to the film industry's constant evolution, reflecting both the possibilities and challenges of integrating technology into the creative process. As we look back, it's clear that this period was not just about spectacle for its own sake but about expanding the horizons of cinematic storytelling, enabling filmmakers to explore new worlds and tell stories that resonate with audiences across generations.

"Jurassic Park" (1993)

Steven Spielberg's "Jurassic Park" stands as a pivotal moment in the history of CGI, blending groundbreaking visual effects with captivating storytelling. The film's portrayal of dinosaurs, brought to life through a combination of CGI and animatronics, set a new standard for realism in cinema, making audiences truly believe in the possibility of these prehistoric creatures walking the Earth again. The innovative use of computer-generated imagery allowed for dynamic, lifelike movements that were previously unattainable, particularly in scenes featuring the T-Rex and the velociraptors. "Jurassic Park" not only showcased the potential of digital effects to enhance cinematic storytelling but also ignited the public's interest in dinosaurs, leading to a resurgence in paleontological research.

> *"And if we're not careful, they're gonna be here after. We're gonna have to adjust to new threat that we can't imagine. We've entered a new era. Welcome to Jurassic World."*

"Terminator 2: Judgment Day" (1991)

James Cameron's "Terminator 2: Judgment Day" revolutionized the use of CGI in filmmaking with its creation of the T-1000 character, a villain capable of morphing its shape and healing its injuries instantly. The seamless integration of CGI with practical effects and live-action footage marked a significant leap forward in visual effects technology, offering audiences an experience that was both visually stunning and narratively compelling. The film's innovative use of CGI set a new benchmark for future action movies and established James Cameron as a filmmaker willing to push the boundaries of technology to tell his stories.

"I'll be back"

"The Matrix" (1999)

"The Matrix" by the Wachowskis introduced audiences to a dystopian world where reality is a simulated illusion, employing groundbreaking CGI to visualize its complex themes. The film's signature "bullet time" effect, which allowed the action to slow down while the camera moved at normal speed, created a visual spectacle that has been widely imitated and referenced in popular culture. This effect, along with the film's innovative use of CGI to depict the digital world of the Matrix, challenged traditional filmmaking techniques and influenced a wide range of genres, from action and science fiction to philosophical dramas.

"You take the blue pill - the story ends, you wake up in your bed and believe whatever you want to believe. You take the red pill - you stay in Wonderland and I show you how deep the rabbit hole goes."

"Titanic" (1997)

James Cameron's "Titanic" combined historical narrative with state-of-the-art CGI to recreate the tragic sinking of the RMS Titanic. The film's use of digital effects to depict the ship and its final hours was unprecedented, blending seamlessly with live-action scenes and detailed set designs. "Titanic's" visual storytelling, supported by CGI, allowed audiences to connect with the historical event in a deeply emotional way, contributing to its massive box office success and numerous awards. The film's achievements in visual effects demonstrated the power of CGI to convey grand historical narratives and complex human emotions.

"Toy Story" (1995)

"Toy Story," directed by John Lasseter and produced by Pixar Animation Studios, marked a significant milestone in film history as the first feature-length film created entirely with computer-generated imagery. This innovation in animation brought characters to life with depth, personality, and emotion, setting a new standard for storytelling in animated films. "Toy Story's" success laid the groundwork for the future of animation, proving that CGI could be used to tell engaging, heartwarming stories that resonate with both children and adults. The film's impact on animation and its pioneering use of CGI technology have made it a beloved classic and a landmark in cinematic history.

"To infinity and beyond"

The phrase "To infinity and beyond!" encapsulates Buzz Lightyear's adventurous spirit. It represents pushing beyond the limits, exploring the unknown, and the boundless possibilities of imagination and adventure

Trivia Tidbits

- For "Jurassic Park," a team of paleontologists was consulted to ensure the dinosaurs' movements and sounds were as accurate as possible, blending science with cinematic creativity.

- "Terminator 2: Judgment Day" extensively utilized computer-generated imagery for the T-1000, but it also employed practical effects, including sophisticated puppetry and makeup for the more complex scenes.
- "The Matrix" introduced the concept of "wire-fu" to Western audiences, a technique that combines wire work with martial arts, enhancing the film's action sequences beyond traditional CGI effects.
- The sinking of the Titanic was simulated using a combination of digital effects and a massive set built to scale, which was partially submerged to recreate the historic event for "Titanic."
- "Toy Story" animators spent countless hours studying the movements and textures of real toys, incorporating these observations into the CGI models to give them a lifelike appearance.
- Spielberg decided not to use CGI dinosaurs exclusively after seeing a test footage that blended animatronics with digital effects, leading to the groundbreaking visual approach of "Jurassic Park."
- The "liquid metal" effect of the T-1000 in "Terminator 2" was one of the earliest uses of CGI to create a completely computer-generated character in a feature film.
- "The Matrix" was inspired by Japanese animation and cyberpunk literature, which influenced its visual style and the use of CGI to create the film's distinctive digital world.
- "Titanic's" depiction of the ship's interiors involved meticulous research and the recreation of the Titanic's furnishings and decorations using both CGI and historically accurate replicas.
- To maintain the illusion of the toys' world, "Toy Story" creators implemented a 'toy's eye view,' using low camera angles throughout the film to reflect the perspective of the characters.

- "Jurassic Park's" T-Rex rain scene was almost cut due to concerns that the animatronic dinosaur would not function properly when wet, but the scene ultimately became one of the film's most memorable moments.
- James Cameron's insistence on practical effects for "Terminator 2" meant that many of the film's stunts were performed live, with CGI used sparingly to enhance the realism.
- "The Matrix" utilized groundbreaking visual effects to create the illusion of the actors performing impossible feats, blending CGI with live-action in ways that had never been done before.
- "Titanic" employed underwater filming and digital effects to recreate the haunting images of the sunken ship, blending historical accuracy with cinematic storytelling.
- The voices of "Toy Story" characters were recorded early in the production process, allowing animators to tailor the characters' mouth movements and expressions to match the voice actors' performances precisely.

Questions

Who provided the voice for Woody in "Toy Story"?
- A) Tom Hanks
- B) Tim Allen
- C) Billy Crystal

In "Jurassic Park," which character famously says, "Life finds a way"?
- A) John Hammond
- B) Dr. Ian Malcolm
- C) Dr. Alan Grant

Which song does the T-800 use to signal John Connor in "Terminator 2: Judgment Day"?
- A) "Bad to the Bone"
- B) "You Could Be Mine"
- C) "Born to Be Wild"

What is the name of the ship that Morpheus captains in "The Matrix"?
- A) Nebuchadnezzar
- B) Zion
- C) Osiris

For which song did Celine Dion win an Oscar for Best Original Song from "Titanic"?
- A) "My Heart Will Go On"
- B) "Because You Loved Me"
- C) "The Power of Love"

In "Jurassic Park," which dinosaur is the first to be fully seen by the park visitors?
- A) Velociraptor
- B) Brachiosaurus
- C) Tyrannosaurus Rex

The "I'll be back" line is associated with which "Terminator" film?
- A) Terminator 3: Rise of the Machines
- B) Terminator 2: Judgment Day
- C) Terminator

Which character in "The Matrix" betrays the group to Agent Smith?
- A) Cypher
- B) Trinity
- C) Morpheus

"Titanic" was filmed at which location?
- A) Mediterranean Sea
- B) Pacific Ocean
- C) Atlantic Ocean

"Toy Story" features a toy astronaut named:
- A) Buzz Lightyear
- B) Woody
- C) Mr. Potato Head

"Jurassic Park" was based on a novel by which author?
- A) Michael Crichton
- B) Stephen King
- C) J.K. Rowling

What is the profession of Sarah Connor in "Terminator 2: Judgment Day"?
- A) Veterinarian
- B) Nurse
- C) Waitress

In "The Matrix," what color pill does Neo take to learn the truth?
- A) Red
- B) Blue
- C) Green

"Titanic" director James Cameron is known for also directing:
- A) Avatar
- B) Inception
- C) The Lord of the Rings

The antagonist of "Toy Story" is:
- A) Stinky Pete
- B) Lotso
- C) Sid

Answers

A) Tom Hanks
- Tom Hanks' brother, Jim Hanks, has often voiced Woody for various "Toy Story" video games and merchandise.

B) Dr. Ian Malcolm
- Jeff Goldblum improvised many of his lines, including some of Dr. Malcolm's most memorable quotes.

B) "You Could Be Mine"
- The song "You Could Be Mine" by Guns N' Roses was specifically chosen for its themes that align with John Connor's rebellious character.

A) Nebuchadnezzar
- The name Nebuchadnezzar is a reference to the biblical king known for his dreams, fitting the film's themes of reality and illusion.

A) "My Heart Will Go On"
- Celine Dion recorded "My Heart Will Go On" in one take, and it became one of the best-selling singles of all time.

B) Brachiosaurus
- The Brachiosaurus scene was one of the first to blend CGI with live-action, creating a sense of wonder and realism.

C) Terminator
- The "I'll be back" line has been used in some form in almost every "Terminator" film as a recurring catchphrase.

A) Cypher
- Joe Pantoliano, who played Cypher, wore sunglasses designed specifically to reflect the characters he was speaking to, enhancing the sense of betrayal.

B) Pacific Ocean
- The wreck scenes were filmed in a specially constructed tank, one of the largest ever built for a film, to simulate the Atlantic's icy waters.

A) Buzz Lightyear
- Buzz Lightyear's name was inspired by astronaut Buzz Aldrin, the second man to walk on the moon.

A) Michael Crichton
- Steven Spielberg acquired the rights to the novel before it was even published, after hearing about it from Crichton directly.

C) Waitress
- Linda Hamilton underwent extensive physical training for her role in "T2," showcasing Sarah Connor's transformation into a warrior.

A) Red
- The choice between the red and blue pills has become a cultural metaphor for choosing between a harsh truth and blissful ignorance.

A) Avatar
- James Cameron wrote a scriptment for "Avatar" before "Titanic," but waited years for technology to catch up to his vision for the film.

c) Sid
- Sid is Pixar's first villain, and his character was designed to subvert the typical childhood innocence associated with toys.

Cult Classics: "The X-Files" and "Buffy the Vampire Slayer

The 1990s were a golden era for television, birthing a number of shows that would go on to achieve cult status, among them "The X-Files" and "Buffy the Vampire Slayer." Both series broke new ground in the science fiction and fantasy genres, respectively, blending clever storytelling, rich character development, and innovative special effects to explore themes of alienation, power, and the struggle between good and evil. Their influence extended well beyond their original broadcast, inspiring a new generation of television writers and directors and cementing their place in pop culture history.

"The X-Files," created by Chris Carter, debuted in 1993 and ran for eleven seasons. The show followed FBI agents Fox Mulder (David Duchovny) and Dana Scully (Gillian Anderson) as they investigated unsolved and often unexplainable cases involving paranormal phenomena. Mulder's quest to uncover the truth about extraterrestrial life, driven by the abduction of his sister, and Scully's skepticism grounded in her scientific and medical background, provided a dynamic and engaging narrative. The series was notable for its "Monster of the Week" episodes alongside a larger, more complex mythology arc concerning government conspiracies and alien colonization. "The X-Files" not only captivated audiences with its blend of horror, science fiction, and drama but also introduced iconic phrases such as "The truth is out there" and "Trust no one," reflecting the show's overarching themes of skepticism and belief.

"Buffy the Vampire Slayer," created by Joss Whedon, premiered in 1997 and lasted for seven seasons. The series centered on Buffy Summers (Sarah Michelle Gellar), a young woman chosen to battle against vampires, demons, and other forces of darkness, with the help of her friends, the so-called "Scooby Gang." "Buffy" was praised for its witty dialogue, emotional depth, and innovative storytelling, including the use of allegory to tackle social issues. The show explored themes of empowerment, friendship, and the pains of growing up, making it a seminal work in the portrayal of strong female characters on television. Episodes like "Hush" and "Once More, With Feeling" demonstrated the series' creative ambition, experimenting with format and genre conventions to critical acclaim.

Both "The X-Files" and "Buffy the Vampire Slayer" have left a lasting legacy, influencing countless shows in the genres of science fiction, fantasy, and horror. They fostered dedicated fan communities that remain active, discussing theories, creating fan fiction, and hosting conventions. The series have been subject to academic analysis, credited with changing the landscape of television in the 1990s and early 2000s by demonstrating the potential for genre series to offer deep, meaningful commentary on the human condition. Their continued popularity in syndication and streaming platforms speaks to the enduring appeal of their stories and characters, proving that their impact on pop culture and television storytelling will be felt for generations to come.

"The X-Files" ventured into the unknown, combining elements of science fiction, horror, and thriller genres. Its success lay in the compelling dynamic between its two leads: the believer, Agent Mulder, and the skeptic, Agent Scully. This dynamic provided a platform for exploring a wide array of themes, from government conspiracy and alien abduction to spirituality and human nature. The show's ability to oscillate between standalone monster-of-the-week episodes and a complex overarching mythology allowed it to appeal to both casual viewers and those looking for a deeper narrative.

"Buffy the Vampire Slayer" redefined what a teenage drama could be, infusing the coming-of-age story with elements of fantasy and horror. Buffy Summers, as the Slayer, was a subversion of traditional female roles in genre storytelling, combining strength and vulnerability in a way that resonated with audiences. The series was celebrated for its witty dialogue, emotional depth, and for tackling serious issues such as addiction, abuse, and loss, all within the framework of its supernatural setting.

Beyond these titans of genre television, the 1990s produced other notable series that have achieved cult status:

- "Charmed": Premiering in 1998, "Charmed" followed the lives of the Halliwell sisters, who discover they are powerful witches destined to fight against evil. The show combined elements of fantasy, drama, and humor, exploring themes of sisterhood, feminism, and morality, and has retained a dedicated fanbase.
- "The Outer Limits" and "Tales from the Crypt": Both of these anthology series offered viewers a collection of standalone episodes, each exploring unique stories of horror, science fiction, and dark fantasy. Their ability to attract top-tier talent and to tell provocative and often morally complex tales contributed to their lasting appeal.

Did You Know? The Outer Limits known for its exploration of the unknown and the extraordinary. The show first aired in 1963 and was created by Leslie Stevens. The original series ran until 1965, but "The Outer Limits" was revived in 1995, continuing to captivate audiences with new stories until its conclusion in 2002. Both incarnations of the show are celebrated for their thought-provoking narratives, innovative special effects for their times, and their ability to blend speculative science fiction with moral and philosophical questions.

"The Outer Limits" episodes often started with a "Control Voice" narration, setting the tone for the story's exploration of themes related to humanity, ethics, and the boundaries of science and technology. This distinctive opening and the show's memorable stories have left a lasting impact on the science fiction genre and have inspired countless other works in television, film, and literature.

True or False Questions

.True or False: "The X-Files" was exclusively about extraterrestrial life and UFO sightings.

True or False: "Buffy the Vampire Slayer" featured an episode entirely devoid of dialogue.

True or False: "Charmed" was initially conceived as a spin-off of "Buffy the Vampire Slayer."

True or False: "The Outer Limits" was a reboot of a series from the 1960s with the same name.

True or False: "Tales from the Crypt" was based on a series of 1950s comic books.

True or False: Both "The X-Files" and "Buffy the Vampire Slayer" were set in the same fictional universe.

Answers

False: While "The X-Files" prominently featured extraterrestrial life and UFO sightings, it also explored a wide range of paranormal phenomena, including cryptids, supernatural events, and government conspiracies, making the series much more diverse in its subject matter.

True: "Buffy the Vampire Slayer" featured an episode titled "Hush" in its fourth season, which is almost entirely devoid of dialogue. This episode is highly acclaimed for its unique storytelling approach and received several award nominations, showcasing the series' innovative use of visual storytelling.

False: "Charmed" was not conceived as a spin-off of "Buffy the Vampire Slayer." Although both shows share themes of supernatural elements and strong female leads, "Charmed" was developed independently and focuses on the lives of three sisters who are powerful witches.

True: "The Outer Limits" is indeed a reboot of a classic science fiction series that originally aired in the 1960s. The reboot aired in the 1990s and continued the tradition of presenting self-contained episodes that explore various sci-fi and speculative fiction themes.

True: "Tales from the Crypt" was based on a series of horror comic books from the 1950s published by EC Comics. The show retained the comic series' blend of horror, dark humor, and moral lessons, often featuring a moral or twist ending.

False: "The X-Files" and "Buffy the Vampire Slayer" were not set in the same fictional universe. Each show has its own distinct setting and mythology, with "The X-Files" focusing on paranormal investigations within a somewhat realistic contemporary world, and "Buffy the Vampire Slayer" centered around a fictional California town plagued by supernatural activity.

The Rise of Premium Cable: HBO's Golden Age

The 1990s marked a pivotal shift in the television landscape with the rise of premium cable networks, most notably HBO (Home Box Office). This era, often referred to as HBO's Golden Age, redefined what could be achieved on the small screen, offering viewers content that was more complex, edgier, and more sophisticated than what was traditionally broadcast.

HBO distinguished itself by delivering high-quality, original programming that pushed boundaries in terms of narrative depth, character development, and production values. This transformative period laid the groundwork for what many would later call the "Golden Age of Television."

HBO's strategy was to provide content that couldn't be found elsewhere, catering to niche audiences with diverse tastes. This included a wide array of programming, from groundbreaking series and documentaries to exclusive movies and live sporting events. The freedom from traditional network constraints allowed HBO to explore mature themes, use explicit language, and depict violence and sexual content with an honesty that was unprecedented on television. Shows like "The Sopranos" and "Sex and the City" became cultural phenomena, not just for their content, but for their innovative storytelling and complex characters. These series, among others, elevated the status of television as a medium capable of rivaling even the best that cinema had to offer.

The success of HBO during this period was instrumental in changing the business model for cable television. Subscription-based revenue meant that HBO didn't rely on advertising dollars, freeing it from the need to cater to mass audiences or to avoid offending advertisers. This model allowed for risk-taking and creativity, leading to content that was both critically acclaimed and commercially successful. The network's ability to attract top-tier talent, from award-winning actors to visionary directors and writers, was key to its success. This era also saw the rise of the "TV auteur," with creators like David Chase ("The Sopranos") and Alan Ball ("Six Feet Under") becoming household names.

HBO's impact extended beyond its programming. The network's success challenged other cable and broadcast networks to raise their standards, leading to a proliferation of high-quality shows across the television spectrum. It also paved the way for other premium and streaming services, like Showtime and Netflix, to invest in original content. The network's approach to storytelling and its focus on character-driven narratives have become the gold standard for television drama and comedy.

Reflecting on HBO's Golden Age, it's clear that the network's contributions were not just to the realm of entertainment but to the cultural discourse as a whole. Shows from this era tackled social issues, explored the human psyche, and presented a reflection of society with nuance and depth. HBO's legacy is one of innovation and excellence, having forever changed how stories are told on television and how those stories are consumed by audiences worldwide.

Following this rich tradition, HBO and other cable networks have continued to produce shows that capture the imagination of audiences around the globe. Here are six significant shows from the premium cable space during the 90s that left an indelible mark on television:

- Oz (1997-2003): Created by Tom Fontana, "Oz" is considered a trailblazer for modern television drama. Set in an experimental unit of a maximum-security prison, the series offered an unflinching look at the lives of its inmates and staff, exploring themes of justice, survival, and morality. "Oz" was notable for its diverse ensemble cast, complex characters, and its willingness to address controversial issues head-on.
- The Larry Sanders Show (1992-1998): A satirical television sitcom created by Garry Shandling and Dennis Klein, "The Larry Sanders Show" provided a behind-the-scenes look at the late-night talk show world. Celebrated for its sharp wit, the series was a precursor to the mockumentary style that would become popular in later years. It blended fiction with real-life celebrities playing exaggerated versions of themselves, blurring the lines between reality and entertainment.
- Tales from the Crypt (1989-1996): Based on the 1950s EC Comics series of the same name, "Tales from the Crypt" was an anthology horror series that featured various macabre stories, often with a twist ending. The show was known for its campy humor, gory content, and the iconic Crypt Keeper, who introduced each episode.
- The Kids in the Hall (1989-1995): A Canadian sketch comedy show produced by Lorne Michaels, "The Kids in the Hall" featured a troupe of comedians performing various skits and characters. The show was celebrated for its surreal humor, unique characters, and its willingness to push boundaries, particularly in its portrayal of gender and sexuality.

"I intend to die there. Oh, I don't live there anymore, but that's where I'm going to die. Die in the house where I was born."

- Mr. Show with Bob and David (1995-1998): An American sketch comedy series featuring Bob Odenkirk and David Cross, "Mr. Show" was known for its absurdist humor and satirical take on social and political issues. The show's sketches were interconnected, creating a seamless flow from one bit to the next.
- Dream On (1990-1996): Created by Marta Kauffman and David Crane, "Dream On" followed the life of Martin Tupper, a newly divorced New York City book editor. The show was distinctive for its use of clips from old black-and-white films to represent Martin's inner thoughts and feelings, blending classic cinema with contemporary storytelling.

The Sopranos

"The Sopranos" stands as one of the most influential television series ever created, marking a significant turning point not only for HBO but for the entire landscape of TV drama. Premiering in 1999 and created by David Chase, the show chronicled the life of Tony Soprano (James Gandolfini), a New Jersey-based Italian-American mob boss, as he tried to balance the demands of his criminal organization with those of his family life. The series delved deep into the psyche of its protagonist, utilizing his therapy sessions as a narrative device to explore themes of identity, morality, and the American Dream.

"The Sopranos" was groundbreaking for its complex characters, moral ambiguity, and its portrayal of the mundane alongside the macabre aspects of mob life. It eschewed the glamorization of organized crime seen in much of popular culture, instead offering a gritty, realistic, and often psychologically nuanced view of the life of a mob boss and his associates. The series was notable for its deep exploration of the characters' psyches, particularly through Tony Soprano's introspective and often troubled relationship with his therapist, Dr. Jennifer Melfi (Lorraine Bracco).

The show's narrative complexity, with its multi-layered storylines and rich character arcs, set a new standard for television storytelling, influencing countless dramas that followed. "The Sopranos" demonstrated that TV could be as artistically significant and narratively ambitious as cinema, paving the way for the modern era of prestige television.

Its use of cinematic techniques, including careful framing, attention to visual detail, and a willingness to allow stories to unfold over time, contributed to its perception as a high-quality, novelistic television experience.

Moreover, "The Sopranos" had a profound impact on pop culture and the way stories about crime and family could be told. It inspired a generation of creators and helped establish HBO as a powerhouse of original programming. The series won numerous awards, including 21 Primetime Emmy Awards and five Golden Globe Awards, and it is frequently cited as one of the greatest television series of all time.

Beyond its critical acclaim and influence on television narrative, "The Sopranos" also had a significant cultural impact. It spawned books, video games, and a vast amount of academic writing.

The series' exploration of themes such as mental health, the decline of the American Dream, and the complexities of family and loyalty resonated deeply with audiences and critics alike. Its ending, famously ambiguous and still widely debated, exemplifies the show's ability to challenge and engage viewers, leaving a lasting legacy on the television landscape.

"We bend more rules than the Catholic Church!"

- "The Sopranos" creator David Chase originally envisioned the concept as a feature film about a mobster going to therapy but decided to develop it into a TV series instead.
- James Gandolfini's portrayal of Tony Soprano was widely praised, but he was not the first choice for the role; Chase had initially considered several other actors, including Steven Van Zandt, who eventually played Silvio Dante.
- The show's famous opening sequence, featuring Tony Soprano driving from New York to his home in New Jersey, was filmed with a camera mounted on a truck driving ahead of Gandolfini's car.
- The series was shot on location in New Jersey, making extensive use of real restaurants, shops, and other sites, lending authenticity to its depiction of the state.
- "The Sopranos" is credited with introducing the term "gabagool," a mispronunciation of "capicola," into the American lexicon, reflecting its influence on popularizing Italian-American slang.
- Lorraine Bracco was originally asked to audition for the role of Carmela Soprano but felt more drawn to the character of Dr. Jennifer Melfi, Tony's psychiatrist.
- The series made television history with its portrayal of violence and sexuality, pushing the boundaries of what was considered acceptable on TV and helping to establish HBO's reputation for adult content.
- In preparation for their roles, many of the actors on "The Sopranos" met with real-life members of the Mafia to gain insight into their characters and the world they were portraying.

- "The Sopranos" was one of the first TV shows to use high-definition video cameras for filming, contributing to its cinematic quality.
- The final scene of "The Sopranos," set in a diner with the screen cutting to black, is one of the most talked-about moments in TV history, sparking widespread debate and analysis about its meaning.

Teen Dramas and Sitcoms: "Dawson's Creek" to "The Fresh Prince of Bel-Air

The 1990s and early 2000s were golden years for teen dramas and sitcoms, significantly shaping youth culture and television storytelling. This era introduced audiences to a plethora of series that were not only entertaining but also groundbreaking in their exploration of themes relevant to young people.

Shows like "Dawson's Creek" and "The Fresh Prince of Bel-Air" epitomized this trend, each offering distinct perspectives on adolescence, family, and societal issues, resonating deeply with viewers and leaving a lasting impact on pop culture.

"Dawson's Creek" (1998-2003), created by Kevin Williamson, was a defining teen drama of its time, chronicling the lives, loves, and losses of a group of friends navigating the complexities of adolescence in the fictional town of Capeside, Massachusetts.

The show was lauded for its mature handling of topics such as sexuality, identity, and personal growth, presenting these themes in a way that was both thoughtful and provocative. Its candid portrayal of teenage life broke new ground for network television and paved the way for more nuanced discussions around youth and the challenges they face.

On the comedic front, "The Fresh Prince of Bel-Air" (1990-1996) offered a lighter yet equally impactful take on the coming-of-age story. Centered around Will Smith's character's move from West Philadelphia to the affluent neighborhood of Bel-Air, the show blended humor with poignant commentary on race, class, and family dynamics. It stood out for its charismatic cast, fresh humor, and the way it used comedy to tackle important social issues, making it a beloved staple of '90s television and an important vehicle for cultural commentary.

The era also saw the rise of other significant teen dramas and sitcoms, each contributing in unique ways to the genre's evolution. Shows like "Buffy the Vampire Slayer" combined supernatural elements with teen angst to explore themes of empowerment and identity, while "My So-Called Life" provided a raw and realistic portrayal of teenage life. Sitcoms like "Saved by the Bell" offered lighter takes on high school life, embedding moral lessons amidst the comedy.

These series not only entertained but also mirrored the complexities of growing up, forging a deep connection with audiences that has endured over the years. They challenged conventions, introduced groundbreaking narrative techniques, and opened up conversations about issues previously considered taboo for young viewers. As a result, they played a crucial role in elevating teen-focused storytelling, influencing subsequent generations of TV shows.

Reflecting on this transformative period, it's clear that the legacy of these teen dramas and sitcoms extends far beyond their original run. They have inspired countless creators, shaped the tastes of a generation, and contributed to the broader cultural acceptance of young adult narratives as worthy of serious attention. Their influence is evident in the continued popularity and evolution of the genre, underscoring the enduring power of stories that speak directly to the experiences and challenges of youth.

The theme song of "The Fresh Prince of Bel-Air," performed by Will Smith, is as iconic as the show itself, encapsulating the show's premise and charm within its catchy, upbeat rhythm and clever lyrics.

Now this is a story all about how
My life got flipped turned upside down
And I'd like to take a minute, just sit right there
I'll tell you how I became the prince of a town called Bel-Air

In West Philadelphia born and raised
On the playground is where I spent most of my days
Chillin' out, maxin', relaxin' all cool
And all shootin' some b-ball outside of the school
When a couple of guys who were up to no good
Started makin' trouble in my neighborhood
I got in one little fight and my mom got scared
And said "You're movin' with your auntie and uncle in Bel-Air"
I begged and pleaded with her day after day
But she packed my suitcase and sent me on my way
She gave me a kiss and then she gave me my ticket
I put my Walkman on and said "I might as well kick it"
First class, yo, this is bad

Drinking orange juice out of a champagne glass
Is this what the people of Bel-Air living like?
Hmm, this might be all right
But wait, I hear they're prissy, bourgeois, and all that
Is this the type of place that they should send this cool cat?
I don't think so, I'll see when I get there
I hope they're prepared for the Prince of Bel-Air

Its narrative style, uncommon for TV theme songs of the time, tells the story of a young man's journey from the rough streets of West Philadelphia to the opulent neighborhood of Bel-Air, setting the stage for the cultural and comedic clashes that define the series. The song's appeal lies not just in its catchiness but in its storytelling, efficiently introducing audiences to the character of Will Smith and his new life in Bel-Air within the span of just over a minute.

Its enduring popularity is a testament to its effectiveness in capturing the essence of the show, making it one of the most memorable and beloved TV theme songs of all time.

The theme tune played a significant role in cementing the show's place in pop culture, serving as a portal into the world of Bel-Air for audiences around the globe and instantly transporting anyone who hears its opening lines back to the 1990s, regardless of when they first encountered the series.

Will Smith

The Fresh Prince of Bel-Air, which aired from 1990 to 1996, is a beloved sitcom that catapulted Will Smith to fame and left an indelible mark on 90s pop culture. Smith played a fictionalized version of himself, a street-smart teenager from West Philadelphia who, after getting into a fight, is sent to live with his wealthy aunt and uncle in their Bel-Air mansion. This setup provided a fertile ground for exploring themes of class differences, racial identity, and the clash of cultures, all while maintaining a light-hearted and comedic tone. Smith's character, with his charismatic and often comical adaptation to the upscale lifestyle, served as the show's heart, delivering both laughter and poignant moments across its six-season run.

Will Smith's performance in "The Fresh Prince of Bel-Air" was a significant factor in the show's success. His natural charisma and comedic timing made the character relatable and lovable, ensuring that the show resonated with a broad audience.

Beyond the humor, Smith adeptly handled more serious themes, contributing to memorable episodes that tackled issues like gun violence, drug use, and racial profiling, showcasing his range as an actor.

- Will Smith was almost bankrupt due to unpaid taxes when he was cast in "The Fresh Prince of Bel-Air," making the show a turning point in his life and career.
- The show's theme song, performed by Smith, is one of the most recognizable TV theme songs and was co-written by Quincy Jones, who also served as a producer.
- Smith's character's full name, William "Will" Smith, is his real name, blurring the lines between the actor and his character.
- Initially, Will Smith memorized the entire script for each episode, including other characters' lines, leading to instances where he can be seen mouthing other actors' lines in early episodes.
- "The Fresh Prince of Bel-Air" was nominated for two Golden Globe Awards during its run, including Best Performance by an Actor in a TV-Series - Comedy/Musical for Will Smith.
- The show featured numerous guest stars, including Oprah Winfrey, Don Cheadle, and Tyra Banks, who had a recurring role as Will's girlfriend.
- The mansion's exterior shown in the show is actually located in the Brentwood area of Los Angeles, not Bel-Air.
- The series finale in 1996 drew 30 million viewers, making it one of the most-watched episodes in the show's history.

- Will Smith's on-screen chemistry with James Avery, who played Uncle Phil, was a highlight of the show. Smith has spoken about how Avery was a mentor to him both on and off the screen.
- "The Fresh Prince of Bel-Air" has seen a resurgence in popularity thanks to streaming services, introducing the series to new generations and solidifying its status as a classic sitcom.

After "The Fresh Prince of Bel-Air," Will Smith's career skyrocketed, firmly establishing him as one of Hollywood's leading men. Transitioning from television to the big screen, Smith starred in a string of blockbuster hits that showcased his versatility as an actor. Films like "Independence Day" and "Men in Black" solidified his status as a bankable action star, while roles in "Ali," for which he received an Academy Award nomination for Best Actor, and "The Pursuit of Happyness" demonstrated his prowess in drama. Smith's charm, wit, and everyman appeal have made him a beloved figure in the entertainment industry, with his movies earning billions at the global box office. Beyond his acting career, Smith has also produced films, music, and even ventured into social media, where his engaging content has garnered millions of followers.

Off-screen, Will Smith is a family man, married to actress Jada Pinkett Smith, with whom he shares two children, Jaden and Willow Smith. Both Jaden and Willow have followed in their parents' footsteps, pursuing careers in music and acting. The Smith family is known for their openness about their personal lives, sharing insights into their challenges and successes, which has endeared them even more to the public. In 2022, Will made headlines not for a film role but for an incident at the Oscars involving a slap that was heard around the world. While opinions on the incident vary, it's undeniable that Will Smith, much like his character on "The Fresh Prince of Bel-Air," remains a figure of endless fascination, capable of capturing the world's attention, whether through his performances or personal moments. And just like in his movies, we're all eagerly waiting to see what he does next—hopefully, it involves less slapping and more rapping.

90s Movie Star Quiz

Which actor portrayed the titular character in "Forrest Gump" (1994)?
- A) Kevin Costner
- B) Brad Pitt
- C) Tom Hanks
- D) Harrison Ford

Who won an Academy Award for Best Actress for her role in "Shakespeare in Love" (1998)?
- A) Gwyneth Paltrow
- B) Cate Blanchett
- C) Helen Hunt
- D) Judi Dench

Which actor played Batman in "Batman Returns" (1992)?
- A) Michael Keaton
- B) Val Kilmer
- C) George Clooney
- D) Christian Bale

Who starred as the lead in "The Silence of the Lambs" (1991)?
- A) Meryl Streep
- B) Julia Roberts
- C) Jodie Foster
- D) Nicole Kidman

Which actor became famous for his role in "Titanic" (1997)?
- A) Leonardo DiCaprio
- B) Matt Damon
- C) Johnny Depp
- D) Tom Cruise

Who played the role of Sarah Connor in "Terminator 2: Judgment Day" (1991)?
- A) Sigourney Weaver
- B) Linda Hamilton
- C) Carrie Fisher
- D) Jamie Lee Curtis

Which actress starred in the romantic comedy "Pretty Woman" (1990)?
- A) Sandra Bullock
- B) Julia Roberts
- C) Meg Ryan
- D) Cameron Diaz

Who played the character of Jack Traven in "Speed" (1994)?
- A) Keanu Reeves
- B) Bruce Willis
- C) Sylvester Stallone
- D) Arnold Schwarzenegger

Which actor portrayed Dr. Ian Malcolm in "Jurassic Park" (1993)?
- A) Richard Attenborough
- B) Sam Neill
- C) Jeff Goldblum
- D) Bob Peck

Who won an Academy Award for Best Actor for his role in "Philadelphia" (1993)?
- A) Denzel Washington
- B) Tom Hanks
- C) Brad Pitt
- D) Al Pacino

Which actress played the lead in "La Femme Nikita" (1990)?
- A) Natalie Portman
- B) Anne Parillaud
- C) Milla Jovovich
- D) Bridget Fonda

Who starred as Andy Dufresne in "The Shawshank Redemption" (1994)?
- A) Tim Robbins
- B) Morgan Freeman
- C) Clancy Brown
- D) William Sadler

Which actor is known for his role in "Die Hard: With a Vengeance" (1995)?
- A) Bruce Willis
- B) Samuel L. Jackson
- C) Jeremy Irons
- D) Both A and B

Who played the character of Cher Horowitz in "Clueless" (1995)?
- A) Alicia Silverstone
- B) Stacey Dash
- C) Brittany Murphy
- D) Elisa Donovan

Which actress starred in "Basic Instinct" (1992)?
- A) Sharon Stone
- B) Demi Moore
- C) Kim Basinger
- D) Michelle Pfeiffer

Who played the lead role in "Braveheart" (1995)?
- A) Mel Gibson
- B) Liam Neeson
- C) Russell Crowe
- D) Kevin Costner

Who starred as the lead in "The Sixth Sense" (1999)?
- A) Bruce Willis
- B) Haley Joel Osment
- C) Tony Collette
- D) Both A and B

Which actress played Rose DeWitt Bukater in "Titanic" (1997)?
- A) Kate Winslet
- B) Keira Knightley
- C) Rachel Weisz
- D) Nicole Kidman

Who was the lead actor in "The Matrix" (1999)?
- A) Hugo Weaving
- B) Laurence Fishburne
- C) Keanu Reeves
- D) Joe Pantoliano

Answers

C) Tom Hanks - For his role in "Forrest Gump," Tom Hanks won the Academy Award for Best Actor, marking his second consecutive Oscar win after his performance in "Philadelphia."

A) Gwyneth Paltrow - Gwyneth Paltrow's Oscar acceptance speech for "Shakespeare in Love" is one of the most memorable, notable for her emotional delivery.

A) Michael Keaton - Michael Keaton's portrayal of Batman was initially met with skepticism, but his performance was widely acclaimed, redefining the character for a new generation.

C) Jodie Foster - Jodie Foster's role in "The Silence of the Lambs" earned her an Academy Award for Best Actress, solidifying her status as one of the premier actresses of her time.

A) Leonardo DiCaprio - "Titanic" became the highest-grossing film of its time, catapulting Leonardo DiCaprio to international superstardom.

B) Linda Hamilton - Linda Hamilton underwent intense physical training for her role in "Terminator 2," significantly transforming her physique to play the iconic Sarah Connor.

B) Julia Roberts - "Pretty Woman" was a turning point in Julia Roberts' career, establishing her as a leading lady in Hollywood and earning her an Academy Award nomination.

A) Keanu Reeves - "Speed" was a critical and commercial success that helped to establish Keanu Reeves as a leading action star in Hollywood.

C) Jeff Goldblum - Jeff Goldblum's portrayal of Dr. Ian Malcolm led to the character's return in several sequels due to his popularity.

B) Tom Hanks - With "Philadelphia," Tom Hanks became one of the first actors to win back-to-back Academy Awards for Best Actor.

B) Anne Parillaud - "La Femme Nikita" is considered a cult classic, and Anne Parillaud's performance as the titular character received critical acclaim.

A) Tim Robbins - "The Shawshank Redemption" did not win any of the seven Academy Awards for which it was nominated, but it has since been recognized as one of the greatest films of all time.

D) Both A and B - "Die Hard: With a Vengeance" is the third installment in the Die Hard series and was the highest-grossing film worldwide in 1995.

A) Alicia Silverstone - "Clueless" has become a cultural icon, known for its fashion, quotable dialogue, and impact on 1990s pop culture.

A) Sharon Stone - Sharon Stone's interrogation scene in "Basic Instinct" became one of the most iconic and controversial scenes of the 1990s.

A) Mel Gibson - Mel Gibson not only starred in but also directed "Braveheart," which won five Academy Awards, including Best Picture and Best Director. "Braveheart" is known for its historical inaccuracies, but Mel Gibson's performance and direction were praised for their emotional depth and epic scope.

D) Both A and B - "The Sixth Sense" is famous for its twist ending, which has been widely parodied and referenced in popular culture.

A) Kate Winslet - Kate Winslet received her second Academy Award nomination for her role in "Titanic," establishing her as a leading actress of her generation.

A) Keanu Reeves - "The Matrix" is renowned for its groundbreaking visual effects and philosophical underpinnings, redefining the science fiction genre.

The 2000s: The Digital Revolution in TV and Cinema

The dawn of the 2000s brought with it the digital revolution, reshaping the landscape of television and cinema in profound ways. This decade saw the golden age of TV drama, with shows like "The Sopranos" and "Breaking Bad" offering complex narratives and deeply developed characters, elevating the medium to new heights. Reality TV dominated the airwaves, from "Survivor" to "American Idol," reflecting a growing appetite for unscripted, real-life entertainment. The fantasy and superhero surge, exemplified by "Harry Potter" and "The Dark Knight," marked a significant trend in cinema, bringing epic tales and comic book heroes to the forefront of pop culture.

The sitcom evolution continued with hits like "The Office" and "30 Rock," while the rise of streaming services began to change how audiences consumed content, offering a new way to watch and a wider array of choices. Animated successes, from "Shrek" to "Finding Nemo," showcased the leaps in animation technology and storytelling, and epic film trilogies like "The Lord of the

Rings" captivated audiences with their scale and spectacle. The 2000s were a decade of technological innovation, genre expansion, and a shift towards more immersive and complex storytelling, setting the stage for the future of entertainment in the digital age.

TV Drama: "The Wire" to "Breaking Bad"

The transition from the late 1990s into the 2000s marked a renaissance period for TV drama, heralding a new era defined by complex storytelling, deep character development, and a willingness to tackle societal issues with nuance and depth.

Two shows that exemplify this golden age of television drama are "The Wire" and "Breaking Bad," each taking the medium to new heights and leaving a lasting impact on both audiences and the television landscape.

"The Wire," created by David Simon and premiering on HBO in 2002, explored the many facets of Baltimore, Maryland, from its drug-infested streets to the halls of political power. Unlike traditional crime dramas, the series delved deep into the systemic issues facing American cities, including the failure of the war on drugs, the struggles of the working class, and the complexities of the criminal justice system.

With its richly drawn characters representing every level of the city's hierarchy, "The Wire" presented a detailed and unsentimental portrait of urban life. Its realistic portrayal of Baltimore, driven by Simon's own experiences as a police reporter, and its refusal to provide easy answers or moralistic judgments, made it one of the most critically acclaimed TV dramas of all time.

"Breaking Bad," created by Vince Gilligan and airing on AMC from 2008 to 2013, followed the transformation of Walter White (Bryan Cranston), a high school chemistry teacher turned methamphetamine manufacturing drug lord, as he descends into the criminal underworld. The series was celebrated for its moral complexity, exploring themes of identity, morality, and consequence with a depth rarely seen in television. Cranston's performance, along with Aaron Paul's portrayal of his former student and business partner Jesse Pinkman, received widespread acclaim, anchoring the series' exploration of character and the human capacity for change. "Breaking Bad" was notable for its tight narrative, meticulous attention to detail, and its ability to keep audiences captivated with each twist and turn.

oth "The Wire" and "Breaking Bad" pushed the boundaries of what television could achieve in terms of storytelling and character development. They showcased television's potential to offer narratives as rich and complex as those found in literature or cinema, challenging audiences to engage with difficult questions about society, morality, and the human condition. These series have had a profound influence on the TV drama genre, inspiring a new generation of shows that seek to explore the complexities of life with the same depth and nuance.

Detailing "The Wire"

"The Wire," created by David Simon and premiering in 2002, stands as a towering achievement in television, offering an unflinching examination of Baltimore's institutional landscapes. Across its five seasons, the show meticulously dissected the city's drug trade, port system, government and bureaucracy, educational institutions, and media. This multi-faceted approach painted a comprehensive picture of urban America's challenges and systemic failures, distinguishing "The Wire" for its ambition and scope. Unlike other crime dramas of its time, "The Wire" delved into the complexities and interconnectedness of societal issues, presenting a narrative that was as informative as it was compelling.

David Simon, leveraging his background as a former police reporter for The Baltimore Sun, imbued the series with a sense of authenticity and realism rarely seen on television. His intimate understanding of the city's intricacies allowed "The Wire" to portray its characters and settings with depth and nuance. The show's commitment to realism was further enhanced by its use of local actors and real locations, which added to the immersive experience of watching the series.

The narrative structure of "The Wire" was revolutionary, with each season focusing on a different segment of Baltimore's infrastructure, thereby layering the city's portrait with each episode. This structure allowed the series to explore the cyclical nature of societal issues and the often-futile efforts to address them. The show's ability to weave these complex themes into engaging storytelling was a testament to Simon's vision and the writing team's execution.

Central to "The Wire's" narrative were its characters, who were drawn with incredible complexity and humanity. From the streets to the schools, from the police department to the political offices, each character served as a lens through which the audience could understand the broader societal issues at play. Characters such as Jimmy McNulty, portrayed by Dominic West, offered insight into the police department's inner workings and its often problematic relationship with the communities it served. Omar Little, brought to life by Michael K. Williams, became one of television's most memorable characters, challenging stereotypes about criminals and moral ambiguity.

The show's portrayal of the drug trade through characters like Avon Barksdale (Wood Harris) and Stringer Bell (Idris Elba) provided a nuanced view of criminal enterprises, highlighting the economic desperation and systemic neglect that fuel the drug market. Meanwhile, characters involved in the city's political sphere, such as Tommy Carcetti (Aidan Gillen), showcased the complexities of governance and the often-compromised efforts to improve the city.

"The Wire" was not just a television show; it was a socio-political treatise on the state of urban America, wrapped in the guise of a crime drama. Its critical acclaim and enduring legacy underscore its importance not only as entertainment but as a profound commentary on society. The series challenged viewers to rethink their perceptions of crime, punishment, and social justice, making it one of the most significant contributions to television in the 21st century.

"The Pawns, Man, In The Game, They Get Capped Quick. They Be Out The Game Early."

Trivia Tidbits

- President Barack Obama named "The Wire" his favorite TV show, specifically praising Omar Little as his favorite character.
- Many of the show's cast members, including Felicia "Snoop" Pearson, were actual residents of Baltimore, some with real-life experiences similar to the characters they played.

- The character of Bubbles was based on a real-life individual from Baltimore, whose life story was shared with David Simon while he was reporting for The Baltimore Sun.
- "The Wire" never won an Emmy Award, despite its critical acclaim and impact on television drama.
- The series used authentic Baltimore slang and dialect, contributing to its realism and authenticity.
- Creator David Simon envisioned the show as a "visual novel," aiming to tell a complete story over the course of its five seasons.
- The show's theme song, "Way Down in the Hole," was performed by a different artist each season, including Tom Waits (who wrote the song), The Blind Boys of Alabama, and Steve Earle.
- David Simon made a cameo in the final episode of the series as a reporter in the Baltimore Sun newsroom.
- The role of Detective Jimmy McNulty was Dominic West's first major American television role.
- Michael K. Williams got the scar on his face, which became a defining physical trait for Omar Little, during a bar fight on his 25th birthday.
- The character of Omar Little is one of President Obama's favorite TV characters.
- To maintain the show's authenticity, former Baltimore police officer Ed Burns co-wrote and produced the series, sharing his experiences and insights.
- The Wire's title refers not only to surveillance technology used by the police but also to the interconnected, invisible barriers within the city's institutions.
- Although critically acclaimed, "The Wire" struggled with ratings throughout its original run, only gaining a larger audience and recognition after concluding.

- The series extensively explored the impact of the drug trade on schools in its fourth season, a storyline that was inspired by the real-life experiences of Ed Burns as a public school teacher.

"You Come At The King, You Best Not Miss."

Breaking Down "Breaking Bad"

"Breaking Bad," created by Vince Gilligan, is an epic narrative that details the descent of a mild-mannered high school chemistry teacher, Walter White, into the depths of the criminal underworld as he becomes a methamphetamine manufacturer and drug lord. The transformation of Walter White, played with masterful nuance by Bryan Cranston, is at the heart of the series. It's a story about desperation, morality, and the lengths to which someone will go when pushed to their limits. White's initial motive—securing his family's financial future after being diagnosed with terminal lung cancer—quickly spirals into a dark tale of power, greed, and destruction.

At the beginning of the series, Walter teams up with a former student, Jesse Pinkman, portrayed by Aaron Paul, to enter the meth production business. Their partnership is fraught with tension, tragedy, and betrayal, yet it forms the emotional core of the show. Jesse's complex relationship with Walter oscillates between loyalty, fear, and hatred, providing a compelling

"Yeah, Science!!"

dynamic that explores themes of fatherhood, mentorship, and redemption. The series is celebrated for its moral complexity and the way it poses challenging questions about good and evil, choices and consequences.

"Breaking Bad" is notable for its tight narrative structure, with each season building upon the last to escalate the stakes and deepen the character arcs. The show's meticulous attention to detail, both in the scientific aspects of meth production and the depiction of the drug trade, lends it an authenticity that immerses viewers in Walter's increasingly perilous world. The series also employs innovative cinematography and visual storytelling techniques, using color, landscape, and symbolic imagery to enhance the narrative and develop its characters.

Supporting characters, such as Skyler White (Anna Gunn), Hank Schrader (Dean Norris), and Saul Goodman (Bob Odenkirk), add depth and complexity to the story, representing different facets of morality and the consequences of Walter's actions. Skyler's struggle with Walter's secrets and her own moral compromises make her a contentious yet critically important character.

Hank, Walter's brother-in-law and a DEA agent, embodies the law's pursuit of justice, adding a cat-and-mouse element to the plot. Saul Goodman, a lawyer who represents the criminal underworld's colorful yet dangerous side, provides comic relief while also highlighting the corruption and ethical ambiguity within the legal system.

"Breaking Bad" pushed the boundaries of television storytelling, proving that a serialized narrative could achieve the depth and complexity of a novel. It has been widely regarded as one of the greatest television series of all time, thanks in part to its resolution, which provided a satisfying and thought-provoking conclusion to Walter White's journey. The series did not shy away from depicting the consequences of Walter's choices, ultimately holding him accountable for his actions in a way that resonated with viewers and critics alike.

The cultural impact of "Breaking Bad" is significant, inspiring a dedicated fan base, critical acclaim, and a successful prequel series, "Better Call Saul." The show's influence extends beyond entertainment, sparking discussions about ethics, the American healthcare system, and the nature of evil. Its legacy is evident in the way it has shaped subsequent television dramas, setting a high bar for character development, narrative innovation, and moral complexity.

"Breaking Bad" received numerous awards, including 16 Primetime Emmy Awards. Bryan Cranston's portrayal of Walter White earned him four Emmy Awards for Outstanding Lead Actor in a Drama Series. Aaron Paul's portrayal of Jesse Pinkman garnered him three Emmy Awards for Outstanding Supporting Actor in a Drama Series, reflecting the critical acclaim for the show's performances.

"I am the one who knocks."

The quote "I am the one who knocks" from "Breaking Bad" is a defining moment for Walter White's character, symbolizing his complete transformation from a sympathetic protagonist to a formidable antagonist. Spoken in a heated conversation with his wife, Skyler, this line encapsulates Walter's descent into villainy and his acceptance of his role as a danger to others, rather than a victim of circumstance. It signifies a shift in the narrative, where the audience is compelled to re-evaluate their allegiance to Walter. Initially rooting for him due to his desperate circumstances, viewers are confronted with the reality that

Walter has become the very threat he once sought to protect his family from.

This moment is pivotal, as it underlines the series' exploration of morality, power, and identity. Walter's assertion of being "the one who knocks" is not just a declaration of his dominance in the drug trade but also a rejection of any remaining semblance of his former, morally upright self. It challenges viewers to consider the complexities of rooting for an anti-hero who has willingly embraced his darker nature for the sake of power and control.

The brilliance of "Breaking Bad" lies in its ability to present characters like Walter White, who, despite their egregious actions, are deeply human and relatable. The series invites the audience to empathize with Walter's initial motives, only to gradually reveal the consequences of his choices, forcing a reckoning with the ethical dilemmas at its core. Walter's journey prompts viewers to question the nature of villainy and heroism, making "I am the one who knocks" a memorable quote that reflects the show's nuanced portrayal of its characters' moral ambiguities.

This exploration of complex characters like Walter White, who blur the lines between hero and villain, has significantly influenced television storytelling. "Breaking Bad" demonstrated that characters with morally gray areas offer a richer, more engaging narrative experience, encouraging audiences to grapple with their perceptions of right and wrong.

Did You Know? Bryan Cranston gained widespread recognition for his role as Hal, the quirky and eccentric father in the television sitcom "Malcolm in the Middle." The show aired from 2000 to 2006 and showcased Cranston's comedic talents

Critically Acclaimed Episodes

"Ozymandias" (Season 5, Episode 14)

Considered one of the greatest episodes in television history, "Ozymandias" showcases the culmination of Walter White's actions and the fallout for his family. The episode is a devastating look at the consequences of Walt's empire crumbling around him. Themes of power, loss, and the inevitability of consequences are explored in depth, making it a turning point in the series. "Ozymandias" is actually a very famous poem. The poem concerns the discovery of a semi-destroyed and decaying statue of Ramesses II, also known as Ozymandias, and shows how power deteriorates and will not last forever.

> *"My name is Ozymandias, King of Kings; /Look on my Works, ye Mighty, and despair!"* ...
> *"Nothing beside remains."* ...
> *"Round the decay / Of that colossal Wreck, boundless and bare / The lone and level sands stretch far away."* ...
> *"The hand that mocked them, and the heart that fed"*

"Felina" (Season 5, Episode 16)

The series finale, "Felina," wraps up Walter White's journey in a manner that many fans found deeply satisfying. It ties up loose ends, brings full circle the transformation of Walt from a high school chemistry teacher to a drug kingpin, and concludes his relationships with other key characters. The episode explores themes of redemption, legacy, and the inescapable nature of one's actions.

"Face Off" (Season 4, Episode 13)

This episode is a high point in the series for its dramatic tension and the showdown between Walt and his nemesis, Gus Fring. The cleverly executed plot twists and the ultimate confrontation are both shocking and satisfying, highlighting themes of rivalry, strategy, and survival.

Gustavo "Gus" Fring, portrayed with chilling precision by Giancarlo Esposito, stands out as one of the most formidable antagonists in "Breaking Bad." A mastermind of both the methamphetamine trade and the owner of the fast-food chain Los Pollos Hermanos, Gus presents himself to the world as a respectable business owner and philanthropist. However, beneath this veneer of respectability lies a calculating, ruthless drug lord who maintains a tight grip on his empire with a blend of fear and loyalty.

Gus's ability to navigate both the legitimate and criminal worlds with equal finesse makes him a unique and memorable character in the series. His role as Walter White's adversary is pivotal, bringing out Walt's own capacity for strategic thinking and moral flexibility. The chicken shop, Los Pollos Hermanos, serves as a front for his drug operations, symbolizing Gus's talent for hiding in plain sight and manipulating those around him to maintain his power and control. The showdown in "Face Off" not only signifies the climax of Walt and Gus's intricate game of cat and mouse but also marks a turning point in Walt's transformation, emphasizing the series' exploration of the thin line between good and evil.

"Crawl Space" (Season 4, Episode 11)

"Crawl Space" is renowned for its intense ending and the incredible performance by Bryan Cranston. The episode delves into the psychological decline of Walter White, as his plans begin to unravel, and he finds himself trapped by his own decisions. Themes of desperation, entrapment, and madness are central.

"Fly" (Season 3, Episode 10)

Trivia Tidbits

- Often considered a controversial episode due to its bottle episode format, "Fly" is a deep dive into the psyche of Walter White. The episode focuses on Walt and Jesse attempting to kill a fly that's contaminating their meth lab, serving as a metaphor for Walt's guilt and his need for control. It explores themes of obsession, guilt, and the search for purity in a corrupt world.
- "Breaking Bad" inspired a successful spin-off prequel, "Better Call Saul," focusing on the character Saul Goodman before he became Walter White's lawyer.
- A feature film sequel, "El Camino: A Breaking Bad Movie," was released in 2019, following Jesse Pinkman's life immediately after the series finale.
- The series' title, "Breaking Bad," is a southern colloquialism that means turning to a life of crime or immorality.
- Bryan Cranston got a real "BrBa" tattoo on his finger the day of filming the final episode to commemorate his time on the show.
- The iconic blue meth was actually made from rock candy to ensure it was safe for the actors to handle.

- The pizza toss scene in "Caballo Sin Nombre" was achieved in one take, leading to Bryan Cranston being praised for his unexpected pizza-throwing skills.
- Aaron Paul used the word "bitch" 54 times throughout the series, becoming one of Jesse Pinkman's signature catchphrases.
- "Breaking Bad" is the highest-rated TV series on IMDb, maintaining a near-perfect score.
- The show's creators made a fake documentary as an April Fool's joke, claiming "Breaking Bad" was a prequel to "The Walking Dead."
- Giancarlo Esposito, who played Gus Fring, prepared for his role by researching real drug lords and studying their mannerisms and psychology.
- "Breaking Bad" used the Albuquerque, New Mexico, setting to its advantage, incorporating the city's unique landscapes and culture into the show's identity.
- The series won the Primetime Emmy Award for Outstanding Drama Series twice, in 2013 and 2014.
- The DEA provided training to Bryan Cranston and Aaron Paul to ensure the meth cooking scenes were depicted with scientific accuracy.
- Vince Gilligan admitted that the writing team often wrote themselves into corners, not knowing how characters would escape situations, adding to the show's suspense.
- A "Breaking Bad" themed coffee shop opened in Istanbul, offering fans a taste of the show's atmosphere, complete with chemistry sets for brewing coffee.
- One interesting fact about Bryan Cranston's life is that before becoming an actor, he worked as a video producer for a non-profit organization. He also worked as a waiter and a security guard to support himself while pursuing his acting career.

Reality TV Domination: "Survivor" to "American Idol"

The late 1990s and early 2000s marked a transformative period in television history, heralding the rise of reality TV as a dominant genre. This era introduced audiences to a new form of entertainment that blurred the lines between reality and fiction, offering viewers an unprecedented look into the lives, talents, and endurance of ordinary and extraordinary people alike. Among the multitude of reality shows that captured the public's imagination, "Survivor" and "American Idol" stood out, not only for their popularity but also for their impact on television programming and pop culture at large.

"Survivor," which premiered in 2000, quickly became a cultural phenomenon. The show's premise—stranding a group of strangers on a deserted island to compete in challenges for a cash prize while forming alliances and voting each other off—captivated viewers with its blend of strategy, social dynamics, and survival skills. "Survivor" was groundbreaking in its use of the reality competition format, setting the template for countless shows that followed. Its success demonstrated the audience's appetite for unscripted drama and real-life stakes, making it a staple of 21st-century television.

On the other hand, "American Idol," debuting in 2002, took a different approach by focusing on talent over survival. The show sought to discover the next big music superstar through nationwide auditions, with contestants performing in front of a panel of judges and the American public voting for their favorites. "American Idol" was not just a talent competition; it was a platform that transformed unknown artists into stars, influencing the music industry and redefining the concept of celebrity in the modern era. The show's format, including the interactive element of audience voting, was innovative and has been replicated in various forms around the world.

Both "Survivor" and "American Idol" were more than just entertainment; they were social phenomena that engaged millions of viewers, sparking discussions in living rooms, workplaces, and online forums. These shows were among the first to leverage the power of the internet for audience engagement, from online voting to fan communities and social media discussions, thus amplifying their impact beyond the television screen.

The success of "Survivor" and "American Idol" opened the floodgates for the reality TV genre, leading to an explosion of reality programming that included competition shows, docu-series, and lifestyle programs. This era of reality TV domination transformed television networks' programming strategies, as reality shows proved to be cost-effective alternatives to scripted content, capable of drawing large audiences and significant advertising revenue.

Moreover, reality TV's emphasis on "ordinary" people facing extraordinary situations or showcasing exceptional talents democratized fame and challenged traditional notions of celebrity. It provided viewers with relatable stories of triumph, failure, perseverance, and talent, often inspiring audiences with its portrayal of the human spirit.

In retrospect, the rise of reality TV with landmark shows like "Survivor" and "American Idol" marked a significant shift in entertainment and culture. These shows not only entertained millions but also influenced television production, viewer engagement, and the very nature of fame and success in the 21st century, cementing their place in the annals of TV history.

- The Amazing Race (2001-Present) - This reality competition takes teams around the world in a race for a million-dollar prize. The show combines travel adventure with challenges that test teams' physical and mental endurance, problem-solving skills, and ability to work together under pressure.
- Big Brother (1999-Present) - Originating in the Netherlands, "Big Brother" places a group of contestants, known as housemates, in a specially constructed house isolated from the outside world. They're continuously monitored by live television cameras as well as personal audio microphones. The public, as well as housemates, vote to evict each other until one remains to claim the cash prize.
- The Apprentice (2004-Present) - Launched in the US, this reality show features a group of aspiring businessmen and women competing for the chance to work for billionaire mogul Donald Trump's company (in its original version). The series is known for its intense boardroom sessions, culminating in Trump's iconic dismissal phrase, "You're fired."
- Project Runway (2004-Present) - A reality show centered around fashion design. Contestants compete against each other to create the best clothes and are restricted in time, materials, and theme. Their designs are judged, and one or more designers are eliminated each week.
- RuPaul's Drag Race (2009-Present) - This American reality competition television series is produced by World of Wonder for Logo TV and, later, VH1. The show documents RuPaul in the search for "America's next drag superstar." It has brought drag culture to mainstream audiences and has expanded globally with several international versions.
- A fun fact about "The Apprentice" is that the show was originally created by British producer Mark Burnett. The Apprentice in the UK features business magnate Sir Alan Sugar, and still runs even today!

- MasterChef (1990-Present) - Originally started in the UK, "MasterChef" is a competitive cooking show television format. Amateur and home chefs compete in cooking challenges judged by professional chefs and cooking experts. Due to its success, it has been adapted in numerous countries around the world, each with its own version of the competition.

Controversy

While reality TV has become a staple of entertainment, captivating audiences worldwide, it has not been without its share of controversy and criticism. These issues range from questions about the authenticity of the content to concerns about the psychological impact on participants and viewers alike. Here's an exploration of some of the controversies surrounding reality TV:

A common critique of reality TV is the extent to which the content is scripted or manipulated by producers. Shows have been accused of creating artificial drama through editing or by placing participants in contrived situations to elicit dramatic responses. This manipulation raises questions about the "reality" of reality TV, blurring the lines between genuine behavior and performance for the camera. For example, "The Apprentice" faced scrutiny over how much of the drama was orchestrated by producers to keep viewers engaged.

The psychological impact on participants is another area of concern. The pressure of competition, constant surveillance, and subsequent public scrutiny can take a toll on contestants' mental health. Shows like "Big Brother" and "Survivor" have faced criticism for the intense psychological environment they create, potentially exacerbating stress and conflict among participants for entertainment value.

The duty of care reality shows have towards their contestants has become a topic of discussion, urging producers to ensure support systems are in place.

Reality TV often thrives on conflict, sensationalism, and personal drama, leading to accusations of exploiting individuals' vulnerabilities for entertainment.

This exploitation can sometimes extend to using participants' personal struggles, such as addiction or financial difficulties, as plot points, raising ethical concerns about the commodification of personal suffering.

Critics argue that reality TV can influence societal norms and values negatively, promoting materialism, superficiality, and unhealthy body images, particularly among young viewers. Shows that focus on lavish lifestyles, appearance, and instant fame can skew perceptions of success and happiness. "The Real Housewives" franchise and similar programs have been critiqued for glamorizing excess and conflict.

Reality TV has also been criticized for its representation of race, gender, and sexuality. Early seasons of shows like "Survivor" and "The Amazing Race" were criticized for lack of diversity and perpetuating stereotypes. Although there has been progress in recent years with shows like "RuPaul's Drag Race" celebrating LGBTQ+ culture, the industry continues to grapple with ensuring diverse and respectful representation.

Despite these controversies, reality TV remains hugely popular, offering viewers a mix of entertainment, escapism, and the occasional educational content. The genre's evolution continues to reflect broader social and cultural shifts, adapting to audience demands for more authenticity, diversity, and ethical considerations in production practices.

- "Big Brother" (UK) Season 5 in 2004 featured a massive fight among contestants, leading to police intervention. This event drew public attention to the psychological pressures of reality TV.
- In "Survivor" Season 7 (Pearl Islands), contestant Jonny Fairplay lied about his grandmother's death to gain sympathy and strategic advantage, sparking debates about ethics in game play.
- "American Idol" Season 2 contestant Corey Clark was disqualified for failing to disclose a prior arrest, raising questions about background checks and contestant vetting processes.
- "The Apprentice" (US) frequently came under fire for Donald Trump's harsh treatment of contestants, particularly his catchphrase "You're fired," which stirred discussions about workplace bullying.
- "Project Runway" Season 3 saw designer Jeffrey Sebelia accused of outsourcing his sewing work, highlighting issues of fairness and integrity in competition.
- "The Amazing Race" Season 15 featured a controversial watermelon slingshot task that went viral when a contestant was accidentally hit in the face, sparking discussions about safety on reality shows.
- "RuPaul's Drag Race" faced backlash for its use of the term "She-mail" in Season 6, leading to accusations of transphobia and a public apology from the showrunners.
- In "MasterChef" (US) Season 3, contestant Josh Marks suffered from mental health issues post-show and tragically passed away, prompting conversations about the aftercare of reality TV participants.
- Survivor" Season 14 (Fiji) faced criticism for its "Haves vs. Have Nots" concept, where one tribe was given abundant resources while the other was left with almost nothing, highlighting issues of fairness and ethics in game design.

- "The Real World" (San Francisco) in 1994 was groundbreaking for its portrayal of Pedro Zamora, an openly gay man living with AIDS, but also faced criticism for exploiting his condition for ratings.
- "Jersey Shore" (2009-2012) was criticized for its portrayal of Italian-American stereotypes, with some cultural organizations accusing the show of promoting negative images.
- "Hell's Kitchen" Season 2 contestant Keith Greene accused Gordon Ramsay of favoritism and sexism during his exit, which ignited a discussion about the treatment of contestants by judges.

During Shilpa Shetty's stint on Celebrity Big Brother 5 in the UK, she faced racial discrimination and bullying from fellow contestants, particularly from fellow housemates Jade Goody, Danielle Lloyd, and Jo O'Meara.

The incidents occurred primarily due to cultural differences and insensitive remarks made by some housemates. Shilpa endured derogatory comments about her Indian heritage, including being referred to as "Shilpa Poppadom" and being mocked for her accent and cooking.

These actions sparked widespread outrage and condemnation both inside and outside the Big Brother house, leading to a significant public outcry and media attention. Shilpa handled the situation with grace and dignity, addressing the issues diplomatically.

The controversy surrounding Shilpa's treatment on the show ignited discussions about racism, cultural sensitivity, and bullying in the media and society at large. Shilpa's victory in Celebrity Big Brother 5 served as a powerful platform for her to advocate for diversity, tolerance, and understanding.

The Fantasy and Superhero Surge: "Harry Potter" and "The Dark Knight"

The late 1990s and early 2000s marked the beginning of a significant surge in the popularity of fantasy and superhero genres in both film and literature, fundamentally transforming popular culture. This era introduced audiences to vast, immersive worlds and complex characters who continue to captivate millions worldwide. Central to this surge were two iconic franchises: "Harry Potter," born from the pen of J.K. Rowling, and "The Dark Knight" trilogy, directed by Christopher Nolan. Both franchises not only achieved monumental commercial success but also garnered critical acclaim, setting new standards for storytelling, visual effects, and character development in their respective genres.

"Harry Potter," beginning with "The Philosopher's Stone" in 1997, quickly became a literary phenomenon. Rowling's imaginative storytelling, combined with a richly detailed universe of magic, appealed to readers of all ages, blurring the lines between children's and adult literature.

The subsequent film adaptations, starting in 2001, brought the magic of Hogwarts to the screen, capturing the hearts of a global audience and igniting a renewed interest in fantasy cinema. The series' exploration of themes such as friendship, courage, and the battle between good and evil resonated deeply with readers and viewers, contributing to its enduring popularity.

On the other hand, Nolan's "The Dark Knight" trilogy, commencing with "Batman Begins" in 2005, redefined the superhero genre. Moving away from the often campy portrayals of comic book characters, Nolan presented a darker, more realistic interpretation of Batman, set against the backdrop of a gritty, morally ambiguous Gotham City. The trilogy's second installment, "The Dark Knight" (2008), was particularly notable for its complex narrative, thematic depth, and Heath Ledger's iconic performance as the Joker. Nolan's films were praised for their philosophical underpinnings, exploring themes of justice, fear, and the potential for heroism in a corrupt world.

Both "Harry Potter" and "The Dark Knight" trilogy benefited from advancements in special effects and CGI, allowing filmmakers to bring fantastical elements and superheroic feats to life with unprecedented realism.

These technological innovations, combined with compelling storytelling, created immersive experiences that expanded the possibilities of cinema as a medium.

Moreover, the success of "Harry Potter" and "The Dark Knight" had a significant impact on the entertainment industry, leading to a surge in the production of fantasy and superhero content. Studios and networks, recognizing the commercial potential of these genres, invested in adaptations of existing properties and the development of original content, resulting in a diverse array of films and television shows that continue to dominate the cultural landscape.

In addition to their entertainment value, both franchises sparked discussions about societal issues, morality, and the human condition, highlighting the capacity of fantasy and superhero stories to reflect and critique real-world concerns. Through their complex characters, intricate worlds, and moral dilemmas, "Harry Potter" and "The Dark Knight" trilogy elevated genre storytelling, demonstrating its potential to engage, challenge, and inspire audiences.

In conclusion, the fantasy and superhero surge of the late 1990s and 2000s, epitomized by "Harry Potter" and "The Dark Knight," marked a pivotal moment in popular culture. These franchises not only set new standards for their genres but also influenced a generation of storytellers and fans, leaving a lasting legacy that continues to shape the entertainment industry today.

Harry Potter

"Don't let the Muggles get you down."
— Ron Weasley

The "Harry Potter" series, spanning seven books and eight films, emerged as a defining cultural phenomenon of the 2000s, captivating a global audience and leaving an indelible mark on the landscape of fantasy literature and cinema. J.K. Rowling's creation of the "Harry Potter" universe was not just a masterclass in world-building; it was a pioneering effort in long-term storytelling that spanned both literature and film, intertwining the fate of its characters with the lives of its readers and viewers.

From the outset, Rowling had a clear vision for the narrative arc of her series, meticulously planning the journey of her protagonist, Harry Potter, from an orphan living in a cupboard under the stairs to the hero of the wizarding world. This attention to detail and forethought allowed for a complex, interconnected plot that evolved over the series' seven books, each installment building on the last to culminate in a richly satisfying conclusion. Rowling's ability to weave intricate plot lines, foreshadow future events, and develop characters over time showcased her prowess as a storyteller and set a new standard for serialized narrative in children's literature.

The transition from page to screen was a monumental task, with the film adaptations beginning in 2001 and concluding in 2011. The filmmakers, starting with Chris Columbus and followed by Alfonso Cuarón, Mike Newell, and David Yates, worked closely with Rowling to ensure that the essence of her books was captured on film. This collaboration was crucial in maintaining the series' integrity, ensuring that the magical world fans had imagined was faithfully brought to life. The decision to cast relatively unknown actors in the leading roles of Harry, Ron, and Hermione was a strategic one, allowing audiences to grow and identify with the characters without the distraction of pre-existing celebrity personas. Daniel Radcliffe, Rupert Grint, and Emma Watson became the faces of their characters, aging with them over a decade of filmmaking and embodying the journey from childhood to adulthood.

The impact of "Harry Potter" on the film industry was profound, influencing the approach to franchise filmmaking. The series' commercial and critical success demonstrated the viability of long-term storytelling across multiple films, encouraging studios to invest in other large-scale adaptations and cinematic universes.

The meticulous planning, casting continuity, and adherence to the source material in the "Harry Potter" films became a blueprint for future franchises.

Rowling's engagement with her fans set a precedent for author involvement in film adaptations. Her active participation in the screenwriting process and her approval of casting decisions ensured that the films remained true to her vision. Additionally, Rowling's use of the internet to communicate with fans and expand the "Harry Potter" universe beyond the books and films fostered a sense of community and engagement unparalleled in literary history.

Yer a wizard Harry."
— Rubeus Hagrid

The series' thematic depth, exploring issues such as loss, prejudice, and the corruption of power, resonated with a diverse audience. Rowling's storytelling was not just about magic and adventure; it was a commentary on the human condition, making the series relevant to readers and viewers of all ages. The emotional depth and universal themes of "Harry Potter" contributed to its lasting appeal, encouraging readers and viewers to revisit the series and find new layers of meaning with each encounter.

In reflecting on the creation and impact of "Harry Potter," it is clear that Rowling's series was more than a literary and cinematic achievement; it was a cultural milestone that redefined the possibilities of storytelling across mediums. The planned approach to character development, the meticulous world-building, and the seamless transition from books to films not only enchanted millions but also inspired a new generation of storytellers to dream big and imagine new worlds. The legacy of "Harry Potter" continues to influence the fantasy genre and the entertainment industry, underscoring the power of a well-told story to capture the hearts and minds of people around the world.

"The Boy Who Lived"

Harry Potter (Daniel Radcliffe): The Boy Who Lived, Harry's journey from an orphan living under the stairs to the hero who defeats Voldemort is the series' heart. Radcliffe brought vulnerability, bravery, and authenticity to Harry, growing alongside the character.

Hermione Granger (Emma Watson): Hermione's intelligence, moral compass, and fierce loyalty make her an indispensable part of the trio. Watson embodied Hermione's strength and complexity, becoming a role model for girls worldwide.

Ron Weasley (Rupert Grint): The series' comic relief and loyal friend, Ron's journey is about overcoming insecurities and embracing bravery. Grint's portrayal added depth to Ron's character, showcasing his growth and vulnerabilities.

Albus Dumbledore (Richard Harris, Michael Gambon): The wise and powerful Headmaster of Hogwarts, Dumbledore guides Harry with his wisdom. Harris initially brought a gentle strength to Dumbledore, and after his passing, Gambon continued the role with a bit more eccentricity and dynamism.

Severus Snape (Alan Rickman): A complex character, Snape's true loyalties are a key mystery. Rickman's performance was nuanced, capturing Snape's bitterness, bravery, and hidden depth.

Voldemort (Ralph Fiennes): The series' main antagonist, Fiennes gave Voldemort a terrifying presence, embodying the character's cruelty and quest for power, making him a memorable villain.

Sirius Black (Gary Oldman): Harry's godfather and a complex figure, Oldman's portrayal of Sirius added layers of warmth, depth, and tragedy, highlighting his significance in Harry's life.

Luna Lovegood (Evanna Lynch): Known for her eccentricities and pure heart, Lynch's portrayal of Luna was spot-on, capturing her whimsical yet insightful nature.

Neville Longbottom (Matthew Lewis): Neville's evolution from a timid boy to a courageous hero is significant. Lewis's transformation mirrored Neville's, marking him as a symbol of growth and bravery.

Draco Malfoy (Tom Felton): Harry's rival at Hogwarts, Felton's Draco was more than just a villain; he brought out the character's internal conflict and the pressures he faced.
Ginny Weasley (Bonnie Wright): Ginny grows from Ron's younger sister to a strong, independent witch. Wright's portrayal highlighted Ginny's courage and her pivotal role in the series.

Fred and George Weasley (James and Oliver Phelps): The twins provided comic relief but also had moments of seriousness. The Phelps twins captured Fred and George's mischief, loyalty, and entrepreneurial spirit.

Minerva McGonagall (Maggie Smith): McGonagall, portrayed by Smith, was the stern yet fair professor who had a deep care for her students, exemplifying strength and integrity.

Rubeus Hagrid (Robbie Coltrane): Hagrid's warmth and unconditional loyalty to Harry and his friends were brought to life by Coltrane's heartfelt performance.

Dolores Umbridge (Imelda Staunton): Perhaps one of the most hated characters, Staunton's portrayal of Umbridge was chillingly effective, capturing her cruelty and tyranny within the Ministry and Hogwarts.

"I hope you're pleased with yourselves. We could all have been killed — or worse, expelled. Now if you don't mind, I'm going to bed." — Hermione Granger

"Do not pity the dead, Harry. Pity the living, and, above all those who live without love." – Albus Dumbledore

Are you a Wizard or a Muggle? Quiz

What is the core function of the Room of Requirement?
- A) To serve as Dumbledore's office
- B) To provide what the seeker needs
- C) To store dangerous artifacts

Who originally owned the Elder Wand before Dumbledore?
- A) Gellert Grindelwald
- B) Tom Riddle
- C) Severus Snape

What potion does Harry take to successfully retrieve a memory from Slughorn?
- A) Amortentia
- B) Felix Felicis
- C) Polyjuice Potion

Which magical creature is NOT found in the Forbidden Forest?
- A) Centaurs
- B) Acromantulas
- C) Basilisks

What spell is used to conjure the Dark Mark?
- A) Morsmordre
- B) Avada Kedavra
- C) Expelliarmus

Who is the Half-Blood Prince?
- A) Sirius Black
- B) Severus Snape
- C) Remus Lupin

What is the name of the Goblin who helps Harry break into Gringotts?
- A) Griphook
- B) Gornuk
- C) Bogrod

Which Hogwarts house did Moaning Myrtle belong to?
- A) Ravenclaw
- B) Hufflepuff
- C) Slytherin

Who destroys the final Horcrux?
- A) Neville Longbottom
- B) Harry Potter
- C) Ron Weasley

What form does Hermione's Patronus take?
- A) Rabbit
- B) Otter
- C) Cat

Which object is NOT a Deathly Hallow?
- A) Marauder's Map
- B) The Resurrection Stone
- C) The Cloak of Invisibility

What class does Professor Trelawney teach?
- A) Potions
- B) Divination
- C) Transfiguration.

Who can see Thestrals?
- A) Only those who have mastered a Patronus
- B) Only those who have seen death
- C) Only pure-blood wizards

Where is the entrance to the Chamber of Secrets located?
- A) In the Forbidden Forest
- B) Underneath the Whomping Willow In
- C) Moaning Myrtle's bathroom

What is the effect of the Imperius Curse?
- A) Causes unbearable pain
- B) Controls the victim's actions
- C) Kills the victim instantly

Answers

B) To provide what the seeker needs
The Room of Requirement changes its interior based on the needs of the person who invokes it, making it one of Hogwarts' most mysterious and useful rooms.

A) Gellert Grindelwald
Grindelwald, a dark wizard defeated by Dumbledore in 1945, was a previous master of the Elder Wand, one of the Deathly Hallows known for its allegiance to the wizard who disarmed its last owner.

B) Felix Felicis
This "liquid luck" potion grants the drinker a day of good fortune, used by Harry to successfully retrieve Slughorn's true memory regarding Horcruxes.

C) Basilisks
The Forbidden Forest is home to many magical creatures, but basilisks are not among them; the only known basilisk in the series resides in the Chamber of Secrets.

A) Morsmordre
This spell conjures the Dark Mark, the symbol of Lord Voldemort and his Death Eaters, used to mark their presence or claim responsibility for acts of terror.

B) Severus Snape
Snape, known as the Half-Blood Prince, used this moniker due to his mixed blood status and his mother's maiden name, Prince.

A) Griphook
Griphook assists Harry, Ron, and Hermione in breaking into Bellatrix Lestrange's vault at Gringotts, highlighting the complicated relationship between wizards and goblins.

A) Ravenclaw
Moaning Myrtle, a ghost haunting the girls' bathroom, was a student in Ravenclaw house before her death caused by the basilisk.

A) Neville Longbottom
Neville destroys the final Horcrux, Nagini, using the Sword of Gryffindor during the Battle of Hogwarts, playing a crucial role in Voldemort's defeat.

C) Otter
Hermione's Patronus, an otter, reflects her playful and intelligent nature; Patronuses are unique to each witch or wizard and are conjured as a protection against Dementors.

A) Marauder's Map
The Marauder's Map, while magical, is not a Deathly Hallow. The Deathly Hallows consist of the Elder Wand, the Resurrection Stone, and the Cloak of Invisibility, items bestowed with unique powers.

B) Divination
Professor Trelawney teaches Divination at Hogwarts, offering students insights into the future, though her predictions are often met with skepticism.

Only those who have seen death
The ability to see Thestrals, a breed of winged horses, is granted only to those who have witnessed death firsthand, symbolizing an understanding of mortality.

C) In Moaning Myrtle's bathroom
The entrance to the Chamber of Secrets is hidden in Moaning Myrtle's bathroom, requiring a Parseltongue command to open.

B) Controls the victim's actions
The Imperius Curse is one of the Unforgivable Curses, allowing the caster to exert control over the victim, forcing them to obey the caster's commands without question.

The Dark Knight

"He's the hero Gotham deserves, but not the one it needs right now. So we'll hunt him. Because he can take it. He's not our hero. He's a silent guardian, a watchful protector, a Dark Knight."

The "Dark Knight" trilogy, directed by Christopher Nolan, marked a revolutionary turn in the superhero genre, introducing audiences to a darker, more nuanced portrayal of Gotham City and its iconic protector, Batman. This series, particularly with its second installment, "The Dark Knight" (2008), is celebrated for its complex storytelling, thematic depth, and character development, setting it apart from traditional superhero narratives.

Christopher Nolan's approach to the trilogy was to ground the superhero story in a level of realism and psychological complexity not previously seen in comic book adaptations. He reimagined Batman not just as a vigilante hero but as a deeply conflicted character, wrestling with issues of justice, morality, and his own inner demons. This grounded portrayal of Batman, along with the trilogy's exploration of the consequences of vigilantism and the thin line between heroism and extremism, resonated with audiences and critics alike, elevating the perception of what a superhero film could be.

"The Dark Knight," the trilogy's centerpiece, is particularly noted for its exploration of chaos, order, and anarchy, personified by the character of the Joker, brilliantly portrayed by Heath Ledger. Ledger's performance brought a level of unpredictability and menace to the role, making the Joker not just a villain but a force of nature that challenges Batman's very ideology. The film delves into the moral ambiguities of Batman's vigilantism and the Joker's anarchistic philosophy, engaging the audience in a philosophical debate about good, evil, and the nature of heroism.

Heath Ledger's untimely death shortly before the film's release cast a shadow over its reception but also cemented his performance as a legendary portrayal that would define the character for generations. Ledger posthumously won the

Academy Award for Best Supporting Actor, a testament to his impactful and haunting embodiment of the Joker.

The "Dark Knight" trilogy's success sparked a renaissance in superhero cinema, influencing studios to adopt a darker, more serious tone in their own comic book adaptations.

Nolan's films demonstrated that superhero stories could be both commercially successful and critically acclaimed, blending action and spectacle with deep thematic content. This has led to an era where superhero narratives dominate the box office, though not without criticism that the market has become oversaturated with similar stories, sometimes at the expense of originality and variety in mainstream cinema.

Despite the proliferation of superhero movies, the "Dark Knight" trilogy remains a benchmark for excellence within the genre. Its influence can be seen in the emphasis on character-driven storytelling and the integration of real-world themes into the fantastical elements of superhero lore.

Nolan's trilogy has not only redefined Batman for a new age but has also challenged filmmakers and audiences to expect more from their heroes, both on the screen and in the complex world they reflect.

"You Either Die A Hero Or You Live Long Enough To See Yourself Become The Villain"

Pop Culture and Marketing Campaign

The "Dark Knight" trilogy, particularly "The Dark Knight," has had a profound impact on pop culture, embedding itself into the collective consciousness with its memorable characters, quotable lines, and philosophical underpinnings. The portrayal of Batman and the Joker has influenced not just other films and television series but also comic books, video games, and broader discussions about heroism and villainy in the modern world. The trilogy's exploration of themes such as justice, chaos, and the duality of human nature resonates deeply with audiences, making it a frequent subject of analysis in academic circles, fan forums, and even political discourse.

> *"Smile, because it confuses people. Smile, because it's easier than explaining what is killing you inside. As you know, madness is like gravity...all it takes is a little push."*

The marketing campaign for "The Dark Knight" was innovative and immersive, setting a new standard for film promotion. It included viral marketing strategies that engaged fans directly, such as scavenger hunts, online games, and websites that expanded on the film's narrative universe. One notable campaign involved a faux political campaign for Harvey Dent, complete with campaign materials and a website. These efforts built tremendous anticipation for the film, creating a sense of involvement and investment in the storyline before its release.

The campaign's success demonstrated the potential of interactive marketing to enhance the movie-going experience, a strategy that has since been adopted and expanded upon by other franchises.

The impact of Heath Ledger's Joker on pop culture has been particularly significant. His portrayal became iconic, inspiring countless imitations, tributes, and discussions about the nature of villainy.

The character's anarchic philosophy and memorable catchphrases have been referenced in various media, reflecting the character's enduring appeal and the depth of Ledger's performance. The Joker has become a symbol of chaos and a critique of societal norms, embodying the complex interplay between society and its outliers.

Moreover, the trilogy's influence extends to the superhero genre itself, prompting a shift towards darker, more complex narratives in both cinema and television.

The success of Nolan's approach encouraged filmmakers to explore the psychological depth of their characters, leading to a wave of films that examine the moral complexities and personal costs of heroism. This trend has contributed to the genre's maturity, allowing for stories that challenge audiences and provoke thoughtful discussion.

The "Dark Knight" trilogy also played a pivotal role in the evolution of marketing strategies for blockbuster films. By creating an immersive and interactive promotional experience, the trilogy demonstrated the effectiveness of engaging directly with the audience, fostering a deeper connection to the film's content and characters. This approach has influenced the marketing of subsequent blockbusters, highlighting the importance of audience engagement in the digital age.

True or False Questions

True or False: "The Dark Knight" was the first film in Christopher Nolan's Batman trilogy.

True or False: Heath Ledger posthumously won an Oscar for his role in "The Dark Knight Rises."

True or False: The viral marketing campaign for The Dark Knight included a real phone number hidden in a movie trailer.

True or False: "Batman Begins" features the villain Scarecrow, who uses fear toxin to terrorize Gotham City.

True or False: The Joker's makeup in "The Dark Knight" was inspired by traditional clown makeup.

True or False: Harvey Dent becomes Two-Face during "The Dark Knight Rises."

True or False: "The Dark Knight" was the highest-grossing film of 2008 worldwide.

True or False: Christian Bale performed all of his own stunts in the trilogy.

True or False: The Batmobile used in the trilogy is officially called the Tumbler.

True or False: "The Dark Knight" trilogy was entirely shot in Chicago, representing Gotham City.

True or False: The theme music for "The Dark Knight" was composed by Hans Zimmer and James Newton Howard.

True or False: A real decommissioned aircraft was used and destroyed in the filming of "The Dark Knight Rises."

True or False: "The Dark Knight" was the first Batman film to feature the Batcave.

True or False: The character of Ra's al Ghul is revealed to be the true identity of Henri Ducard in "Batman Begins."

True or False: The Dark Knight trilogy introduced the character of Robin, who takes over as Batman at the end of "The Dark Knight Rises."

Answers

- False: "Batman Begins" (2005) was the first film in Christopher Nolan's Batman trilogy, introducing audiences to Nolan's darker, more realistic take on the Batman story.
- False: Heath Ledger posthumously won an Oscar for his role as the Joker in "The Dark Knight," not "The Dark Knight Rises."
- True: The viral marketing campaign for "The Dark Knight" was extensive and included a real phone number in a trailer that led fans to further clues about the movie.
- True: "Batman Begins" features the villain Scarecrow, played by Cillian Murphy, who uses a fear toxin as his weapon against Gotham City.
- False: The Joker's makeup in "The Dark Knight" was designed to look smeared and chaotic, resembling war paint more than traditional clown makeup, to match the character's anarchic nature.
- False: Harvey Dent becomes Two-Face in "The Dark Knight," not "The Dark Knight Rises," after half of his face is disfigured.
- True: "The Dark Knight" was the highest-grossing film of 2008 worldwide, showcasing the immense popularity and impact of Nolan's take on the Batman saga.
- False: While Christian Bale performed many of his own stunts, not all stunts were performed by him due to the dangerous nature of some scenes.
- True: The Batmobile in Nolan's trilogy is known as the Tumbler, a heavily armored vehicle used by Batman in his fight against crime in Gotham City.
- False: While much of "The Dark Knight" trilogy was filmed in Chicago, other locations, including London, Hong Kong, and Pittsburgh, were also used to represent Gotham City.

- False: While much of "The Dark Knight" trilogy was filmed in Chicago, other locations, including London, Hong Kong, and Pittsburgh, were also used to represent Gotham City.
- True: Hans Zimmer and James Newton Howard collaborated on the score for "The Dark Knight," creating a memorable and impactful musical backdrop for the film.
- True: A real decommissioned aircraft was indeed used and destroyed in the filming of "The Dark Knight Rises," demonstrating Nolan's preference for practical effects over CGI.
- False: The Batcave makes its appearance in "Batman Begins," serving as Batman's headquarters beneath Wayne Manor.
- True: The character of Ra's al Ghul, played by Liam Neeson, is revealed to be the true identity of Henri Ducard in "Batman Begins," serving as a mentor and later antagonist to Bruce Wayne.
- False: While "The Dark Knight Rises" introduces a character named Robin John Blake, played by Joseph Gordon-Levitt, he discovers the Batcave at the film's end, hinting at the legacy of Batman rather than taking over as Batman.

Did You Know? Christian Bale is known for his remarkable physical transformations for various roles throughout his career. For his role as Batman in Christopher Nolan's "Batman Begins" (2005), Bale underwent a significant weight gain. Prior to being cast as Batman, Bale had drastically lost weight for his role in "The Machinist" (2004), where he weighed about 120 pounds (54 kg). He then had to bulk up to fit the physicality expected of Batman, gaining around 100 pounds (45 kg) to reach about 220 pounds (100 kg), showcasing a muscular and imposing figure suitable for the Caped Crusader. Bale mentioned his diet routine in an interview, highlighting the simplicity and discipline of his food intake"I had a very simple diet: I ate salads and I ate tuna. That's it. If you eat tuna and salads, you get lean".

The Sitcom Evolution Continues: "The Office" to "30 Rock"

The early 2000s witnessed a notable evolution in the sitcom genre, with shows like "The Office" and "30 Rock" redefining comedic storytelling on television. These series moved away from traditional multi-camera setups and live studio audiences, embracing single-camera formats that allowed for a more intimate, nuanced style of comedy. "The Office," an adaptation of Ricky Gervais's British series, used a mockumentary format to explore the everyday lives of office employees, blending cringe comedy with touching moments of human connection. "30 Rock," created by and starring Tina Fey, provided a behind-the-scenes look at a fictional live sketch comedy show, celebrated for its quick-witted humor and eccentric characters. Both shows were critical in shaping the landscape of modern sitcoms, influencing a generation of comedy writers and creators.

Additional shows that contributed to the sitcom evolution include:

- "Parks and Recreation" (2009-2015): This mockumentary-style series focused on the quirky employees of the Parks Department in the fictional town of Pawnee, Indiana. Amy Poehler's portrayal of Leslie Knope became iconic. The series is known for creating the "Galentine's Day" holiday, celebrating female friendships on February 13th.
- "Arrested Development" (2003-2019): Known for its complex narratives and unique humor, this show chronicled the dysfunctional Bluth family. It was one of the first to be revived by Netflix due to fan demand. The show utilized a narrator, voiced by executive producer Ron Howard, to provide context and humor.

- "Modern Family" (2009-2020): This series broke new ground by portraying a diverse and non-traditional family structure through a mockumentary lens. It won the Emmy for Outstanding Comedy Series five times consecutively. The show is notable for its portrayal of a gay couple as main characters, contributing to increased LGBTQ+ representation on television.
- "It's Always Sunny in Philadelphia" (2005-Present): Famous for its politically incorrect humor and antihero characters who run an Irish bar. It's one of the longest-running live-action comedy series in American television history.
- "Community" (2009-2015): Set in a community college, known for its meta-humor and pop culture references, including a notable paintball episode that paid homage to action movies. The show's creator, Dan Harmon, went on to co-create the popular animated series "Rick and Morty."

The Office

"Well, well, well... how the turntables..."

"The Office," initially created by Ricky Gervais and Stephen Merchant for British television, was adapted for an American audience by Greg Daniels in 2005. The adaptation retained the mockumentary style of the original, focusing on the day-to-day operations of the Dunder Mifflin Paper Company in Scranton, Pennsylvania. This format allowed for a unique blend of humor and pathos, often blurring the lines between comedy and drama. The American version expanded on the concept by extending the show's run and developing a broader ensemble cast, which enabled deeper exploration of characters and their relationships.

Unlike the UK version's two seasons, the American "The Office" spanned nine seasons, offering more time to develop and evolve its characters and storylines.

This longer run allowed for significant character growth and arcs that were not possible in the original's more concise format. The show excelled in creating relatable, flawed characters whose personal and professional lives provided a rich source of comedy and occasionally heartfelt moments.

- Michael Scott (Steve Carell), the bumbling yet well-meaning regional manager whose lack of self-awareness and desperate need for approval drive much of the show's humor.
- Jim Halpert (John Krasinski) and Pam Beesly (Jenna Fischer), whose slow-burning romantic relationship becomes a central storyline, offering viewers a heartwarming portrayal of love in the workplace.
- Dwight Schrute (Rainn Wilson), the eccentric beet farmer and salesman whose intense loyalty to the company and bizarre personal life provide endless comedic material.
- Kelly Kapoor (Mindy Kaling) and Ryan Howard (B.J. Novak), who exemplify the show's ability to satirize contemporary workplace issues and relationships.

The adaptation also tailored the show's humor to suit American sensibilities while maintaining the original's essence. Elements of cringe comedy were balanced with moments of sincerity, making the characters endearing despite their flaws.

The American version's success is attributed to its ability to be both universally relatable and specifically attuned to the nuances of American office culture.

The adaptation process from the UK to the US version of "The Office" involved keeping the mockumentary format but expanding the scope and depth of the character ensemble. This allowed for a broader exploration of themes such as workplace dynamics, personal ambition, and the search for identity within the confines of a seemingly mundane office environment. The American "The Office" stands as a testament to the adaptability and enduring appeal of the original concept, successfully translating its humor and humanity for a new audience and becoming a cultural touchstone in its own right.

> *"Would I rather be feared or loved? Easy. Both. I want people to be afraid of how much they love me."*

The Funniest Skits

- Dwight's Fire Drill (Season 5, Episode 14, "Stress Relief: Part 1"): Dwight's extreme fire safety demonstration leads to chaos, including Angela throwing her cat into the ceiling and Stanley having a heart attack. This skit showcases the show's ability to combine physical comedy with character-driven humor.
- Jim Impersonates Dwight (Season 3, Episode 20, "Product Recall"): Jim comes to work dressed as Dwight, complete with glasses and a mustard-colored shirt, mimicking his mannerisms and catchphrases. Dwight's indignant response, "Identity theft is not a joke, Jim!" is a classic line from the show.
- Michael's "That's What She Said" (Various Episodes): Michael Scott's inappropriate and untimely use of the phrase "That's what she said" became one of the show's running jokes, highlighting his character's lack of social awareness and contributing to some of the series' funniest moments.

- **The Dundies (Season 2, Episode 1, "The Dundies")**: The annual Dundie Awards, hosted by Michael at a local Chili's, is full of awkward and hilarious moments, including Pam getting banned from Chili's for being overly intoxicated. This episode showcases the show's ability to blend cringe humor with genuine warmth.
- **Kevin's Famous Chili (Season 5, Episode 26, "Casual Friday")**: The cold open where Kevin brings in his famous chili only to spill it all over the office floor is both tragic and hilarious, encapsulating the character's well-meaning but clumsy nature.
- **Asian Jim (Season 9, Episode 3, "Andy's Ancestry")**: In a classic Jim prank, he convinces Dwight that he has been Asian all along, with actor Randall Park playing "Asian Jim" and family photos on Jim's desk altered to include Park. Dwight's confusion and eventual acceptance highlight the show's clever use of situational comedy.
- **Prison Mike (Season 3, Episode 9, "The Convict")**: To convince the office that working there is better than being in prison, Michael invents his alter ego "Prison Mike," complete with a bandana and a New York accent. The absurdity of Michael's performance and the employees' reactions make it a standout skit.
- **The Lip Dub (Season 7, Episode 1, "Nepotism")**: The office decides to create a lip dub to "Nobody but Me" by The Human Beinz as a fun way to start the season. The entire sequence, full of energy and ridiculous moments, highlights the cast's chemistry and the show's willingness to embrace the absurd.
- **Oscar's Southern Accent (Season 5, Episode 13, "Stress Relief Part 2")**: When Michael forces Oscar to do a southern accent during a murder mystery game, Oscar's exaggerated and reluctant performance is a highlight of the episode, showcasing the ensemble's comedic talents.

- Parkour (Season 6, Episode 1, "Gossip"): The office's attempt at parkour, led by Michael, Andy, and Dwight, results in a series of failed stunts culminating in Andy jumping into a refrigerator box. This skit illustrates the show's ability to incorporate physical comedy effectively.

"The Office" not only became a staple of American television for its humor and heart but also garnered critical acclaim throughout its run. The series won numerous awards, including the Primetime Emmy Award for Outstanding Comedy Series, solidifying its status as a critical darling. Its mockumentary style, which was relatively fresh to American audiences at the time, influenced a wave of similar sitcoms that sought to replicate its success.

The show's ability to tackle everyday workplace issues with humor and sensitivity contributed to its widespread appeal. Critics lauded "The Office" for its ensemble cast, with Steve Carell's portrayal of Michael Scott often receiving particular praise for his ability to balance the character's absurdity with moments of genuine pathos. The series was also commended for its development over time, transitioning from cringe comedy to a more heartfelt exploration of its characters' lives, making it a touchstone of 2000s television.

The impact of "The Office" extended far beyond its initial run, launching the careers of its cast into new heights. John Krasinski, who played Jim Halpert, has since directed critically acclaimed films such as "A Quiet Place" and its sequel, showcasing his versatility and talent beyond acting. Jenna Fischer (Pam Beesly) and Rainn Wilson (Dwight Schrute) have also enjoyed continued success in television and film, leveraging their fame from the show to explore a variety of creative projects. Perhaps most notably, the series has maintained a significant cultural presence thanks to streaming platforms, introducing new generations to Dunder Mifflin's unique office dynamic. Its enduring popularity is a testament to the show's quality and the deep connection it forged with its audience, proving that "The Office" is more than just a sitcom—it's a cultural milestone that defined an era of television.

Trivia Tidbits

- "The Office" originally aired on NBC from March 24, 2005, to May 16, 2013, spanning nine seasons and 201 episodes.
- The show's setting, Scranton, Pennsylvania, was chosen by Greg Daniels because his wife's family hails from the area, adding a layer of authenticity to the setting.
- The iconic opening theme song was composed by Jay Ferguson and played by The Scrantones.
- "The Office" was almost canceled after its first season due to low ratings, but it was saved partly because of Steve Carell's rising fame from "The 40-Year-Old Virgin."
- The computers on set were fully functional, and cast members often used them for internet browsing and emailing during scenes.
- Rainn Wilson, who played Dwight Schrute, originally auditioned for the role of Michael Scott.
- Pam's watercolor painting of the office building's exterior was created by the show's production artist.
- Many of the series' episodes were directed by cast members, including John Krasinski, who directed three episodes.
- "The Office" filmed its company picnic episode at the same location where the movie "MAS*H" was shot.
- The Dunder Mifflin logo and many of the props used on the show have become popular merchandise items among fans.

- The series finale saw the return of Steve Carell as Michael Scott, despite initial statements that he would not be making an appearance.
- Phyllis Smith, who played Phyllis Vance, was initially an assistant casting director for the show before being cast in her role based on her readings with other actors during auditions.

The Rise of Streaming Services: A New Way to Watch

The landscape of television and film consumption underwent a seismic shift with the rise of streaming services, a change that has redefined how we watch, what we watch, and even when we watch. This digital revolution began in earnest in the late 2000s, with Netflix transitioning from a DVD rental service to streaming, heralding a new era for entertainment consumption. In this transformation, Netflix, originally a plucky upstart sending DVDs through the mail, became the harbinger of doom for the once-ubiquitous Blockbuster video rental stores. The tale of Netflix's rise and Blockbuster's fall is not just a story of technological innovation but also a cautionary tale of what happens when companies fail to adapt to changing consumer behaviors.

Netflix's pivot to streaming in 2007 was a game-changer. It offered convenience, accessibility, and an all-you-can-watch model that was unheard of at the time. Suddenly, the idea of driving to a store, browsing through aisles of DVDs, and then facing the dreaded late fees became as outdated as the VHS tapes that once lined those store shelves. Blockbuster, slow to recognize the potential of streaming and burdened by its brick-and-mortar business model, found itself outmaneuvered. The once-dominant chain filed for bankruptcy in 2010, a victim of Netflix's disruption and its own inertia. The irony of Blockbuster having the opportunity to buy Netflix early on and passing it up is a delicious detail that history will never let it live down, a business blunder of epic proportions that is often cited in "what could have been" discussions.

The rise of streaming services like Netflix, Amazon Prime Video, Hulu, and later Disney+, HBO Max, and others, signaled not just the end of video rental stores but also a fundamental change in the television industry. The "binge-watch" culture, enabled by the release of entire seasons at once, altered viewing habits, making "waiting for next week's episode" an antiquated notion. This change in consumption has led to the demise of traditional TV's reign, prompting debates on whether "TV is dead." While broadcast and cable TV still exist, their dominance and cultural impact have waned in the face of streaming's flexibility and breadth of content.

Streaming services have democratized content creation, providing a platform for stories and voices that might not have found a home in the traditional TV landscape. This has led to an explosion of diversity in content, genres, and storytelling styles, contributing to what many call a new "Golden Age of Television." The traditional barriers to entry for creators have been lowered, resulting in a richer, more varied entertainment landscape that better reflects the complexity of the world we live in.

The rise of streaming has not been without its challenges. The overwhelming choice of content can lead to decision fatigue, the phenomenon of "streaming wars" has prompted concerns about market saturation, and the shift to digital has raised questions about digital rights, royalties, and the sustainability of content creation in the streaming model. Furthermore, the nostalgia for the communal aspect of scheduled TV watching has given rise to "watch parties" and live-tweeting events, proving that even as technology changes, the human desire for shared experiences remains.

As we look to the future, the landscape of streaming continues to evolve, with new players entering the market and traditional media companies scrambling to adapt. The streaming revolution has not just killed Blockbuster; it has rewritten the rules of the entertainment industry, proving that adaptability, innovation, and understanding of consumer behavior are key to survival in the digital age. And as for TV, it hasn't died; it's just changed channels, moving from the living room set to any device, anywhere, anytime, proving that the more things change, the more the couch remains our favorite place to escape the world.

- Netflix originally shipped DVDs in standard jewel cases before developing their iconic custom mailers to reduce shipping costs and damages.
- Hulu, initially a joint venture between several major media companies, including NBC Universal and Fox, was launched in 2007, aiming to offer a legal alternative to online TV show piracy.
- Amazon entered the streaming scene with Amazon Prime Video in 2006 as Amazon Unbox, but it wasn't until it was bundled with Prime membership that it gained significant traction.
- The first Netflix Original Series, "House of Cards," premiered in 2013, marking the beginning of Netflix's venture into original content production, which drastically changed its business model and the industry's landscape.
- Disney+ announced its entry into the streaming market in 2017 and launched in 2019, quickly becoming a major player due to its library of Disney classics, Marvel films, Star Wars series, and more.
- The term "Netflix and Chill" started as a simple way to describe an evening watching Netflix but quickly evolved into internet slang for a casual romantic or sexual encounter.

- HBO Max, launched in May 2020, combined HBO's premium content with a vast library from WarnerMedia, including Warner Bros., New Line Cinema, and DC content, aiming to compete directly with other streaming giants.
- The final Blockbuster store, located in Bend, Oregon, became a nostalgic tourist attraction and is still operational.
- In an effort to combat password sharing, Netflix began testing features in 2021 that would prompt users suspected of using a shared password to verify their account through a text or email code.
- The "streaming wars" have led to an unprecedented amount of original content production, with streaming services spending billions annually to capture viewers' attention and distinguish themselves in a crowded market.

Did You Know? Blockbuster was founded on October 19, 1985, in Dallas, Texas. It was established by David Cook as a stand-alone mom-and-pop video rental store. Over the years, it expanded into a national chain, featuring video game rentals, DVD-by-mail, streaming, video on demand, and cinema theatre. This marked the beginning of a new era in home entertainment, with Blockbuster becoming a dominant player in the video rental industry for several decades.

Blockbuster, at its peak, operated in over 17 countries around the world. This global expansion included the United States, Canada, Mexico, the United Kingdom, Australia, and several countries across Europe, South America, and Asia. Blockbuster's presence in these countries represented the company's ambition to dominate the home video rental market internationally.

Animated Success: "Shrek" to "Finding Nemo"

The turn of the millennium marked a golden era for animated films, with studios delivering stories that charmed not just children but adults alike. This period saw a significant evolution in animation techniques and storytelling, with "Shrek" and "Finding Nemo" standing out as iconic examples that redefined the genre.

Released in 2001, "Shrek" was a game-changer. Produced by DreamWorks Animation, it was a direct challenge to the traditional fairy tale narrative, offering a satirical take that delighted audiences with its humor, heart, and a groundbreaking blend of animation techniques. "Shrek" introduced a level of adult humor and pop culture references that hadn't been prominently featured in animated films before, making it a hit across different age groups. The film's success lay not just in its technical achievements, which were considerable, but in its ability to subvert expectations. It presented a world where the ogre was the hero, the princess didn't need saving, and the villain was far from formidable. "Shrek" went on to win the first-ever Academy Award for Best Animated Feature, firmly establishing DreamWorks as a major player in animation and sparking a franchise that would continue to captivate audiences for years.

Two years later, in 2003, Pixar Animation Studios released "Finding Nemo," a film that would set a new standard for emotional depth and visual beauty in animation. Following the underwater journey of Marlin, a clownfish, as he searches for his son Nemo, the film was praised for its rich storytelling, memorable characters, and stunning portrayal of ocean life.

"Finding Nemo" was a testament to Pixar's ability to combine cutting-edge technology with heartfelt narratives, creating a world that was immersive and emotionally resonant. The film's exploration of themes such as family, trust, and overcoming fear resonated with viewers worldwide, making "Finding Nemo" one of the highest-grossing animated films of its time and earning it an Academy Award for Best Animated Feature.

These films, along with others from the era, benefited from advances in computer-generated imagery (CGI), allowing animators to create more detailed and expressive characters and environments than ever before. This period was characterized by a willingness to experiment and push the boundaries of what animation could achieve, both in terms of visual aesthetics and narrative complexity.

Moreover, "Shrek" and "Finding Nemo" demonstrated the potential of animated films to serve as platforms for exploring contemporary issues and themes in a way that was accessible to both children and adults. They showed that animation was not just a medium for telling children's stories but a versatile art form capable of conveying complex messages and evoking a wide range of emotions.

The success of these films also had a significant impact on the industry, encouraging studios to invest more in animated features and to explore new stories and characters. The 2000s saw an explosion of creativity in animation, with films exploring everything from superhero families and culinary rats to toys and cars, each bringing something unique to the genre.

In reflecting on the legacy of "Shrek," "Finding Nemo," and their contemporaries, it's clear that this era was a pivotal moment in the history of animated film. These stories expanded the audience for animation, challenged conventional storytelling, and leveraged technological advancements to create cinematic experiences that were visually spectacular and emotionally compelling. They left an indelible mark on the genre, influencing the direction of animated films for years to come and cementing their place as classics in the pantheon of animation.

Pixar Animation Studios continued to lead the charge in CGI animation, building on the success of "Toy Story" with films like "Monsters, Inc." (2001) and "WALL-E" (2008). These films not only showcased Pixar's pioneering animation technology but also their commitment to storytelling, character development, and thematic depth, addressing themes from friendship and fear to environmental conservation and the human condition.

DreamWorks Animation emerged as a formidable competitor with "Shrek" (2001), a film that challenged traditional fairy tale narratives and introduced a more irreverent, adult-friendly humor to family animation. Following its success, DreamWorks produced other notable films such as "Madagascar" (2005) and "Kung Fu Panda" (2008), which combined visually stunning animation with engaging, heartwarming stories.

Blue Sky Studios entered the animation scene with "Ice Age" (2002), a film that combined humor, adventure, and a touch of prehistoric cool. Its success led to a lucrative franchise, showcasing Blue Sky's ability to create compelling characters and worlds, despite being a smaller player in the industry.

Sony Pictures Animation made its mark with "Cloudy with a Chance of Meatballs" (2009), an adaptation of the beloved children's book that impressed audiences with its imaginative story and vibrant animation style. The studio's innovative approach to visual storytelling and humor set the stage for future successes.

Nickelodeon Movies, in collaboration with Paramount Pictures, contributed to the animation boom with films like "The SpongeBob SquarePants Movie" (2004), expanding its popular TV brand into the cinematic realm. The film's success demonstrated the potential for television-based animated properties to make a significant impact on the big screen.

Laika, an animation studio known for its stop-motion films, debuted with "Coraline" (2009), offering audiences a visually stunning and slightly eerie adventure that stood out for its craftsmanship and storytelling. Laika's commitment to the art of stop-motion animation offered a distinct alternative to the CGI-dominated landscape.

Trivia Tidbits

- "Monsters, Inc." introduced the concept of "scream energy," cleverly flipping the script on the classic monster-under-the-bed trope by making monsters afraid of children.
- The fur technology developed for Sulley in "Monsters, Inc." involved simulating over 2.3 million individual hairs, a groundbreaking feat at the time.
- "WALL-E" was celebrated for its minimal dialogue in its first half, relying heavily on visual storytelling to convey its narrative.
- "Shrek" was the first film to win the Academy Award for Best Animated Feature, a category introduced in 2001.
- The character of Shrek was initially meant to be voiced by Chris Farley, who recorded nearly all of the dialogue before his untimely death.
- "Madagascar" features a group of zoo animals who end up on the island of Madagascar, with the film's success spawning several sequels and a spin-off featuring the penguins.

- "Kung Fu Panda" incorporated traditional Chinese martial arts, and its production involved the team taking martial arts classes to ensure authenticity.
- "Ice Age" is known for its character Scrat, a saber-toothed squirrel, whose quest for an acorn became a recurring comedic element throughout the series.
- "Cloudy with a Chance of Meatballs" was Phil Lord and Christopher Miller's directorial debut, who would go on to direct "The Lego Movie."
- The film's unique animation style was inspired by the work of children's book illustrators, blending a cartoonish aesthetic with dynamic 3D animation.
- "The SpongeBob SquarePants Movie" expanded the lore of the TV series, taking SpongeBob and Patrick on a quest beyond Bikini Bottom.
- The film featured David Hasselhoff in a memorable cameo, blending live-action with animation.
- "Coraline" was based on Neil Gaiman's novella of the same name and required the creation of 28 different Coraline puppets to capture the range of the character's emotions.
- The film used a blend of stop-motion animation and 3D printing to create the faces of the characters, allowing for detailed facial expressions.
- "Coraline" was the first stop-motion animated feature to be shot entirely in 3D, enhancing its eerie and immersive atmosphere.
- "Monsters, Inc."'s Boo was initially named "Mary" in the film's early scripts, a nod to her voice actress, Mary Gibbs.
- "Shrek's" soundtrack, featuring Smash Mouth's "All Star," became iconic, contributing significantly to the film's pop culture impact.
- "Kung Fu Panda's" Po was specifically designed to challenge traditional hero stereotypes, focusing on an unlikely hero's journey.

- "Ice Age's" directors cited the influence of classic buddy movies and silent film era comedies on the film's humor and dynamics.
- "The SpongeBob SquarePants Movie" marked the first time the TV show's characters were brought to the big screen, necessitating a higher level of detail in the animation to suit cinematic release.

Coraline

"Coraline," written by Neil Gaiman and later adapted into a successful animated film, captivated audiences with its eerie atmosphere and haunting storyline. The tale follows Coraline Jones, a young girl who discovers a parallel world that initially seems like a dream come true but quickly turns into a nightmare.

One of the main elements that scared kids in "Coraline" was the concept of the Other Mother. At first glance, she appears as a loving and attentive mother figure, but she gradually reveals herself to be a sinister entity with button eyes who seeks to trap Coraline in the alternate reality forever.

The Other Mother's transformation from warm and caring to cold and threatening unsettled many young viewers, tapping into a primal fear of the uncanny and the unknown.

Additionally, the Other World itself, with its distorted and twisted versions of reality, created a sense of unease. From the eerie button-eyed inhabitants to the unsettling emptiness of the landscape, the setting of "Coraline" served as a playground for nightmares.

Furthermore, the themes of isolation and the loss of identity resonated with children, as Coraline struggles to navigate a world where she feels alone and misunderstood.

Overall, "Coraline" scared kids by tapping into primal fears, such as the fear of the unknown, the loss of identity, and the unsettling feeling of being trapped in a nightmarish reality.

Monsters, Inc

"Monsters, Inc.," released in 2001 by Pixar Animation Studios, introduced audiences to a captivating world where the city of Monstropolis is powered by the screams of human children. At the heart of this world are Sulley and Mike, employees at Monsters, Incorporated, the corporation responsible for generating power by scaring children.

However, the film transcends its whimsical premise, exploring themes of friendship, fear, and the ethical implications of exploiting others for energy.

At its core, "Monsters, Inc." is a story about the unlikely friendship between Sulley, the company's top scarer, and Boo, a little girl who accidentally finds her way into the monster world.

This relationship challenges the long-held belief in Monstropolis that children are toxic and to be feared, highlighting the power of understanding and empathy to bridge worlds. The film cleverly reverses the typical monster-under-the-bed narrative, portraying the monsters themselves as complex characters with their own fears and vulnerabilities. This shift encourages audiences, particularly children, to question their own fears and consider the perspectives of those different from themselves.

The theme of fear as a source of power is central to "Monsters, Inc.," presenting a subtle critique of how societies can exploit individuals to sustain their way of life. The monsters' reliance on children's screams as an energy source serves as a metaphor for real-world issues, such as the exploitation of natural resources and the ethical costs of energy consumption. The film's resolution, discovering that laughter is a more potent and sustainable energy source than screams, suggests a more harmonious way of living that benefits both monsters and humans. This shift from fear to joy not only resolves the energy crisis in Monstropolis but also offers a commentary on the importance of seeking alternative, ethical solutions to societal problems.

"Monsters, Inc." also delves into themes of corporate greed and the moral dilemmas faced by individuals within large organizations. The film's antagonist, Randall, and the company's CEO, Mr. Waternoose, are willing to go to great lengths, including kidnapping and endangering children, to keep the company afloat.

This storyline prompts viewers to consider the consequences of valuing profit over ethics and the responsibility of individuals to challenge corrupt practices. Through its compelling narrative, vibrant characters, and thoughtful themes, "Monsters, Inc." not only entertains but also encourages audiences to reflect on the impact of their actions on others and the world around them.

Madagascar

Madagascar, released in 2005 by DreamWorks Animation, stands out for its comedic take on the story of four animals from the Central Park Zoo who unexpectedly find themselves stranded on the island of Madagascar. The film explores themes of freedom, friendship, and adapting to change, all while providing a hearty dose of humor through its colorful and endearing characters.

At the heart of "Madagascar" are Alex the lion, Marty the zebra, Melman the giraffe, and Gloria the hippopotamus. Each character brings a unique perspective to the group's dynamic, reflecting individual fears, aspirations, and the value of community. The film cleverly uses the animals' misadventures to highlight the contrast between life in the wild and the comforts of captivity, challenging both the characters and the audience to reconsider notions of home and freedom.

One of the most memorable aspects of "Madagascar" is its humor, which appeals to both children and adults. The film is packed with witty dialogues, slapstick comedy, and cultural references that keep viewers engaged and entertained. The introduction of the penguins, who plot their own escape with military precision, adds another layer of comedy, making them fan favorites and earning them their own spin-off series and movies.

"Madagascar" also addresses the theme of identity, as the main characters, especially Alex, struggle with their instincts when faced with the realities of life outside the zoo. This internal conflict adds depth to the narrative, allowing for moments of introspection amid the laughter. The lush, vibrant setting of Madagascar itself serves as a backdrop for the exploration of this theme, showcasing the beauty and diversity of the natural world.

The critical and commercial success of "Madagascar" led to the development of a franchise, including sequels, a spin-off featuring the penguins, and various short films. The series has been praised for its animation quality, voice acting, and the way it balances humor with touching moments of friendship and self- discovery.

"Madagascar" not only entertained audiences around the globe but also sparked conversations about the importance of understanding and embracing differences, making it a memorable addition to the landscape of 2000s animation.

Epic Film Trilogies: "The Lord of the Rings" and Beyond

The early 2000s heralded a golden era for epic film trilogies, with "The Lord of the Rings" (2001-2003) setting the standard for cinematic storytelling, visual effects, and the successful adaptation of beloved literary works. Directed by Peter Jackson, this trilogy brought J.R.R. Tolkien's rich fantasy world to life, capturing the hearts and imaginations of audiences worldwide. Through its intricate plot, complex characters, and groundbreaking special effects, "The Lord of the Rings" trilogy redefined the fantasy genre, demonstrating the potential for epic storytelling on the big screen.

At the core of its success was Jackson's unwavering commitment to authenticity and detail, from the creation of entire languages to the meticulous construction of Middle-earth's diverse landscapes and cultures. The trilogy's narrative, centered around the quest to destroy the One Ring, wove together themes of friendship, sacrifice, and the struggle between good and evil, resonating with viewers of all ages. The ensemble cast, featuring Elijah Wood, Ian McKellen, Viggo Mortensen, and many others, brought depth and humanity to their roles, further immersing audiences in Tolkien's world.

"The Lord of the Rings" trilogy was not only a commercial triumph but also a critical darling, earning numerous Academy Awards, including Best Picture for its final installment, "The Return of the King." Its success paved the way for other epic film trilogies and series, inspiring filmmakers to tackle ambitious projects and push the boundaries of what was possible in cinema.

Following in the footsteps of "The Lord of the Rings," other trilogies captured the public's attention in the 2000s:

- "The Matrix" Trilogy (1999-2003): Beginning with a groundbreaking blend of philosophy, action, and special effects, the Wachowskis' series explored themes of reality, freedom, and human potential, becoming a cultural touchstone.
- "Pirates of the Caribbean" Trilogy (2003-2007): This swashbuckling adventure, led by Johnny Depp's iconic portrayal of Captain Jack Sparrow, combined humor, action, and supernatural elements, reviving the pirate genre.
- "Spider-Man" Trilogy (2002-2007): Directed by Sam Raimi and starring Tobey Maguire, this series brought the web-slinging superhero to life, balancing spectacular action sequences with the personal growth and challenges of Peter Parker.
- "The Bourne Trilogy (2002-2007): Matt Damon starred as Jason Bourne, an amnesiac spy, in this series that redefined the spy thriller genre with its realistic action and exploration of identity and morality.

These trilogies, along with "The Lord of the Rings," not only dominated the box office but also left a lasting impact on popular culture, inspiring a generation of filmmakers and setting new benchmarks for storytelling, character development, and cinematic spectacle. The early 2000s were indeed a renaissance for epic film trilogies, each bringing its unique flavor to the era's cinematic landscape.

The Lord of The Rings

"Even the smallest person can change the course of the future."

"The Lord of the Rings" trilogy, directed by Peter Jackson, stands as a monumental achievement in the history of cinema, encapsulating the essence of J.R.R. Tolkien's epic fantasy saga with unprecedented fidelity and scale. The trilogy – comprising "The Fellowship of the Ring" (2001), "The Two Towers" (2002), and "The Return of the King" (2003) – is celebrated for its deep narrative complexity, fully realized world, and the emotional depth of its characters, setting a new standard for epic filmmaking.

At the heart of the trilogy's success was its meticulous adaptation process. Jackson and his team, including screenwriters Fran Walsh and Philippa Boyens, undertook the Herculean task of condensing Tolkien's expansive lore into a coherent cinematic narrative while retaining the story's emotional core and thematic richness. They succeeded in weaving the diverse threads of Middle-earth's history, cultures, and languages into a tapestry that was both accessible to newcomers and deeply satisfying to long-time fans of the books.

The trilogy's production was a landmark in film technology and craftsmanship. Weta Workshop, the special effects and prop company co-founded by Jackson, pioneered advancements in CGI, makeup, and costume design to bring the inhabitants of Middle-earth to life. Gollum, voiced and performed through motion capture by Andy Serkis, became a symbol of the trilogy's technical ingenuity, seamlessly blending animation and live-action to create a character of complex emotions and motivations.

Moreover, the trilogy's filming in New Zealand, with its lush landscapes and dramatic vistas, was instrumental in bringing the beauty and danger of Middle-earth to vivid life. The natural scenery became as much a character in the films as the actors themselves, with iconic locations such as the rolling hills of the Shire and the imposing peaks of Mordor capturing the imagination of viewers around the world.

The cultural impact of "The Lord of the Rings" trilogy is profound, influencing not only the fantasy genre but also the broader landscape of entertainment. Its commercial and critical success demonstrated the viability of high-fantasy adaptations, paving the way for subsequent films and television series within the genre. The trilogy's exploration of themes such as the corrupting influence of power, the importance of friendship and courage, and the indomitable spirit of good in the face of overwhelming evil resonated with audiences globally, reinforcing the timeless nature of Tolkien's work.

"The Lord of the Rings" trilogy's legacy extends beyond its cinematic achievements. It revitalized interest in Tolkien's writings, contributed to a surge in tourism to New Zealand, and inspired a new generation of creatives across various media. Its accolades, including 17 Academy Awards across the three films, cement its status as one of the greatest and most influential film projects ever undertaken. In the years since its release, the trilogy has endured as a benchmark of storytelling ambition and cinematic magic, a testament to the power of a well-told epic to enchant, inspire, and endure.

"One ring to rule them all, one ring to find them, one ring to bring them all and in the darkness bind them."

Frodo Baggins (Elijah Wood)

Frodo, the humble Hobbit and ring-bearer, is the heart of the quest to destroy the One Ring. Elijah Wood's portrayal captured Frodo's innocence and the weight of his burden.

- Trivia: Elijah Wood sent in his audition tape wearing a homemade Hobbit costume, showcasing his dedication to the role.
- Director Peter Jackson believed Wood's eyes conveyed the depth needed for Frodo's character.
- Frodo's internal struggle with the Ring's corruption was enhanced by subtle CGI in his eyes, a detail that underscored his battle with temptation.

Gandalf (Ian McKellen)

The wise wizard Gandalf, played by Ian McKellen, guides the Fellowship with his knowledge and power. McKellen's performance added gravitas and warmth to the character.

- Trivia: McKellen kept one of Gandalf's staffs and his sword, Glamdring, as mementos from the filming.
- The actor used platforms and forced perspective to appear taller than his co-stars.
- McKellen recorded dialogue for the Battle of Helm's Deep under a bridge in New Zealand to capture the echo effect realistically.

"The World Is Not In Your Books And Maps, It's Out There"

Aragorn (Viggo Mortensen)

The ranger destined to be king, Aragorn's journey from obscurity to monarch is central to the trilogy. Mortensen's rugged portrayal and physical commitment brought authenticity to the role.

- Trivia: Mortensen did many of his own stunts, adding to Aragorn's realism.
- He carried his character's sword with him off-camera to get accustomed to its weight.
- Mortensen spontaneously broke a toe while kicking a helmet for a scene, using the pain to fuel his performance.

Legolas (Orlando Bloom)

The elf prince Legolas, known for his archery skills and agility, was played by Orlando Bloom. Bloom brought an ethereal yet dynamic presence to the character.

- Trivia: Bloom auditioned for Faramir but was cast as Legolas instead.
- The actor performed many of his own stunts, including a scene where he mounted a horse from behind without using his hands.
- Bloom took archery lessons to prepare for the role, enhancing his portrayal's authenticity.
- Despite suffering a cracked rib during a fall from a horse, Bloom continued filming without significant delays, showcasing his dedication to the role.
- Orlando Bloom's casting as Legolas led to his international breakthrough, significantly boosting his career and making him a household name worldwide.

Gimli (John Rhys-Davies)

Gimli the Dwarf, portrayed by John Rhys-Davies, adds humor and heart to the Fellowship. His unlikely friendship with Legolas is a highlight of the series.

- Trivia: Rhys-Davies suffered allergic reactions to his prosthetic makeup but persevered through the filming.
- The actor also voiced the Ent, Treebeard, showcasing his versatility.
- A running joke about Gimli's height required creative camera angles and props to maintain the illusion of his stature.

"You shall not pass!"

Gandalf's Stand Against the Balrog on the Bridge of Khazad-dûm: "You shall not pass!" Gandalf's confrontation with the Balrog is one of the trilogy's most iconic scenes, highlighting his bravery and self-sacrifice. It's a visually stunning moment that demonstrates the power of darkness they're fighting against, and Gandalf's fall into the abyss marks a significant emotional low point for the Fellowship.

The Fellowship's Formation at Rivendell

This pivotal scene brings together representatives from Middle-earth's races to form the Fellowship of the Ring. It's a defining moment that underscores the theme of unity and cooperation among disparate groups to combat a common enemy. The picturesque setting of Rivendell and the solemnity of the gathering emphasize the gravity of their mission.

The Battle of Helm's Deep
This epic battle sequence in "The Two Towers" is a masterpiece of tension, pacing, and visual effects. It showcases the desperation and courage of the defenders of Rohan against overwhelming odds. The battle's scale, combined with personal stories of bravery, loss, and survival, makes it a central piece of the trilogy's narrative.

Gollum's Internal Struggle
Gollum's conversation with his reflection in the water, where he battles between his Smeagol and Gollum personas, offers a deep dive into his tortured psyche. It's a key moment that humanizes a conflicted character, making him both pitiable and tragic, and emphasizes the corrupting influence of the One Ring.

The Destruction of the One Ring
The culmination of Frodo's journey at Mount Doom is a moment fraught with tension and desperation. Frodo's final struggle to let go of the Ring, followed by Gollum's intervention leading to the Ring's destruction, is a cathartic release for the audience and characters alike. It symbolizes the end of a long struggle, the victory of good over evil, and the power of even the smallest characters to change the course of the future.

The Lighting of the Beacons
This visually stunning sequence in "The Return of the King" captures the urgent call for help across the kingdoms of Middle-earth. The lighting of the beacons from Gondor to Rohan is a powerful symbol of hope and solidarity, rallying allies to come to Gondor's aid against the forces of Sauron. The sweeping cinematography that follows the chain of fires across mountain peaks not only highlights the films' breathtaking landscapes but also reinforces the theme of unity and the importance of standing together in the face of darkness.

Trivia Tidbits

- The Fellowship's Casting Could Have Been Different: Nicolas Cage was offered the role of Aragorn, but he turned it down due to family obligations.
- Real-Life Languages Influenced Elvish: Tolkien, a philologist, constructed the Elvish languages, Quenya and Sindarin, with influences from Finnish and Welsh, respectively.
- A Massive Prop Count: Over the course of filming, the production used approximately 48,000 props.
- Hobbit Feet Took Time: It took up to an hour and a half each day to apply the prosthetic Hobbit feet to actors.
- Viggo Mortensen's Singing: Aragorn's actor, Viggo Mortensen, performed his own singing in "The Return of the King," showcasing his versatile talents.
- Sean Bean's Fear of Flying: Bean, who played Boromir, is afraid of flying. For remote shoot locations, he would hike in costume to avoid helicopter rides.
- A Miniature or "Bigature" World: The trilogy made extensive use of miniatures, or "bigatures," for scenes involving locations like Minas Tirith, often built in incredible detail but on a smaller scale.
- Gandalf's Fireworks Dragon: The dragon firework at Bilbo's birthday party was inspired by Tolkien's own artwork.
- The Fellowship's Tattoo Bond: The main cast members got a tattoo of the word "nine" in Elvish to commemorate their time filming the trilogy.
- Weather Challenges: A flash flood destroyed one of the sets, specifically the bridge at the Ford of Bruinen, which required a rebuild for the scene.
- Extended Editions Add Depth: The extended editions of the trilogy add a total of 2 hours and 6 minutes to the film series, fleshing out character backstories and plot details.

- The Scale of Helm's Deep: The Helm's Deep set was built on a dry quarry, which allowed for the epic scope of the battle scenes to be filmed with hundreds of extras.
- A Cameo by the Director: Peter Jackson appears in all three movies in cameo roles, including as one of the Rohirrim soldiers at Helm's Deep.
- Andy Serkis' Dual Role: In addition to playing Gollum, Andy Serkis also provided the movements for the Witch-King of Angmar in a pivotal battle scene.
- The Leaves of Lothlórien: Each leaf in the Elven cloaks given to the Fellowship was handmade and intricately woven, symbolizing the painstaking attention to detail throughout the trilogy's production.

Sailing into the New Millennium: The "Pirates of the Caribbean" Saga

At the dawn of the 21st century, a new franchise emerged from the depths of cinematic imagination, marrying swashbuckling adventure with supernatural lore to create an unforgettable experience. "Pirates of the Caribbean," inspired by the Disneyland theme park ride, debuted in 2003 with "The Curse of the Black Pearl," introducing audiences to a world where pirates, cursed treasures, and oceanic myths come to life. This film series, spanning five installments, rejuvenated the pirate genre and anchored its place in the hearts of viewers around the globe.

The success of "Pirates of the Caribbean" was anchored by Johnny Depp's iconic portrayal of Captain Jack Sparrow, a character whose eccentricity, cunning, and charm have become synonymous with the series. Depp's performance, which earned him an Academy Award nomination, redefined pirate archetypes and became a cultural phenomenon. Alongside Depp, the series boasted a talented cast including Orlando Bloom as the honorable Will Turner, Keira Knightley as the spirited Elizabeth Swann, and Geoffrey Rush as the formidable Captain Barbossa, creating a dynamic ensemble that contributed to the films' appeal.

At the helm of "The Curse of the Black Pearl" was director Gore Verbinski, whose vision brought the fantastical world of the Caribbean seas to vivid life. The film's blend of action, humor, and romance, set against the backdrop of stunning visual effects and epic set pieces, struck a chord with audiences, proving that tales of piracy could captivate the modern viewer. The movie's storyline, revolving around the cursed crew of the Black Pearl, introduced a supernatural element to the pirate narrative, setting the stage for the adventures that would follow in the sequels.

"Pirates of the Caribbean" not only revitalized the pirate genre but also demonstrated the potential of theme park attractions as sources for cinematic inspiration.

The franchise's success led to a surge in pirate-themed media, from television shows to video games, rekindling interest in pirate lore and history. Furthermore, the series had a significant impact on the Disney brand, reinforcing its ability to produce blockbuster films outside of its traditional animation domain.

The series' legacy is marked by its influence on pop culture, from Captain Jack Sparrow's inclusion in various forms of media and merchandise to the revitalization of pirate folklore in the public consciousness. "Pirates of the Caribbean" remains a testament to the enduring appeal of adventure on the high seas, blending historical myth with modern storytelling to create a saga that continues to enchant and entertain.

- Johnny Depp's portrayal of Jack Sparrow was initially met with skepticism from Disney executives, who were unsure about his eccentric interpretation of the character.
- The character of Jack Sparrow was inspired by the Rolling Stones guitarist Keith Richards, who later played Jack's father, Captain Teague, in the series.
- The original Disneyland attraction, "Pirates of the Caribbean," which inspired the movie series, was the last theme park ride overseen by Walt Disney himself before his death.
- "The Curse of the Black Pearl" was the first Disney film to receive a PG-13 rating, due to its action sequences and dark themes.
- Before Johnny Depp was cast as Jack Sparrow, actors such as Jim Carrey, Hugh Jackman, and Robert De Niro were considered for the role.
- The ship used for the Black Pearl in the films was originally named the Sunset, a floating platform that was transformed into the iconic pirate ship.
- "Pirates of the Caribbean: Dead Man's Chest" set a record at the time for the highest-grossing opening weekend, with $136 million in the United States.
- The eyeball that frequently pops out of the skull of Captain Barbossa's pet monkey is a CGI effect, not a practical one.
- For his role as Davy Jones, Bill Nighy wore a special motion capture suit and was never actually in makeup or costume on set, contrary to what the final CGI character might suggest.
- The famous line, "But why is the rum gone?" was improvised by Johnny Depp during filming.
- Orlando Bloom, who played Will Turner, learned to sword fight for his role, adding realism to his character's duels and battles.
- Keira Knightley was only 17 years old when she was cast as Elizabeth Swann and had to have a guardian accompany her to all the film shoots due to her age.

- The Kraken, seen in "Dead Man's Chest," required over 50 different CGI tentacles for its various scenes, each controlled by individual animators.
- The wedding scene in "At World's End" between Will Turner and Elizabeth Swann was filmed in one continuous shot amidst a chaotic battle scene.
- The compass that Jack Sparrow uses, which points to what he wants most, is a real navigational tool known as a "gimbal compass," but its magical properties are, of course, purely fictional.

Captain Jack

Captain Jack Sparrow, portrayed with unparalleled flair by Johnny Depp, is arguably the soul of the "Pirates of the Caribbean" series. From his first appearance, staggering onto the docks of Port Royal, Sparrow captivated audiences with his wit, unpredictability, and a moral compass that, while not always pointing north, reliably guides him through treacherous waters.

Depp's inspiration for Sparrow's character came from a blend of rock stars like Keith Richards and the cartoon skunk Pepé Le Pew, resulting in a pirate who is both a strategist and a charmer, navigating the Caribbean with an almost supernatural luck.

Jack Sparrow's appeal lies in his complexity; he is neither hero nor villain but occupies the grey area in between. His loyalty is as fluid as the seas he sails, making him an unpredictable yet invaluable ally. His quest for freedom and aversion to authority make him a relatable figure, embodying the spirit of rebellion and independence that defines the pirate lore. Yet, despite his self-serving nature, Sparrow often finds himself doing the right thing, whether out of a sense of adventure, a hidden moral code, or pure happenstance.

Depp's portrayal brought depth to what could have been a straightforward pirate character, infusing Sparrow with a sense of humor, vulnerability, and intelligence that resonated with viewers.

This characterization, combined with Depp's physical comedy and impeccable timing, turned Captain Jack Sparrow into an icon of the silver screen, earning him a place in the annals of cinematic history.

The character's impact on pop culture is immense, influencing fashion, language, and even attitudes towards piracy. Jack Sparrow's influence extends beyond the films, inspiring Halloween costumes, fan fiction, and a dedicated fan base that spans generations.

His quotes and mannerisms are instantly recognizable, a testament to Depp's lasting legacy as the captain of the Black Pearl.

In exploring the character of Jack Sparrow, "Pirates of the Caribbean" delves into themes of freedom, loyalty, and the price of ambition, making the series more than just a collection of pirate tales. It's a journey into the heart of what it means to be a pirate, with Jack Sparrow as the perfect, if unorthodox, guide. Through deception, wit, and a touch of madness, Sparrow embodies the chaos and charm of pirate life, securing his place as one of cinema's most beloved rogues.

"Not all treasure is silver and gold, mate."

Cult TV Hits: "Lost" and "Firefly"

The early 2000s witnessed the emergence of several television series that, despite their varying degrees of mainstream success, left indelible marks on the landscape of popular culture and amassed dedicated fanbases. Among these, "Lost" and "Firefly" stand out for their unique storytelling, genre-blending elements, and the fervent communities they inspired, embodying the essence of what it means to be a cult TV hit.

"Lost," created by J.J. Abrams, Damon Lindelof, and Jeffrey Lieber, premiered in 2004 and ran for six seasons. The series begins with the crash of Oceanic Flight 815 on a mysterious tropical island, setting the stage for an expansive narrative that intertwines the survivors' personal backstories with the enigmatic nature of the island itself. "Lost" was groundbreaking for its nonlinear storytelling, complex characters, and blending of genres — incorporating elements of drama, science fiction, and supernatural mystery. The show's commitment to character-driven narratives, combined with its overarching mysteries (such as the smoke monster, the Dharma Initiative, and the nature of the island), spurred intense speculation and theory-crafting among its audience. "Lost" was both praised and criticized for its ambiguous and philosophical finale, but its impact on television storytelling and fan engagement remains undisputed.

On the other side of the spectrum lies "Firefly," created by Joss Whedon. Premiering in 2002, this space western series was set in the year 2517 and followed the crew of the Serenity, a "Firefly-class" spaceship, as they navigated the fringes of space on the run from the authoritarian regime of the Alliance. Despite its premature cancellation after just one season of 14 episodes, "Firefly" garnered a passionate fanbase, known as "Browncoats," who praised the show for its character development, dialogue, and the fusion of western and sci-fi elements. The series addressed themes of freedom, loyalty, and the impacts of war, resonating deeply with viewers. The demand from fans eventually led to the production of a feature film, "Serenity" (2005), which provided closure to the series' story arcs.

Both "Lost" and "Firefly" exemplify the characteristics of cult TV hits: original and compelling storytelling, richly developed characters, and the ability to foster strong, engaged communities.

Their legacies continue to influence television production, demonstrating the potential for genre-blending narratives and the importance of fan support. These shows underscore the shifting dynamics of television consumption in the early 2000s, where dedicated fandoms could champion underappreciated gems or debate the finer points of complex narratives, laying the groundwork for the next generation of cult favorites.

"Lost" Trivia:

The initial concept for "Lost" was significantly different, envisioned as a castaway-themed reality show.
The character of Jack Shephard was supposed to die in the pilot, but this was changed to keep Matthew Fox as a leading character.
The series finale is one of the most-watched TV episodes, with an estimated 13.5 million viewers in the U.S. alone.
The show's creators had a rule called "no dreams, no hallucinations," to maintain the narrative's integrity.

"Lost" featured a complex ARG (Alternate Reality Game) called "The Lost Experience," which expanded the show's mythology.

The number sequence 4, 8, 15, 16, 23, 42 played a recurring and significant role throughout the series, appearing in various contexts and stirring fan theories.

Several characters were named after famous philosophers, including John Locke, Desmond David Hume, and Rousseau.

The Dharma Initiative was inspired by real-world scientific projects and utopian communities.

The series utilized an actual decommissioned plane for the crash site in the pilot episode.

"Lost" won the Emmy for Outstanding Drama Series for its first season in 2005.

"Firefly" Trivia:

"Firefly" was aired out of order by Fox, contributing to its initial low ratings and eventual cancellation.

The show included subtle references to the "Alien" franchise, including Weyland-Yutani Corporation logos in certain scenes, as a nod to Joss Whedon's work on "Alien Resurrection."

The cast learned parts of the Chinese language to incorporate into their dialogue, reflecting the show's cultural mash-up.

Nathan Fillion (Captain Malcolm Reynolds) kept the prop of Mal's pistol as a memento from the show.

The "Firefly" universe is devoid of sound in space scenes, adhering to scientific accuracy.

The character of Inara Serra had a largely unexplored backstory involving a terminal illness.

The Battle of Serenity Valley, pivotal to the show's backstory, was named after the ship Serenity itself.

"Firefly" received a posthumous Emmy for Outstanding Special Visual Effects for a Series in 2003.

A fan campaign called "Help Nathan Buy Firefly" gained traction online, aiming to revive the show under Nathan Fillion's leadership, though it was not successful.

"Serenity," the follow-up film, was made possible largely due to fan demand and support, showcasing the power of the show's dedicated fanbase.

Swinging into the New Millennium: Spider-Man's Cinematic Web

At the dawn of the new millennium, the superhero genre began to take shape in the cinematic world, heralding a new era of blockbuster entertainment. Among the vanguard of this movement was "Spider-Man," a film that not only catapulted the web-slinging superhero from comic book pages to the silver screen but also set a precedent for the superhero movies that followed. Directed by Sam Raimi and released in 2002, "Spider-Man" brought to life the story of Peter Parker, a high school student who gains spider-like abilities after being bitten by a genetically modified spider.

The film explores Peter's struggle to balance his dual identity as a regular teenager and a superhero, a theme that resonated with audiences and became a staple of the character's narrative. Tobey Maguire's portrayal of Peter Parker/Spider-Man captured the character's earnestness, intelligence, and the weight of the responsibility that comes with his powers. "With great power comes great responsibility," a line delivered by Peter's Uncle Ben (Cliff Robertson), encapsulates the film's moral core and Spider-Man's guiding principle.

"Spider-Man" delves into Peter's transformation from an awkward, bullied student to a hero of New York City, highlighting his internal conflicts and the challenges he faces in his personal life, especially his love for Mary Jane Watson (Kirsten Dunst) and his friendship with Harry Osborn (James Franco). The film also introduces audiences to one of Spider-Man's most iconic adversaries, the Green Goblin, portrayed with manic intensity by Willem Dafoe. The Goblin's alter ego, Norman Osborn, is Harry's father and Peter's mentor, adding layers of complexity to the hero-villain dynamic.

Sam Raimi's direction combined with the screenplay's faithful adaptation of the Spider-Man lore, striking a balance between action-packed sequences, character development, and humor. The film's success at the box office and among critics underscored the audience's appetite for superhero stories and paved the way for two sequels, "Spider-Man 2" (2004) and "Spider-Man 3" (2007), each further exploring the complexities of Peter's world and his evolution as a superhero.

"Spider-Man" was a milestone in cinematic history, not only for its commercial success but also for its impact on the superhero genre. It demonstrated the potential of comic book movies to tell compelling, character-driven stories that appeal to a wide audience. The film's innovative visual effects, especially the depiction of Spider-Man swinging through the skyscrapers of New York, set a new standard for action sequences. Moreover, it played a crucial role in the rise of Marvel's cinematic presence, laying the groundwork for the expansive Marvel Cinematic Universe that would come to dominate the film industry.

- Tobey Maguire performed many of his own stunts for "Spider-Man," including the iconic cafeteria scene where he catches Mary Jane and the lunch tray items. The scene required numerous takes to get right without any CGI.
- "Spider-Man 2" is considered by many fans and critics to be one of the best superhero movies ever made, largely due to its character-driven plot and the performance of Alfred Molina as Doctor Octopus.

- The train fight scene in "Spider-Man 2" was one of the most complex sequences to film, involving both practical effects and CGI to create the illusion of a high-speed battle atop a moving subway train.
- For "Spider-Man 3," Thomas Haden Church underwent a significant physical transformation to play Sandman, including gaining weight and undergoing extensive makeup sessions to achieve the character's distinct look.
- The black suit Spider-Man wears in "Spider-Man 3" is a direct nod to the "Venom" storyline from the comics, which was eagerly anticipated by fans before the movie's release.
- "Spider-Man" was the first film to gross over $100 million in its opening weekend, setting a new standard for blockbuster openings.
- Director Sam Raimi originally wanted to include the Vulture as a villain in "Spider-Man 3," but studio pressure led to the inclusion of Venom instead.
- J.K. Simmons' portrayal of J. Jonah Jameson, the editor-in-chief of the Daily Bugle, was so well-received that he reprised his role in later Spider-Man films, even across different cinematic universes.
- The iconic upside-down kiss between Spider-Man and Mary Jane in the first film won the MTV Movie Award for Best Kiss in 2003.

"With great power comes great responsibility."

"The ones I love will always be the ones who pay."

Questions

What motivates Peter Parker to become Spider-Man?
- A) A desire for fame
- B) The death of Uncle Ben
- C) A school science project

Who is Peter Parker's first main antagonist as Spider-Man?
- A) Doctor Octopus
- B) Sandman
- C) The Green Goblin

What is Mary Jane Watson's dream in the "Spider-Man" series?
- A) To become a doctor
- B) To become an actress
- C) To become a photographer like Peter

How does Peter Parker initially use his Spider-Man abilities?
- A) Stops a bank robbery
- B) Competes in a wrestling match
- C) Performs in a circus

In "Spider-Man 2," what causes Doctor Octopus to turn to a life of crime?
- A) The death of his wife
- B) Mind control by a villain
- C) Exposure to a radioactive spider

Which character discovers Peter Parker's secret identity in "Spider-Man 2"?
- A) Mary Jane Watson
- B) Harry Osborn
- C) J. Jonah Jameson

In "Spider-Man 3," what substance amplifies Peter Parker's aggressive tendencies?
- A) A special serum developed by Oscorp
- B) The Venom symbiote
- C) A rare spider venom

What triggers the birth of Sandman in "Spider-Man 3"?
- A) A failed Oscorp experiment
- B) Exposure to a nuclear reactor
- C) Falling into an experimental particle accelerator

Answers

1. B) The death of Uncle Ben

Uncle Ben's famous last words to Peter, "With great power comes great responsibility," become Spider-Man's guiding principle throughout the series.

2. C) The Green Goblin

The Green Goblin, or Norman Osborn, is not only Peter's first major antagonist but also the father of his best friend, Harry Osborn, adding a deeply personal conflict to their battles.

3. B) To become an actress

Mary Jane's career ambitions play a significant role in her character development, reflecting her struggle for independence and success outside of her relationship with Peter.

4. B) Competes in a wrestling match

Peter's initial use of his powers in a wrestling match to win money showcases his naivety and the youthful impulsiveness that he must overcome to become a hero.

5. A) The death of his wife
The tragic loss of Doctor Octopus' wife during a demonstration of his fusion reactor is the catalyst for his descent into madness and villainy, highlighting the theme of grief and revenge.

6. A) Mary Jane Watson
Mary Jane discovering Peter's secret identity adds complexity to their relationship, challenging the boundaries between his dual lives as Peter Parker and Spider-Man.

7. B) The Venom symbiote
The Venom symbiote's influence on Peter emphasizes the theme of internal conflict and the dangers of letting anger and vengeance take control.

8. C) Falling into an experimental particle accelerator
Sandman's accidental transformation in a particle accelerator experiment gone wrong not only gives him his powers but also introduces the theme of unintended consequences and the idea that villains are sometimes created by accident.

"Mamma Mia! Here We Go Again: A Joyous Journey Through Song"

*I've been cheated by you since I don't know when
So I made up my mind, it must come to an end
Look at me now, will I ever learn
I don't know how, but I suddenly lose control
There's a fire within my soul*

"Mamma Mia!" erupted onto the big screen in 2008, delivering a whirlwind of joy, music, and color that captured the hearts of audiences worldwide. Based on the 1999 musical of the same name, which itself was built around the iconic hits of ABBA, the film intertwines the timeless tunes of the Swedish pop sensation with a heartwarming narrative of love, family, and self-discovery.

Set against the idyllic backdrop of a Greek island, "Mamma Mia!" invites viewers to a cinematic celebration that feels like a sun-soaked holiday peppered with the irresistible urge to sing along.

At the heart of "Mamma Mia!" is the story of Sophie Sheridan (Amanda Seyfried), a young bride-to-be on a quest to discover the identity of her father before her wedding day. Unbeknownst to her mother, Donna (Meryl Streep), Sophie invites three of Donna's former lovers, each potentially her father, to the wedding, unraveling a tapestry of past romances and present-day reunions. This simple yet compelling premise serves as the perfect stage for a musical journey that is both nostalgic and freshly invigorating.

The film's narrative cleverly integrates ABBA's discography, with songs like "Dancing Queen," "SOS," and "Mamma Mia" not just serving as background music but propelling the story forward and deepening the emotional resonance of the characters' journeys. The musical numbers, characterized by their vibrant choreography and infectious energy, transform the film into a celebratory spectacle that encourages viewers to embrace life's spontaneity and joys.

Meryl Streep's performance as Donna is a standout, showcasing her versatility and vocal prowess. Streep brings depth and vitality to the role, making Donna a relatable and endearing character whose past adventures and present challenges resonate with viewers. The chemistry among the cast, including Pierce Brosnan, Colin Firth, and Stellan Skarsgård as the trio of potential fathers, adds a layer of humor and warmth to the film, creating a sense of camaraderie and shared history that enriches the narrative.

"Mamma Mia!" is more than just a musical; it's a celebration of womanhood, friendship, and the enduring bonds between mothers and daughters. The film explores themes of identity, belonging, and the search for personal and familial connections, all while maintaining a light-hearted and uplifting tone. It's a testament to the film's storytelling and musical arrangements that these themes resonate amid the exuberant song and dance numbers.

The success of "Mamma Mia!" led to the release of a sequel, "Mamma Mia! Here We Go Again," in 2018, which continued to charm audiences with its dual timeline narrative, exploring Donna's youth while advancing the present-day storyline. Together, the films create a vibrant, joyous universe that celebrates the universal appeal of ABBA's music and the timeless themes of love and family.

In conclusion, "Mamma Mia!" stands as a cinematic gem that transcends the typical musical genre, offering a delightful escape into a world where music, laughter, and love reign supreme. Its ability to connect with audiences across generations through the timeless appeal of ABBA's songs and the universal experiences it portrays cements its place in the hearts of viewers and as a standout film of the 2000s.

> *"Mamma mia, here I go again*
> *My, my, how can I resist you?*
> *Mamma mia, does it show again*
> *My, my, just how much I've missed you?"*

Trivia Tidbits

- The film's location, the Greek island of Skopelos, became a major tourist attraction after the movie's release, drawing fans who wanted to visit the real-life settings of their favorite musical numbers.
- Benny Andersson, one of ABBA's original members, makes a cameo in the film. He's seen playing the piano during the "Dancing Queen" scene.
- The cast recorded their own vocals, and a month-long workshop was held before filming to perfect their performances, highlighting the commitment of actors who were not traditionally singers.
- Meryl Streep performed her own stunts during the "Money, Money, Money" sequence, where she's seen jumping on a bed.
- "Mamma Mia!" became one of the highest-grossing films in the UK at the time of its release, proving the enduring appeal of ABBA's music and the star power of the cast.

- The sequel, "Mamma Mia! Here We Go Again," features a posthumous appearance by Donna (Meryl Streep) and introduces Lily James as the young Donna in flashbacks, offering a new perspective on the character's backstory.
- Pierce Brosnan, despite receiving criticism for his singing voice, expressed that participating in "Mamma Mia!" was one of the best experiences of his career.
- The movie's costume designers created vibrant and flamboyant outfits that paid homage to ABBA's iconic stage costumes, blending 70s flair with the film's picturesque setting.
- "Mamma Mia!" was Phyllida Lloyd's directorial debut in film, having previously directed the stage version of the musical.
- The original stage musical's creator, Judy Craymer, conceived the idea for "Mamma Mia!" after recognizing the theatrical potential in ABBA's songs, specifically "The Winner Takes It All," which she felt had a dramatic narrative quality.

- During the end credits, the cast performs a high-energy medley of ABBA songs, encouraging audiences to stay in their seats and sing along, creating a concert-like experience.
- Amanda Seyfried, who plays Sophie, learned to play the piano for her role in the sequel, showcasing her musical talents beyond singing.
- The film's title comes from ABBA's 1975 hit song "Mamma Mia," which is featured prominently in the movie.
- The production used the real chapel of Agios Ioannis Prodromos on Skopelos for the wedding scene, which is now a popular site for fans and tourists.
- "Mamma Mia!" inspired a surge in interest for other jukebox musicals and films, demonstrating the successful fusion of popular music with narrative storytelling.

Questions

1. What is the name of Sophie's mother in "Mamma Mia!"?
   A) Donna
   B) Rosie
   C) Tanya

2. Which ABBA member makes a cameo in the film "Mamma Mia!"?
   A) Anni-Frid Lyngstad
   B) Benny Andersson
   C) Björn Ulvaeus

3. How many potential fathers does Sophie invite to her wedding?
   A) Two
   B) Three
   C) Four

4. Which ABBA song is NOT featured in "Mamma Mia!"?
   A) "Waterloo"
   B) "Fernando"
   C) "The Winner Takes It All"

5. Where is "Mamma Mia!" primarily set?
   A) A Spanish villa
   B) A Greek island
   C) An Italian vineyard

6 What event is Sophie planning in "Mamma Mia!"?
   A) Her 18th birthday party
   B) Her wedding
   C) Her graduation celebration

Answers

1. A) Donna
Meryl Streep played Donna Sheridan, Sophie's free-spirited mother who runs a hotel on a Greek island. Streep's performance included several song numbers, showcasing her vocal talents.

2. C) Björn Ulvaeus
Björn Ulvaeus makes a brief cameo appearance during the wedding scene. Both he and Benny Andersson were involved in the production of the film's music.

3. B) Three
Sophie invites three men, believing one of them might be her father. The storyline creates a heartwarming exploration of family and identity.

4. B) "Fernando"
"Fernando" was not featured in the first "Mamma Mia!" film but made its way into the sequel, "Mamma Mia! Here We Go Again," sung by Cher.

5. B) A Greek island
The movie is set on the fictional Greek island of Kalokairi, with its picturesque landscapes serving as a stunning backdrop for the musical numbers.

6. B) Her wedding
Sophie's wedding is the central event around which the plot of "Mamma Mia!" revolves, leading to the reunion of Donna with her three former lovers.

Thank you for joining us on this enthralling voyage through the annals of television and film history in "Reels and Revelations: A Journey Through TV and Movies."

As we draw the curtains on this expedition, we hope you've found joy in the kaleidoscopic journey from the vibrant 1960s to the innovative 2000s, a period that witnessed the birth of iconic characters, groundbreaking plots, and the transformative evolution of filmmaking.

Our odyssey through the decades was designed not just to reminisce but to celebrate the monumental shifts, the unforgettable stories, and the magic that have shaped the realms of TV and cinema. We embarked on this adventure together, unraveling the enchantment of each era, from the technicolor dreams of the sixties to the digital marvels of the 2000s, and every pivotal moment in between.

Whether you dove into this compendium as a trivia mastermind aiming to conquer the quizzes or as a casual enthusiast eager to wander through the nostalgic lanes of cinematic and television history, we trust this journey has enriched your appreciation for the art of visual storytelling.

As you close this book, remember that the reels of the past continue to influence the revelations of the future, and your newfound knowledge is now a part of the ongoing legacy of TV and movies. May the trivia you've encountered inspire conversations, spark curiosity, and ignite a deeper passion for exploring the boundless world of screens big and small.

From the depths of our cinephile hearts to yours, thank you for reveling in the wonders of "Reels and Revelations." Until our next adventure, keep the popcorn popping, the screens glowing, and the stories flowing.

Here's to the endless journey through the captivating universe of television and film. Cheers to being quirky, inquisitive, and forever enchanted by the flickering lights of the screen!

BNW
PUBLISH

Join us on your favourite platform, Scan the QR code on your phone or tablet

Printed in Great Britain
by Amazon